ABOVE THE LAW

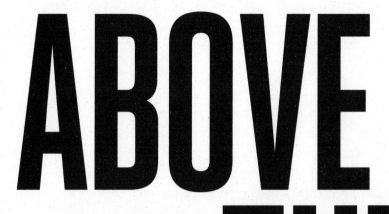

ABOVE THE LAW

The Inside Story of How the Justice Department Tried to Subvert President Trump

MATTHEW WHITAKER

FORMER ACTING U.S. ATTORNEY GENERAL

REGNERY
PUBLISHING
A Division of Salem Media Group

Regnery® is a registered trademark of Salem Communications Holding Corporation

ISBN 978-1-68451-049-8
ebook ISBN 978-1-68451-065-8

LCCN: 2020931895

Published in the United States by

Regnery Publishing
A Division of Salem Media Group
300 New Jersey Ave NW
Washington, DC 20001
www.Regnery.com

Manufactured in the United States of America

10 9 8 7 6 5 4 3 2 1

Books are available in quantity for promotional or premium use. For information on discounts and terms, please visit our website: www.Regnery.com.

To Calvin, Alison, and Lincoln, may your success be on your terms

CONTENTS

FOREWORD

BY CONGRESSMAN DEVIN NUNES OF CALIFORNIA

M att Whitaker's story looks very familiar to me, though I saw it from a different perspective.

In this book, Whitaker relates how he was suddenly thrust into the top position at the Department of Justice during the hysteria of the Russia collusion hoax. From there he had an insider's view of the bizarre scheming of the Mueller team, Rod Rosenstein, and elements of the Intelligence Community (IC) who had essentially declared war on the government they were supposed to be serving.

I witnessed all this from outside the executive branch, as Chairman and then Ranking Member of the House Intelligence Committee. Republicans on the Committee saw very soon after President Trump's election that IC officials were gearing up for some kind of attack on the incoming Trump administration. The compilation of the Intelligence Community Assessment on Russia's election meddling, ordered by President Obama in early December 2016, was the first tip-off. Intelligence agency leaders were reluctant to brief the Committee on their work on the report. Then in mid-December, they suddenly revised their work and assessed that Putin was trying to help Trump win the election. This was a major change to what was then a highly classified assessment, but they refused to inform my committee about it. Instead, they leaked the new assessment to the media in order to help spread to the public the narrative that Trump was a tool of Putin.

What followed was the most egregious attempt to oust a President in American history. As Whitaker explains, when he took charge of the Department of Justice more than two years later, the Russia collusion hoax was still being perpetuated in full force. In Congress I witnessed all the main elements Whitaker describes:

- Unending leaks of classified information
- The mainstream media's abandoning all pretense of objectivity, transforming into an arm of the Resistance, and becoming a leading perpetuator of the collusion hoax
- Demands from Democrats and the entire media that any official who appeared to be interfering with the hoax recuse or resign
- The outlandish conduct of the FBI's Russia investigation, including its murky origins, the FBI's reliance on the bogus Steele dossier, the inexplicable role played by Bruce Ohr, the chief investigators and lawyers showing a fanatical hatred of Trump, the appointment of the Special Counsel as a calculated result of a leak by Jim Comey, and conflicts of interest among the Mueller team
- The zealous prosecution of Trump associates for process crimes while Democrats, who actually were colluding with Russians to produce and spread the Steele dossier, faced no such repercussions

I can only imagine the challenges facing Whitaker as the top official at the DOJ as he tried to lead that department while being surrounded by Resistance operatives trying to sabotage both his leadership and the President's. I had my share of interactions with these types before Whitaker took over. As Committee Republicans were investigating the conduct of the Russia investigation, and in particular the Foreign Intelligence Surveillance Act (FISA) warrant used to spy on Trump associate Carter Page, we were blocked, stonewalled, and obstructed at every turn. Meanwhile, the DOJ and FBI were obviously planting all kinds of fake news stories warning that our oversight efforts were endangering national security and putting lives at risk.

A good example is the memo Whitaker describes that Intelligence Committee Republicans published in February 2018. The memo explained some of the major problems we'd found with the FISA warrant on Carter Page—namely, that the FBI relied on unverified accusations from the Steele dossier. The memo was denounced by the entire mainstream media, fueled by the DOJ's publication of a letter to me claiming they were "unaware" of any wrongdoing related to the Page FISA, that it would be "extraordinarily reckless" of us to publish the memo without letting the DOJ and FBI see it first, and warning me of the "damaging impact" the memo's publication could have on our national security and our intelligence sharing with allies.

Of course, the only thing damaged by these revelations was the reputation of the DOJ and FBI officials who exploited the ridiculous Steele dossier as an excuse to spy on an American citizen. As Whitaker notes, in late 2019 the DOJ Inspector General published a report on the Carter Page FISA that found a stunning degree of malfeasance, especially involving their use of the Steele dossier. One FBI lawyer even doctored an email to disguise the fact that Carter Page had cooperated with another U.S. intelligence agency. The FISA Court then banned numerous agents involved in the Page FISA from making any further submissions to the court.

Remember, these agents' work had been championed by the media for nearly three years while their innocent victim, Carter Page, was widely portrayed as a treasonous Russian asset. In fact, the collusion hoax birthed a whole strange, neo-McCarthyite atmosphere among the left where anyone who wouldn't go along with the hoax was ritually denounced as a Russian puppet.

I was not immune to the attacks. I had publicly advocated a stronger response to Russian aggression since 2014, and in April 2016 I argued on national television that our biggest intelligence failure since 9/11 was our failure to predict Putin's plans and intentions. My hawkish position on Russia has never changed, yet when I began arguing that the Steele dossier was absurd and that there was no evidence of Trump officials' colluding with Putin, I suddenly began getting attacked as a Russian asset by Democrats, left-wing groups, the media, and an army of Twitter bots.

After we voted to publish our FISA abuse memo, NBC News and MSNBC analyst John Heilemann asked an Intelligence Committee Democrat on television, "Congressman Nunes, your chairman—it is suggested not by me but by people who follow these matters closely— could possibly be someone who's been compromised by the Russians. Is that something you consider a possibility?" Being denounced as a Russian stooge for revealing abuses of the FISA process was one of the many surreal elements of this whole episode.

The collusion hoax revealed the total corruption of the mainstream media. They were all-in on the hoax from the beginning, and they freely abandoned basic journalistic standards and ethics to perpetuate the collusion narrative. Whitaker experienced this firsthand. "I was well aware of the partisan politics and the ideological bias of the press," he writes, "but I had no idea the extent to which they would go to damage this president, me, and anyone who supported him or was willing to serve in his administration. I still thought there were some fundamental rules of fairness that almost everyone in positions of power and responsibility followed. I freely confess now: I was wrong."

There is some irony that the collusion hoax ultimately imploded with the report and subsequent testimony of Special Counsel Robert Mueller. The Democrats, the media, and the Deep State all counted on him to end the Trump presidency. And it's clear that's what his team aimed to do. But as Whitaker details, they couldn't create Russian collusion out of nothing, and after a year-long FBI investigation followed by the two-year-long Mueller probe, *nothing* is exactly what they had.

Despite the raft of leaks and "bombshell" media stories about Mueller's team supposedly gathering all sorts of irrefutable collusion evidence, there were signs they had no such evidence even before they issued their report. For example, there was Mueller's February 2018 indictments of the Russian troll farm that had meddled in the 2016 U.S. presidential election. Although the indictments—some of which have now been withdrawn—went into great detail about how the conspirators planned and executed their operation, the Mueller team did not allege that any Americans had conspired with them.

Even before that, there was the Peter Strzok text message from May 19, 2017, two days after Mueller was appointed, in which Strzok texted Lisa Page about the current state of the collusion evidence and whether he should join the Mueller team: "You and I both know the odds are nothing," said Strzok. "If I thought it was likely, I'd be there no question. I hesitate in part because of my gut sense and concern there's no big there there."

This means that when Mueller took over the investigation, he would've learned on his first day that the FBI, after investigating for nearly a year, had found no evidence of a collusion conspiracy. And yet he continued the investigation and the accompanying media circus for nearly another two years—and still found no evidence of collusion.

Whitaker provides a valuable account of the machinations he saw surrounding the Mueller report, or as I call it, the Mueller dossier. He describes the long, inexplicable delay in the Mueller team's filing of their dossier, and then his discovery of what they were doing: having found no collusion conspiracy, they were drafting a "Part II" to the dossier, hoping Congressional Democrats could use it to impeach Trump for obstruction.

With the Mueller team's knowing from the beginning that there was no evidence of a collusion conspiracy, I believe they structured their entire investigation as an obstruction of justice trap. Whitaker's account of the team's underhanded compilation and presentation of the Mueller dossier supports this view. So does the dossier itself, which is packed with groundless innuendos of wrongdoing and, as Whitaker notes, absurdly declares that even though it found no conspiracy, the report "does not exonerate" Trump—thus creating an entirely new legal standard of "not guilty but not exonerated."

The Democrats hoped the insinuations in the Mueller dossier would be enough to move forward with impeachment, which was the goal of the collusion hoax from the beginning. But their hopes were dashed by Mueller's public testimony to the House Judiciary and Intelligence Committees, in which Mueller showed a stunning lack of familiarity with the most basic elements of his own report. He even claimed not to know what Fusion GPS was—the smear merchants paid by the Hillary Clinton campaign and the Democratic National Committee to compile the Steele dossier.

At that point, with their years-long plan for ousting Trump suddenly lying in tatters, the Democrats were sent scrambling for a Plan B. What they ended up impeaching the president for—his phone call with the Ukrainian President—may have been an even more ridiculous pretext than the collusion hoax was. Led by Adam Schiff, the Democrats on the House Intelligence Committee held secret depositions in the basement of the Capitol. Committee Democrats opened the leak floodgates—a habit they perfected during previous interviews for our Russia collusion investigation—and like the obedient lapdogs they are, the media triumphantly blasted out every morsel of propaganda they were being fed. These depositions were used as an audition process, with the most useful witnesses paraded in front of TV cameras in open hearings. But Trump's alleged offense was so convoluted and insulting to the intelligence of the American people that viewership fell as the hearings proceeded. As I said at the time, it's not easy to make a coup attempt boring, but the Democrats found a way.

In the end, despite Speaker Nancy Pelosi, Judiciary Committee Chairman Jerry Nadler, and Schiff all having declared that impeachment could not be partisan, that's exactly what it was, with every House Republican voting against the impeachment bill. Senate Republicans too were unimpressed with the case, which was dismissed fairly quickly.

At some point this tragic episode in American history will pass on to historians. With this book, Matt Whitaker has made a crucial contribution to an accurate accounting of the collusion hoax, especially with his firsthand details of the bizarre final months of the Mueller probe. It's my hope that the creation of a full and truthful account of these deviant events will help prevent them from reoccurring in the future.

JUSTICE TRIUMPHANT VS. JUSTICE DEFEATED

Every American, regardless of personal politics, should be concerned by what I saw happen to President Donald Trump inside the U.S. Department of Justice between 2017 and 2019. No one—no private citizen, no political figure, not even an accused criminal (and I've prosecuted thousands)—should be subjected to such an arrogant abuse of power by federal law enforcement leaders and bureaucrats. The American people and all honest public servants deserve better.

Top officials at the Department of Justice felt so strongly that Donald Trump's election as President in 2016 was unacceptable that they decided—working with congressional Democrats—that they could put themselves above the law and above the Constitution. They overturned bedrock standards of American justice, flouted normal prosecutorial procedures, violated federal rules and policies, and even committed crimes.

Department of Justice officials like former FBI Director James Comey appear to have openly meddled in the 2016 election. They spied on American citizens without proper justification and revealed investigative details about presidential candidates Donald Trump and Hillary

Clinton, as though the Justice Department was tasked with voter education instead of charging and prosecuting criminals. After the election,
Comey and his colleagues at the Justice Department continued their
extracurricular activities—this time to convince voters the man they
elected President was "morally unfit" and ought to be removed from
office. The appointment of Special Counsel Robert Mueller and his team,
whose behavior was totally above the law, was meant to ensure Trump's
impeachment.

Prior to moving in 2017 to Washington, D.C., I had spent my entire
professional career in the Midwest. I didn't have the firsthand experience
to know how to react to President Trump's initial comments about
Washington's "unelected operatives" and "entrenched bureaucrats"—a
so-called "Deep State." I learned it existed by working alongside it and
against it.

I routinely encountered—both directly, and indirectly through their
anonymous leaks to the media—powerful, ambitious individuals who
held themselves above the law and treated Donald Trump, Hillary Clinton, and other Americans in their investigative crosshairs as though they
were below the law. I am joined by others who also believed this culture
existed.

Justice Department Inspector General Michael Horowitz, who was
appointed by President Obama in 2012, found "the implication that
senior FBI employees would be willing to take official action to impact
a presidential candidate's electoral prospects to be deeply troubling and
antithetical to the core values of the FBI and the Department of Justice."[1]
He wrote this in his June 2018 report, issued while I was chief of staff to
the Attorney General of the United States and managing some of these
bad apples.

Horowitz's August 2019 report, described as "blistering" by the *New
York Times*, blasted former FBI Director Comey for setting a "dangerous
example for the over 35,000 current FBI employees—and the many
thousands more former FBI employees" with access to classified information.[2] The report concluded that "Comey's retention, handling, and
dissemination of certain memos violated [Justice] Department and FBI

policies, and his FBI Employment Agreement."[3] These violations were made in order to bring direct political harm to the President of the United States.

My aim in writing this book is not only to encourage greater transparency and accountability in the Department of Justice, but to use the platform I humbly accepted as Acting Attorney General to speak out for the overwhelming majority of law enforcement officers who are scrupulous rule followers and deserving of the public's trust—who are offended by the elite Justice Department leaders who held themselves above the law.

The Justice Department is the only cabinet office named after one of the four cardinal virtues of Greek philosophy and Christian theology (justice, temperance, fortitude, and prudence). To my dismay, it singularly failed to represent that virtue. What I saw happen inside the Justice Department, and what is now documented record, should never happen to another President again.

■ ■ ■

As Special Counsel Robert Mueller's team was drafting their now infamous 448-page "Report on the Investigation into Russian Interference in the 2016 Presidential Election," I was working a few blocks away, at 950 Pennsylvania Avenue, N.W., on the fifth floor of the Justice Department's Washington, D.C., headquarters. From September 2017 through November 2018, I was Attorney General Jeff Sessions's chief of staff. After President Trump requested Sessions's resignation, I was Acting Attorney General from November 7, 2018, through February 14, 2019.

From the moment I joined Sessions's staff, it was no secret that President Trump was frustrated with him, but I was determined that I could work well with both men, and I liked and respected Sessions very much. He was devoted to the Constitution and the rule of law and was a strong supporter of law enforcement. Unfortunately, Sessions's recusal from the ongoing Russia investigation that began in July 2016 would in many ways dominate his tenure.

Sessions understood Washington's bureaucratic ways much better than I did—he warned me that trying to reform the Justice Department was "like firing a bullet into Jello, the bullet never quite gets to the other side." ("Jello" is ballistic gel.) What he meant was that even ideas supported by enthusiasm and senior attention are rarely fully implemented and get worn down by bureaucratic inertia. But I don't know that any experience could have prepared me to navigate the politics of the Justice Department's fourth floor, where Deputy Attorney General Rod Rosenstein had supervision of the Russia investigation. Rod had an unusual verbal maneuverability that helped him appease Republicans and Democrats alike, and he ran a massive office with over a hundred direct reports. Before I arrived, Rod was supervising the Acting Director of the FBI Andrew McCabe who made President Trump an investigative target, and Rod had also appointed former FBI Director Robert Mueller a Special Counsel to investigate alleged collusion between the Trump campaign and Russia. Attorney General Session's recusal from the Russia investigation had the practical effect of disturbing the regular hierarchy of decision-making. My appointment as chief of staff was meant to restore regular order at the Department, which was a hotbed of plotting, back-channeling, and leaking.

There's no doubt that Russia tried to influence the 2016 presidential election. That's business as usual for the Kremlin, which, during the Cold War, had tried to defeat the presidential campaigns of Richard Nixon and Ronald Reagan.[4] We need to guard against such foreign interference, and efforts to safeguard the 2020 elections are already underway. The Departments of Justice and Homeland Security work closely with federal, state, local, and private sector partners, including all fifty states and more than 1400 local jurisdictions, to support efforts to secure election infrastructure and limit risk posed by foreign interference. While I was Acting Attorney General, I joined then–Department of Homeland Security Secretary Kirstjen Nielsen in reviewing attempts at foreign interference. We issued a joint report concluding: "[T]here is no evidence to date that any identified activities of a foreign government or foreign agent had a material impact on the integrity or security of election infrastructure or political/campaign infrastructure used in the 2018 midterm elections for the United States Congress. This finding was informed by a report prepared by the Office of the Director of National Intelligence (ODNI) pursuant to the same Executive Order and is consistent with what was indicated by the U.S. government after the 2018 elections." (See Appendix A for the full report.) But the political meddling within our own government, within the Justice Department, and within the intelligence community poses a far greater threat to Americans than any Russian internet troll farm. Without the rule of law, without respect for the Constitution, without honest administration in the Justice Department, we don't have a republic.

■ ■ ■

I developed a deep affection for the Justice Department during my five and a half years as the U.S. Attorney for the Southern District of Iowa. It was there I discovered how good public service feels—even if it doesn't pay what private sector lawyers can earn. In 2009, President Obama's first Attorney General, Eric Holder, appointed Democrats to replace me and almost every other remaining Bush-appointed U.S. attorney. Fair enough; that's a new President's prerogative, and I gladly welcomed and briefed my successor, Nick Klinefeldt, to ensure a smooth transition. It was in the best interest of the Department and the U.S. Attorney's Office in the Southern District of Iowa that the transition not interrupt the administration of justice.

Now was the perfect time to start my own law practice. I have always had an entrepreneurial spirit, and few law firms were hiring during the Great Recession anyway. I believe there is no more honorable calling than public service, but I wondered whether I would ever have another opportunity to serve my community and country. In the back of my mind, I really doubted that I would have the privilege of serving in any future Republican administration. Setting out on a small business–owner track, I did enjoy the freedom and opportunity that private practice allowed. During the week of the 2012 election, for example, I successfully defended a client at a federal criminal trial while President Obama held a large outdoor rally blocks from the federal courthouse in Des Moines. Five years after leaving the U.S. Attorney's office, I presented myself as a candidate in the Republican primary for U.S. Senate in 2014. (If I had to lose as badly as I did, I'm glad it was to now-Senator Joni Ernst, a dear friend.) Right after that, I put my legal background and passion for public service to work for the nonprofit Foundation for Accountability and Civic Trust, advocating for greater transparency and accountability in government. In that private sector capacity, I was writing op-eds and making occasional television appearances—never imagining my commentary would be held against me or that in a few short years I would be facing off against House Judiciary Chairman Jerrold Nadler, the New York City Democrat engineering President Trump's impeachment.

Contrary to news reports, President Trump didn't locate me in Iowa by channel surfing. Former White House Counsel Don McGahn put the word out that he wanted another attorney to help respond to the Russia investigation. I interviewed for that role in the summer of 2017, but it ultimately went to Ty Cobb—the Washington, D.C., superlawyer who was favored by one of President Trump's personal lawyers, John Dowd. Cobb is a distant cousin of the famous baseball player with the same name, but, more significant, he was a contemporary and friend of Robert Mueller's. A different opportunity for me to serve would soon emerge.

"I recommended him and was very supportive of him for chief of staff for very specific reasons," Leonard Leo, the executive vice-president of the Federalist Society, told CNN. "Jeff Sessions needed a reliable conservative, a strong manager, and someone who had credibility—who had previously served the department.... Whitaker was a very good former U.S. Attorney and is a very good manager. He's a no-nonsense, get-it-done kind of guy."[5]

I remain deeply humbled and very grateful for Leonard Leo and the Federalist Society's faith in me. Their most illustrious members include Chief Justice John Roberts, and Justices Neil Gorsuch, Clarence Thomas, Samuel Alito, and Brett Kavanaugh. The support of the Federalist Society was extremely important because President Trump was almost as new to Washington as I was, and he didn't have an obvious pool of personnel to draw from. He wanted to find solid conservative appointees, and to that end, he relied heavily on recommendations from both the Heritage Foundation and the Federalist Society. The political establishment class—Republican and Democratic—had been shaken to its core by Trump's election, and the resentment was palpable in Washington. Plenty of Republicans disliked him and his "outsider" appointees. A Daily Beast headline gave me a taste of their disdain for the President and anyone associated with him, including myself: "They Hate This Guy: Matt Whitaker Braces for Showdown with Dems."[6] But I also felt plenty of suspicion and hostility from the "insider," "bipartisan" Washington lawyers who felt that positions like mine rightly belonged to them.

As Jeff Sessions' gatekeeper and an outsider to Justice Department politics, my goal was to advance the President's agenda: reducing violent crime, combating international criminal organizations, and supporting law enforcement. We all felt it to be our moral imperative to back the men and women in blue and restore public support for them. I made it a point to walk the halls and meet people, to visit the agencies under the department, and to work out in the FBI gym. I usually walked to the office (until the surreal day when I entered the building as a chief of staff in the morning and left it that night with a security detail and armored Suburban as Acting Attorney General). The overwhelming majority of Justice Department employees I met performed their jobs conscientiously and honorably.

And then there were those who held themselves above the law.

■ ■ ■

"No. No he won't. We'll stop it," Peter Strzok, the FBI's lead agent on the Russia investigation, replied in one of many above the law–attitude texts to fellow FBI agent Lisa Page, who had texted him, "[Trump's] not ever going to become President, right? Right?!" How, I wondered then and now, could an FBI agent lawfully stop the election of a presidential candidate? My eighteen months at the Department of Justice left me with many troubling questions like that.

Why did Acting FBI Director Andrew McCabe write a memorandum of a meeting where Rod Rosenstein suggested—in front of Strzok and Page whom he supervised—secretly wearing a wire to the Oval Office to prove that the President was mentally "incapacitated" and therefore possibly subject for removal from office under the Twenty-Fifth Amendment? Why was a Special Counsel appointed to investigate Russian interference in the election instead of a regular Department of Justice attorney? Why choose Robert Mueller, described by the *Washington Post* in 2017 as "Brothers in Arms" with Jim Comey, whom President Trump had just fired?[7] Why did Rosenstein not recuse himself from the investigation, given that he wrote the memo that Trump cited as providing the grounds for firing Comey?

Why didn't Mueller properly vet the investigators joining the Special Counsel team? Not only did it include Strzok, but Andrew Weissmann who was apparently partisan—he had reportedly attended Hillary Clinton's 2016 election night party and had praised Acting Attorney General Sally Yates's defiance of President Trump's court-approved "travel ban" on several majority-Muslim countries—and had a reputation as a prosecutor willing to give faulty jury instructions to score a win. (Weissmann's conviction of the auditing firm Arthur Andersen was reversed by the U.S. Supreme Court in a stunning 9–0 decision.[8])

Why did Mueller allow the Independent Counsel's office to investigate for another twenty-two months after Strzok conceded to Page, via text in May 2017, "You and I both know the odds are nothing.... there's no big there there."[9] (As the FBI's Deputy Assistant Director of the Counterintelligence Division, Strzok knew well before I arrived in Washington that Trump hadn't colluded with the Russians.)

After Attorney General William Barr provided the public with a four-page summary of Mueller's 448-page report highlighting that there was no evidence that President Trump had committed any crimes, why did Mueller issue a letter of complaint about the summary, erroneously claiming that "a central purpose for which the Department appointed the Special Counsel" was "to assure full public confidence in the outcome of the investigations," when the report did not need to be made public at all?[10] (See Appendix B for the full text of Barr's report.) And why did Mueller go above the law, exceeding his authority by establishing an extralegal standard of prosecutorial "exoneration," instead of making a "traditional prosecutorial judgment"—a recommendation on the basis of the evidence to prosecute or not prosecute—as required?

Similarly bewildering, why did James Comey feel it was within his purview to provide the public with commentary on Hillary Clinton's email investigation, or to store memos in his personal home safe, detailing seven of his conversations with President Trump while he was FBI Director?

Why did Andrew McCabe—who succeeded Comey as FBI Director and was later fired for lying about leaking to the press—feel he was capable of overseeing the investigation into Hillary Clinton's email scandal even though his wife had received $467,500 from a Clinton-related PAC for her 2015 bid for the Virginia Senate? Why did McCabe feel that "the threat" posed by President Trump warranted his leaks to the media that only served to enhance his own reputation, leaks he then blamed on innocent FBI subordinates in the New York field office?[11]

And without evidence that any crime had been committed, why was McCabe allowed to add the President to the Russia investigation the day after Jim Comey was fired? ("I'm being investigated for firing the FBI director by the man who told me to fire the FBI director!" the President tweeted, referring to Rosenstein's memo outlining Comey's mishandling of Hillary Clinton's email investigation.)

Why did Justice Department official Bruce Ohr feel it was okay to shuttle information from his wife's boss, who had been hired by the Democratic National Committee to conduct opposition research on Trump, to Andrew McCabe and Lisa Page at the FBI...even when he knew the information came from former British spy Christopher Steele, a source whom the FBI had itself fired and a foreign national who stated he was "desperate that Donald Trump not get elected"? Why would FBI attorney Kevin Clinesmith alter a government document to inflate the case for wiretapping a Trump campaign member? And why would McCabe and President Barack Obama's Deputy Attorney General Sally

Yates sign off on a foreign intelligence court application to spy on that campaign member, Carter Page, an American citizen, on the basis of the discredited Steele's "dossier," skipping the usual vetting process inside the Department of Justice for such applications?[12] Why, if McCabe or anyone else at the FBI thought the Trump campaign had been breached by Russian efforts, didn't they warn President Trump or his campaign and provide defensive briefings?

There was no way for President Trump to change the culture at the Department of Justice without cleaning house. The FBI Director serves at the pleasure of the President, and firing him when he was breaking with long-standing DOJ policy and tradition is not obstruction of justice. It's evidence of executive leadership and fully within the President's power.

■ ■ ■

Even in ordinary times, the President depends on his Attorney General to pursue his agenda inside the Justice Department. That's why John F. Kennedy chose his brother Robert for the job, and why Barack Obama's Attorney General, Eric Holder, called himself the President's "wingman." Adherence to the law, discretion, and judgment are key parts of law enforcement. A President needs to identify three or four priorities and rely on the Attorney General to elevate those above others. The Attorney General is not the President's private lawyer and, like any other political appointee, serves at the President's pleasure.

Given the extraordinary mutiny fomenting inside the Justice Department after the 2016 presidential election, one could understand why the new President would hope for, at least, guard rails and an endpoint around a Special Counsel investigation. Otherwise, such an investigation could be nearly limitless. "This is the end of my presidency," Trump reportedly told Sessions after he learned that Rosenstein had appointed a Special Counsel. "Everyone tells me if you get one of these Independent Counsels it ruins your presidency… It takes years and years, and I won't be able to do anything."[13] President Trump knew that no matter how innocent he was, the political cost of a special prosecutor's investigation could be crippling. And for most Presidents, it would have been. But not this President. He was energized and would fight back.

My time at the Justice Department overlapped with retired U.S. Marine Corps General John Kelly's tenure as President Trump's White House chief of staff. General Kelly attempted to impose order, discipline, and an organized process for getting things done at the White House. He had been Secretary of Homeland Security and a Four-Star General. He was someone I respected and needed to get along with for the success of the administration. On my first day on the job, he shared with me his frustrations with the Department of Justice. He expected me to improve its management. General Kelly expected that the Justice Department, as an executive branch cabinet office under the President's authority, would advance the President's priorities. And we did, despite all the resistance throughout the Department. Between 2017 and 2019, we had so many important accomplishments, an entire book could be dedicated to the great work of the men and women at DOJ. To give just a few examples, we changed federal regulations to ban the "bump stock" devices that effectively convert legal rifles into illegal machine guns, we convicted El Chapo, we charged the Chinese telecommunications company Huawei with financial fraud and theft of trade secrets, and we sentenced to prison five members of a Mexican sex-trafficking organization that had been trapping young girls in modern day slavery for a decade. Eradicating sex trafficking has been a priority of mine since I became a U.S. Attorney.

I also had the honor of representing the executive branch when I presented the presidential commission of newly confirmed Brett Kavanaugh to the United States Supreme Court at the ornate U.S. Supreme Court chambers. It was an event attended by the who's who of the legal community, including three former Attorneys General, John Ashcroft, Alberto Gonzales, and Michael Mukasey. As is tradition at the Court, DOJ lawyers must wear morning coats. The day before the event—the day I was appointed—Solicitor General Noel Francisco came by to make sure I had the requisite coat and let me borrow one from his office. I appreciated his wise legal counsel, sartorial help, and friendship; he is an example of the Department of Justice at its best. But, according to President Trump's gleeful report, the First Lady noticed that coat did not quite fit my 6'4" former football player's frame.

During my time as chief of staff, when the atmosphere was often tense at the Justice Department, crazy headlines—traceable to leaks from within the building—often strained our relations with the White House. One day in particular I remember General Kelly was so frustrated with the Department of Justice that he snarled at me in the Oval Office. I was at the end of my tether too, and I jokingly challenged him to a fight. I'm thankful we didn't come to blows in the Oval Office (he would have won of course), and both of us continued to work closely on behalf of the American people after that day.

The presidential policy closest to my heart was showing support for local law enforcement, who were suffering a major crisis of morale after eight years of being thrown under the bus by the Obama administration.[14] The number of law enforcement officers committing suicide has been continually rising, exceeding the number killed in the line of duty according to Blue H.E.L.P.[15] So I decided to ask the President for a favor: Would he fly to Kansas City on December 6, 2018, to address the Project Safe Neighborhoods Conference? Project Safe Neighborhoods (PSN) is an initiative at the Department of Justice that focuses federal resources, especially from the Bureau of Alcohol, Tobacco, Firearms, and Explosives (ATF) and U.S. Attorneys' offices, to collaborate with local police departments in neighborhoods experiencing the most serious violent crimes, including those involving guns. PSN cases that would otherwise be handled by local prosecutors are instead prosecuted federally, often resulting in a stiffer sentence for gun crime defendants. This was the only time I asked the President for something directly—admittedly bad form from someone who knows what it's like to be a gatekeeping chief of staff. The President, as one might expect, had many things on his plate, including weathering the latest fake news leaks from the Russia investigation. When I met him at the White House the morning of the conference, he asked in frustration: "Why are we going to Kansas City today? Whitaker, you and the great cops are the only ones I would do this for!" Jared

Kushner and I followed him out to the White House lawn and onto *Marine One* on our way to board *Air Force One.*

Of course, he delivered spectacularly in Kansas City because he genuinely loves the men and women of law enforcement who daily put their lives on the line for the rest of us. Back in Washington, the President made me pay for granting my favor: watching the Dow plunge more than 1400 points between December 4 and 7—concurrent with Senate Democrats' challenging the legality of my status as Acting Attorney General— the President jokingly dubbed it "the Whitaker crash."

Watching President Trump lead, and lead effectively, while under withering attacks from the media, Democrats in Congress, former government officials, and even members of his own Justice Department, was like nothing else I've witnessed or even read about in American history. The traits that so upset his detractors are the very same traits that keep him going. Another President might have resigned, officially or emotionally, under such an unrelenting attack from powerful elites and the Washington establishment. But President Trump, to their apparent astonishment, fights back, and fights back hard. As I weathered the hyper-political atmosphere, I leaned heavily into my faith. Often strangers would approach me and tell me that they were praying for me. I could feel the power of their prayers both for me and for this administration. To this day, that continues to happen. Their continued prayers and my faith carried me through the toughest moments, and I will be forever grateful to the American people for their prayers and support.

What bothered me most, of course, were those members of the executive branch who put their own interests above those of the President and sought to subvert him and subvert the rule of law. These people, who attended some of the nation's best schools, were so blinded by arrogance that they either didn't see or didn't care about their own hypocrisy in abandoning legal and constitutional norms in order to undercut a President they found offensive. Personally, I am offended by a Washington swamp that provides cover for the unethical and potentially illegal actions of a few bureaucratic elites and disregards the mandate handed to President Trump by his decisive victory in the Electoral College. I am worried that these elites and their enablers are trying to criminalize political speech and actions with which they disagree and in the process are destabilizing our Constitution's three coequal branches of government and empowering a permanent Washington oligarchy.

Arrogant disregard for the executive branch is already the hallmark of the Southern District of New York, or the "Sovereign district," as other U.S. Attorneys refer to New York City's seat of federal judicial power, which dreamed up new ways to torment President Trump throughout my tenure at the Department of Justice. As long as the Special Counsel regulation remains on the books, I am convinced that people like James Comey, Andy McCabe, and then–CIA Director John Brennan, people who know how to manipulate the system, will do so to achieve their own political ends.

Inside the Attorney General's conference room are two oil paintings commissioned during the Great Depression. One is called *Justice Triumphant* and the other *Justice Defeated*. They are situated in opposition to each other, and the images have stuck with me. In one, Lady Justice wears a bright white robe as she leads a group of citizens up a mountain with prosperous farms and cities in the background. But it is the drama of the opposite painting, *Justice Defeated*, that really strikes me. Dark and menacing skies above a barren landscape hang over Lady Justice on her knees, head bowed in her hands. She has been defeated by a cruel tyrant, dressed in a black robe, overseeing the enslavement of innocent citizens. It would be the ultimate irony if the Justice Department were abused to defeat the principles of justice itself—due process and the supremacy of the Constitution—but I fear that some of the bureaucratic elite have few qualms about that as long as it serves their partisan interest.

CHAPTER ONE

DOUBLE STANDARDS

H ell can rain down on me, I remember thinking to myself, but under no condition would I allow partisan Democrats, above-the-law Justice Department leakers, and a biased media to deter me or keep me from doing my job. For starters, when I became Acting Attorney General right after the 2018 midterm election, I refused to immediately recuse myself from the Russia investigation. Instead, I went through the Justice Department's normal vetting procedures for determining potential conflicts of interest. Every President is entitled to an Attorney General who can manage the totality of the Justice Department and its investigations.

Though as a private citizen I had been very critical of the Special Counsel regulation, I fully accepted that as Acting Attorney General I should behave impartially towards an investigation already underway; my guidelines would be the Justice Department's mandated rules of fairness and regular order. But those who hated President Trump expected me to behave as unprofessionally as the sainted career officials in the Resistance.

Here is Daily Kos, in a panic, the day I became Acting Attorney General:

Whitaker may have already instituted changes in the Mueller investigation. Significant changes in staffing might be visible. Might. But some of the changes that Whitaker proposed, like severely limiting Mueller's budget or setting the scope of the investigation so that everything other than a handful of actions were off limits, would not. It's not as if Mueller is going to put out a press release, and Whitaker knows that. One sign of Whitaker's effect on the investigation could be— no sign at all. In issuing new indictments, Mueller would likely have to go to Whitaker for approval. It's unclear how this might affect existing indictments already under seal, but if there is a continued ringing silence from the Russia investigation, it could well be because pending actions are going from Whitaker's inbox straight to the circular file.[1]

As soon as I was appointed by President Trump, Democratic Congressman Jerrold Nadler of New York, ranking member and soon to be Chair of the House Judiciary Committee, complained, "Under these conditions, it would be wholly inappropriate for Mr. Whitaker to supervise the Special Counsel investigation given his documented history of opposition to it. The Deputy Attorney General, Rod Rosenstein, should continue to oversee the investigation unhindered...."[2]

New York Democratic Senator Charles Schumer objected to me on similar grounds "heightened by specific expressions of bias against the Special Counsel investigation that Mr. Whitaker made just last year."[3] The media jumped on board and Beltway elitists piled on with commentary. I'm disappointed but not surprised that 400 former Justice Department officials, almost entirely Clinton and Obama era, took the time to sign an open letter protesting my appointment. This became a trend, and in February 2020, 1100 former Justice Department officials signed a letter calling for my highly respected successor William Barr to resign. In my case, Nadler, Schumer, and their allies desperately wanted the Senate-confirmed Deputy Attorney General Rod Rosenstein not only overseeing the Special Counsel investigation but actually to be appointed Acting Attorney General. But appointing an Attorney General is the President's prerogative.

Even the far-Left *Mother Jones* agreed that the President was within his rights to appoint me instead of Rosenstein, pointing out that different rules govern different executive agencies: "Unlike the [Director of National Intelligence] DNI-specific statute, which says the No. 2 official 'shall' serve in the event of a vacancy at the top, the law pertaining to the Justice Department only says the Deputy Attorney General 'may' fill the vacancy. This wiggle room gave Trump a legal advantage, even as Senate Democrats and more than a dozen state Attorneys General argued otherwise."[4]

The Office of Legal Counsel, staffed by some of the smartest, most professional attorneys inside of the government, quickly ruled my appointment was valid, and the U.S. Supreme Court refused to hear challenges to it. But for three weeks, the adjectives "illegitimate" and "invalid" were in practically every media account of my appointment. It was a completely manufactured controversy, but one that dragged my name through the mud and made me consider whether I was willing to go through the Senate confirmation process if the President were to offer me the permanent position.

It was not my time. Better to focus on building the team and leaving the Department in a better place than I had found it in, which I think I did. As soon as I was appointed, my goal was to keep DOJ focused on its priorities, stabilize the Department, and insist that it operate consistent with regular order. To instill confidence, my first order of business was to call all of the U.S. Attorneys, Assistant Attorneys General, and component heads with this same message—that DOJ's priorities remain the same, and we will follow regular order, making the transition to the new Attorney General seamless.

Interestingly, the law validating my temporary appointment absent Senate confirmation was the 1998 Federal Vacancies Reform Act, which President Bill Clinton successfully lobbied Congress to broaden. Chris

Geidner provided a succinct analysis for BuzzFeed on December 9, 2018. It was titled, "Matthew Whitaker Is Now Acting AG Because Congress Gave In to Bill Clinton."[5] He wrote:

> The key change relevant to today's dispute about Whitaker's appointment addressed the [Clinton] administration's concerns about the narrow limits on who could be appointed. A new section was added, specifying that in addition to the first assistant or a Senate-confirmed presidential appointee being able to be acting officers, a wide swath of senior government officials within the agency also could fill in if the President so chose. Specifically, the bill provided that the President could "direct an officer or employee of such Executive agency to perform the functions and duties of the vacant office temporarily in an acting capacity," if the person worked in the agency "for not less than 90 days" in the prior year and the person's pay rate is "equal to or greater than the minimum rate of pay payable for a position at GS–15 of the General Schedule."

There was no doubt that I met the legal requirements. I had been Sessions's chief of staff for more than a year at the Department of Justice and met the pay rate threshold. Moreover, both Schumer and Nadler had voted for the Federal Vacancies Reform Act of 1998 (it was part of a 1999 appropriations bill) when they were both House members.[6] But more important, I had been in the office of the Attorney General more than a year, I fully understood how DOJ operated, and I knew that I could navigate and lead it and its roughly 110,000 employees. It was the honor of a lifetime.

The Vacancy Reform Act double-standard—approved when proposed by a Democrat, condemned when employed by a Republican— was only one of many I would notice inside the Justice Department. Double standards were constantly applied to Trump appointees and used to question their qualifications and alleged conflicts of interest.

■ ■ ■

In the Democrats' version of reality, Jeff Sessions's objectivity as Attorney General was compromised because he had met with Russian Ambassador Sergey Kislyak several times in the same year that Sessions was campaigning for Donald Trump. In his confirmation hearings, Sessions denied having any knowledge of Russian efforts to influence the election. His occasional interactions with Kislyak were so routine for a Senate Foreign Relations Committee member, which he was in 2016, that he didn't even bother to mention them in his confirmation hearings.

A lot has been written about Jeff Sessions's recusal, but as I found out firsthand, recusal is a very personal, fact-driven decision. I can easily imagine the overwhelming pressure he felt from the Obama administration holdovers surrounding him inside the Justice Department between February 8, 2017, when he was confirmed along party lines, and March 2, 2017, when he recused himself. He had less than a month to make one of the most consequential decisions of his life without his full team in place. Of course, President Trump's opponents were thrilled, but Sessions was being held to a blatant double standard.

When my team asked Justice Department officials about how I should be vetted for conflicts of interest as Acting Attorney General, I was told that Session's Obama-era predecessor, Loretta Lynch, simply made a ten-minute phone call to the Department's ethics office and determined she didn't have a conflict of interest overseeing the FBI's investigation of Hillary Clinton's mishandling of classified information on her home email server. Lynch, it should be remembered, had accepted a thirty-minute private meeting with Bill Clinton while his wife was running for President and under FBI investigation. Bill Clinton was the President who had selected Lynch to be a U.S. Attorney in 1999. But

Lynch and her fellow Democrats saw no conflict of interest and no reason why she should recuse herself.

One month later, FBI Director Comey inexplicably announced he wouldn't be prosecuting Hillary Clinton, even though she had been "extremely careless" in handling classified information because "no reasonable prosecutor" would charge her. (Peter Strzok, or someone else using his computer keyboard, replaced the words "gross negligence," which is a chargeable offense under federal law, with "extremely careless," which means the same thing but isn't a chargeable offense.[7])

Lisa Page didn't think that Strzok's close friend and neighbor, federal Judge Rudolph Contreras, who accepted Michael Flynn's guilty plea, needed to recuse himself just because Strzok was the lead agent charging Michael Flynn. "I can't imagine either one of you could talk about anything in detail meaningful enough to warrant recusal," she texted Strzok.

Strzok, who didn't recuse himself and admits he didn't disclose his biased texts that included an "insurance plan" with Page to Mueller when they joined the Special Counsel's team, also didn't disclose his connection to Judge Contreras, who later recused himself from the Flynn case.[8] According to the *Wall Street Journal*:

> Mr. Contreras didn't explain the reasons for stepping aside at such an unusual juncture. It's rare for a judge to recuse himself from a case, especially after overseeing a plea hearing. But the texts exchanged between FBI agent Peter Strzok of the Federal Bureau of Investigation and FBI lawyer Lisa Page, appear to shed light on the decision.[9]

Strzok was terminated by the FBI once his machinations were revealed, though he contends his First Amendment rights were violated because he was merely expressing his personal opinions about President Trump when he texted—on a government phone—that Trump was a "douche" and that he and Page would "stop" him from becoming President.[10]

But there's a significant difference between what you do as a private citizen and what you do as a government official (using a government phone). For instance, when I retweeted a *Philadelphia Inquirer* op-ed titled "Note to Trump's Lawyer: Do Not Cooperate with Mueller's Lynch Mob," and noted it was "worth a read," I was a private citizen living and working in Iowa, not a government official.[11] But a government official, especially one involved in an investigation, should not do or say anything that could be prejudicial to what he is working on. So I agree with Alan Dershowitz's assessment of Strzok: "He should have recused himself. He's a professional. And his failure to recuse himself, I think, is what led to his firing."[12]

Dershowitz feels similarly about Rod Rosenstein, whom Congressman Nadler wanted running the Russia investigation. "[Rosenstein] also creates the impression of bias. Not, again, from personal feelings but because he's a witness in the case, he's the main witness in the case," Dershowitz said. "You can't be the main prosecutor and the main witness in the same case. That creates an obvious conflict of interest."

The *New York Times*, through leaks, shed some light on what was happening at DOJ and the environment that allowed Andrew McCabe to include the President as a target of the investigation: "The President's reliance on his memo [critical of Comey] caught Mr. Rosenstein by surprise, and he became angry at Mr. Trump, according to people who spoke to Mr. Rosenstein at the time. He grew concerned that his reputation had suffered harm. A determined Mr. Rosenstein began telling associates that he would ultimately be 'vindicated' for his role in the matter."[13]

Senate Minority Leader Chuck Schumer warned that "this story must not be used as a pretext for the corrupt purpose of firing Deputy Attorney General Rosenstein in order install an official who will allow the President to interfere with the Special Counsel's investigation."[14]

With Schumer and his fellow Democrats providing cover, neither Rod Rosenstein nor Andrew McCabe felt the need to recuse himself from the investigation. According to the *New York Times,* they each made the case for the other's recusal:

> An atmosphere of mistrust had quickly taken hold at the top levels of law enforcement: Mr. McCabe believed that Mr. Rosenstein should recuse himself from any investigation into Mr. Comey's firing because of his role in it, according to people familiar with Mr. McCabe's thinking. In turn, Mr. Rosenstein and other Justice Department officials questioned whether Mr. McCabe should recuse himself to avoid the appearance of political bias because his wife had run a failed State Senate campaign in Virginia and accepted hundreds of thousands of dollars from a political committee run by a longtime ally of the Clintons.[15]

At Jim Comey's urging, McCabe recused himself from the FBI's investigation into whether donations to the Clinton Foundation influenced Secretary of State Hillary Clinton, but he "did not fully comply" with that recusal in at least three separate occasions according to the 2018 Inspector General report.[16] The report also found that Assistant Attorney General Peter Kadzik never bothered to recuse himself from that investigation, even though he tried to get his son a job on the Clinton campaign and then provided John Podesta, Counselor to President Obama, a "heads up" email about the Justice Department's release of the Clinton emails.[17]

When Andrew Weissmann joined the Special Counsel investigation and became "Mueller's Legal Pit Bull," as a *New York Times* headline boasted, he didn't seem worried that he had written Acting Attorney General Sally Yates to praise her public defiance of President Trump's executive order that sought to protect the nation from foreign terrorists entering the United States on travel visas or as "refugees."[18]

Nor did Weissmann think he needed to recuse himself even though he had donated money to Democratic presidential campaigns, as had six other attorneys on the investigation. At least two of these attorneys had

donated the maximum amount allowable under federal law to Hillary
Clinton's campaign in 2016. The *Wall Street Journal* reported that "Mr.
Weissmann also attended Hillary Clinton's election night party at the
Jacob K. Javits Center in New York, according to people familiar with his
attendance."[19]

In addition to being a donor to Democratic presidential campaigns, a
guest at Hillary Clinton's election night party, and "in awe" of Sally Yates's
mutiny against President Trump, Weissmann the pit bull is notorious for
his win-at-all-costs, scorched earth tactics. "It's pretty clear that Weissmann created a culture in which they presumed that the people they were
investigating were guilty," Tom Kirkendall, a Houston defense lawyer who
represented clients on Enron-related cases, told the *New York Times*.[20]

As the Director of the Justice Department's Enron task force in 2004,
Weissmann gave "faulty jury instructions" to secure the conviction of
Enron's accounting firm, Arthur Andersen, in federal court. The U.S.
Supreme Court reversed that conviction—unanimously and embarrass-
ingly—but not before 85,000 innocent Andersen employees lost their jobs,
30,000 of them in the U.S.

Chief Justice William Rehnquist's rebuke in the 2005 decision, *Arthur
Andersen, L.L.P., v. United States*, zeroes in on Weissmann's intentional
deception:

> The outer limits of this element need not be explored here
> because the jury instructions at issue simply failed to convey
> the requisite consciousness of wrongdoing. Indeed, it is striking
> how little culpability the instructions required. For example,
> the jury was told that, "even if [Andersen] honestly and sin-
> cerely believed that its conduct was lawful, you may find
> [Andersen] guilty."...The instructions also diluted the meaning
> of "corruptly" so that it covered innocent conduct....[21]

That Weissmann did this as a prosecutor for the Department of
Justice is an embarrassment. That the *New York Times* fawned over him

is an embarrassment too: "If Mr. Mueller is the stern-eyed public face of
the investigation, Mr. Weissmann, 59, is its pounding heart, a bookish,
legal pit bull with two Ivy League degrees, a weakness for gin martinis
and classical music, and a list of past enemies that includes professional
killers and white-collar criminals."[22]

But for Weissmann, the *New York Times*, and the "Resistance," the
ends justify the means.

Schumer and Nadler apparently did not care any more than the *New
York Times* did about Weissmann's behavior, which would have gotten
lesser lawyers disciplined for obvious leftist bias. If I had to guess, they
were only worried that I was going to behave—if trusted with power—as
badly as their coterie of anti-Trump allies in the Justice Department.

■ ■ ■

Of course, everyone should be held to the same standard, and government departments need to follow their legally defined roles and
procedures very carefully. But, as longtime professional staff of the
Justice Department privately acknowledged to me, the arrogance char-
acteristic of the Obama administration, personified by his first Attorney
General, Eric Holder, created an above-the-law culture inside the Justice
Department. Senior officials began to flout the rules and were not held
accountable if it served the ends of the administration. Leaking to the
media became rampant. Politics seeped into everything.

As is usually the case, the problem started at the top: Attorney General Eric Holder felt the rules didn't apply to him because he was President Obama's "wingman" with a mission greater than following regular
order at the Justice Department. "Holder has proven to be the most
political Attorney General since Richard Nixon's Attorney General, John
Mitchell," wrote the conservative historian Victor Davis Hanson after
Holder dropped a case against the New Black Panther Party, which was
caught on tape intimidating voters at polling places, and sued Arizona
for enforcing previously unenforced federal immigration laws.[23]

Inspector General Michael Horowitz, himself an Obama appointee, recognized the shift. In 2010, "after several critical reports by my office as inspector general at the Justice Department," he requested "all records" in another internal investigation, and FBI attorneys obstructed his request. "For decades, there was no controversy over what the words 'all records' meant.... This was the first time anyone in the department had asserted that the broad powers of the Inspector General Act did not apply fully to oversight," Horowitz remarked in a 2015 *Washington Post* op-ed.[24] "Over the past thirty-five years, that access has empowered inspectors general to root out government corruption and save U.S. taxpayers billions of dollars."

The FBI attorneys were invoking a form of executive privilege—implying that there were certain Justice Department records that even the Inspector General could not see, and Democrats supported the Obama administration's position. Yet when President Trump took the position that former White House aides have executive branch immunity and can't be subpoenaed to testify before Congress—a perfectly reasonable reading of existing law—Jerry Nadler called that "a shocking and dangerous assertion of executive privilege" and voted to impeach the President for "obstruction of Congress" (which is not a crime).[25]

On the other hand, the Obama administration refused to prosecute crimes that the administration committed. When the Inspector General for the Obama Treasury Department reported in 2013 that, as summarized by CNN, "the Internal Revenue Service deliberately targeted some conservative groups applying for federal tax exempt status, delayed processing their applications, and requested unnecessary information," Holder's Justice Department declined to prosecute anyone, not even for obstruction of justice after former IRS Commissioner Lois Lerner's official emails went "missing" while under investigation (just as Hillary Clinton's would three years later while she was under FBI investigation).[26]

Eric Holder was also an antagonist of law enforcement. When Ferguson, Missouri, police officer Darrell Wilson responded exactly as trained in 2014 and discharged his weapon when robbery suspect Michael Brown tried to seize it, Holder visited Brown's family in Ferguson to express that he was "angry and upset," and he put the Ferguson police department under investigation by the Justice Department Civil Rights Division for, among other things, "discriminatory policing." (Talking out of both sides of his mouth, Holder declined to prosecute Wilson, but I would argue that Holder's above-the-law moral grandstanding is largely responsible for the "Ferguson effect," with 72 percent of police officers more reluctant to stop and question suspicious people than they were in 2014, according to Pew Research.[27])

By late 2018, Holder was unabashedly flying his above-the-law banner as he campaigned for congressional Democrats in the midterm elections: "Michelle [Obama] always says, you know, 'When they go low, we go high.' No. When they go low, we kick them," he told a Georgia audience. "That's what this new Democratic Party is about."[28]

Holder's successor as Attorney General, Loretta Lynch, also lived as though she was above the law, meeting with former President Bill Clinton alone aboard her plane while her staff waited on the tarmac, declining to recuse herself from the Hillary Clinton investigation, and then allegedly instructing James Comey to refer to the FBI's interest in Clinton's emails as a "matter" rather than an "investigation."[29] The Federal Bureau of Matters has a nice ring to it, eh?

Sally Yates, Obama's Deputy Attorney General who was held over as the Acting Attorney General after President Trump's election, should have resigned if she felt she couldn't enforce President Trump's so called "travel ban" executive order, a version of which was ultimately upheld as constitutional by the U.S. Supreme Court. She won praise from partisan Democrats like Andrew Weissmann, who gushed that he was "in awe" of her willingness to subvert the President.[30] But executing the law, not subverting the President, is the proper job of the Attorney General. Yet Yates appeared to believe that she was a member of the anti-Trump Resistance and could use her role at the Justice Department to oppose him. According to the 2018 congressional testimony of former FBI

Deputy General Counsel Trisha Anderson, Yates (and McCabe) signed off on one of the FISA court applications to wiretap Carter Page before she could conduct her usual review of it.[31]

It is reasonable to assume that Obama holdovers like Yates viewed the arrival of Attorney General Jeff Sessions with dread, as he was everything Holder was not: a friend to law enforcement, tough on criminals and illegal immigration, and a stickler for following the rules. His recusal from the Russia investigation was the best thing to happen to the Deep State inside the Justice Department, and the worst thing to happen to the West Wing.

■ ■ ■

"We've got to transfer Ohr! We've got to get the papers signed today—don't let General Sessions leave the office today without signing them!"

I've never seen anyone more frantic than Rod Rosenstein's Principal Deputy was when he came into my office in late 2017.

I didn't know it at that time, but Bruce Ohr had been working within the Justice Department to try to prevent Donald Trump's election and then to try to end his presidency. He had also been working across the hall from the Deputy Attorney General since Rod's arrival in April 2017. A career lawyer at the Justice Department, he was supposed to be working on cases related to the nation's opioid epidemic. He had no official role whatsoever in the Russia investigation. Nevertheless, according to Inspector General Horowitz's December 2019 report, Russia investigators at the FBI "continued to obtain information from Steele through Ohr, who met with the FBI on 13 occasions to pass along information he had been provided by Steele."[32]

The former British spy was once an FBI informant but had since been fired for lying to the Bureau. Steele told Ohr he was "desperate" and "passionate" that Trump not win the election. Four months after Steele approached Ohr in January 2016, Fusion GPS was hired by the Democratic

National Committee's law firm to conduct opposition research on Trump. Fusion was already paying Steele to ask Russians for dirt on Trump; now they started paying Ohr's wife, a Russian linguist, to compile opposition research on Trump. Ohr would continue to meet secretly with Steele for nearly two years. Nellie Ohr and Christopher Steele would produce the only "evidence" Sally Yates would cite to the courts as a reason to spy on Trump campaign volunteers. It was "evidence" bought and paid for by the DNC.[33]

One consequence of Jeff Sessions's recusal from the Russia investigation was that neither he nor I, his chief of staff, knew about Ohr's meetings with FBI counterintelligence or the reason for Rod Rosenstein's Principal Deputy's panic.

■ ■ ■

Once my appointment as Acting Attorney General was a settled matter, it was time to end the speculation as to whether I, like Sessions, would recuse myself from overseeing the Special Counsel investigation. Since Senator Schumer and Congressman Nadler wanted Rod Rosenstein running the investigation, they may have assumed that his goal was compatible with their own. President Trump could have fired Rosenstein after he learned Rosenstein had suggested secretly recording their conversations, but that would have created a huge political distraction.

To determine whether or not I should recuse myself, I submitted to a six-week review by the Office of Deputy Attorney General's senior ethics official, who scrutinized my previous tweets, op-eds, and on-camera appearances and found that "there were no circumstances that would present a conflict of interest under the applicable rules of professional conduct," and that "there was no actual conflict of interest that would bar the Acting Attorney General from supervising the Special Counsel investigation."

Furthermore, the senior ethics official found, "there was not a personal or political relationship between Acting Attorney General Whitaker and any person [meaning President Trump] requiring recusal.... and there was not a personal or business relationship that would require recusal."

But on "optics," I was vulnerable to criticism:

> However, Acting Attorney General Whitaker had made public comments prior to his re-joining the Department that could constitute "circumstances other than those specifically described" and raise an appearance of impartiality issue under the catch-all provision....
>
> Under the appearance of impartiality provision, the ethics rules do not require a formal recommendation from the ethics officials.... The ethics official concluded however, that if a recommendation were sought, they would advise that the Acting Attorney General should recuse himself from supervision of the Special Counsel investigation because it was their view that a reasonable person with knowledge of the relevant facts would likely question the impartiality of the Attorney General. The...ethics official also expressed his view that it was a close call and credible arguments could be made either way.

I appreciated the unofficial opinion and the fact that it was a close call, but there was no actual conflict of interest. In the most comparable "appearance" case that was also a "close call," no recusal was ultimately deemed necessary. In the sixteen months since I had expressed my personal opinions about the Special Counsel regulation and its misapplication to President Trump, I had also expressed my opinion that Robert Mueller was a respected professional and appeared to be adhering to Justice Department guidelines for Special Counsels. I had been a Senate-confirmed U.S. Attorney for five and a half years and the Attorney General's chief of staff for over a year; I was well acquainted with the ethical duties of a federal prosecutor.

A final reason I declined to recuse myself: my team asked the ethics official if any other Attorney General or Acting Attorney

General had ever recused himself or herself because of an "appearance of impartiality." The ethics official couldn't name one.[34] If I had wanted to be popular with Chuck Schumer and Jerry Nadler, I could have been the first. But I refused to set that legally unsupported precedent.[35]

■ ■ ■

Guiding me through the ethics process and what followed was one of the most impressive public servants I have ever worked with: McGregor Scott, the U.S. Attorney for California's Eastern District and a twenty-three-year U.S. Army Reserve veteran who retired a Lieutenant Colonel. "Greg" and I met while we were both serving as U.S. Attorneys in President George W. Bush's administration.

You could say we met in prison: as U.S. Attorneys we toured the U.S. penitentiary "Supermax" location in Florence, Colorado, where the worst of the worst criminals are held under maximum security. For example, that is where "the shoe bomber," "the blind sheik," and Robert Hanssen are held. Greg and I share a passion for the Justice Department at its best: charging criminals and supporting law enforcement. After Eric Holder was selected to be Attorney General, he—like myself and most other Republican U.S. Attorneys—went into private practice. Also like me, he couldn't resist the call to serve when President Trump offered him another appointment as a U.S. Attorney.

I'm thankful that Greg didn't resist my call either because I needed his wisdom and advice. At the request of the White House, Sessions resigned the Wednesday after the 2018 midterm elections. I called Greg Thursday after my brief Supreme Court appearance. By Monday, the Veterans Day holiday, we were having dinner in Washington, D.C., preparing for our first week in the office together. I don't recall if I picked up the check, but I hope I did because I am tremendously grateful for Greg's service, professionalism, wise counsel, friendship, and patriotism, which all proved invaluable.

Optics might not have mattered to Loretta Lynch and Eric Holder, but they mattered to Greg. He worked many long days from a fifth-floor office connected to my chief of staff's suite. Greg helped me maintain a standard of conduct that was above reproach. The Attorney General's office remained unoccupied while I was Acting Attorney General. On December 7, President Trump nominated William Barr to serve as Attorney General, so my task was to lead the Justice Department—including the Special Counsel investigation—until Barr's confirmation on February 14.

Greg recalls the atmosphere at the Justice Department on November 12 as toxic and tense. Many staffers were angry that President Trump had fired Sessions, who was extremely likeable and humble. They were offended that I, a "nobody," was his replacement, however temporary. They were annoyed I wouldn't recuse myself and that I could potentially shut down the Russia investigation, or curtail it, or refuse subpoenas, or fire Robert Mueller. I was prepared to do whatever the right thing was, what justice demanded, to act boldly and let history decide no matter the flak I might take from the media or the Democrats, and no matter how much they would try to damage my reputation.

Ultimately, I didn't take any of the actions they feared. The investigation was practically finished, and it was a big zero, a total waste of time, money, and valuable DOJ resources. Peter Strzok knew this outcome as early as September 2017, when he told Lisa Page, "You and I both know the odds are nothing…there's no big there there." They were only, in desperation, hoping to find something, anything, that might damage the President and lead to his impeachment. Because their case amounted to nothing, it appeared to me that the Mueller team was in no hurry to bring the investigation to a close. Were they waiting for another tweet from the President in order to strengthen their extremely weak attempted obstruction of justice case? Were they waiting for me to shut down their investigation as a possible obstructive act? Were they just trying to keep the political weapon of open investigation aimed at the President and do more damage to his political prospects? Were they waiting for someone on the President's team to make an alleged mistake that could be manipulated into a subjective basis for impeachment, as the Democrats did months later with President Trump's phone call with Ukrainian President Volodymyr Zelensky?

In January 2019, two months before the report was released, Mueller's chief of staff, Aaron Zebley, met with Greg and told him that the Special Counsel had found insufficient evidence of collusion and obstruction to recommend charging the President with any crime. Greg asked Zebley: "Would you recommend charges were it not for Justice Department's Office of Legal Counsel memos (from 1973 and 2000) advising a sitting President can't be indicted?"

Zebley, in a very lawyerly manner, answered, no. (This information from their meeting gave me great confidence as I faced down House Judiciary Committee Chairman Jerry Nadler a few days later.)

The decision to let Greg be the intermediary between the Special Counsel's office and myself was a considered and strategic one. I purposely never met with Mueller, whose investigation was a weapon directed at the President who had appointed me. The Special Counsel regulation does not require a written report after an investigation, but with no lawful ammunition to use against the President, the Special Counsel and his staff took an additional two months to write a 448-page report, highlighting select excerpts for the press and congressional Democrats: "As we stated in our meeting of March 5 and reiterated to the Department early in the afternoon of March 24, the introductions and executive summaries of our two-volume report accurately summarize this Office's work and conclusions," Mueller explained to Barr after pleading, "I am requesting that you provide these materials to Congress and authorize their public release at this time."[36]

In May 2017, when Rosenstein issued a press release announcing his appointment of a Special Counsel, he asserted that, while he had "great confidence" in the "independence and integrity" of Justice Department attorneys who would normally investigate a matter like Russian meddling in the 2016 presidential election, "considering the unique circumstances…I determined that a Special Counsel is necessary in order for the American people to have full confidence in the outcome."[37]

There is nothing in the Special Counsel regulation about appointing a Special Counsel so that "the American people" can have "full confidence in the outcome" of an investigation. But the regulation does specify that if there are conflicts of interest inside the Department of Justice, or "other extraordinary circumstances," it can be "in the public interest" to appoint one.[38]

On March 24, 2019, Attorney General Barr reported to congressional leaders in four succinct pages the "principal conclusions"— in other words, just the legally relevant facts—of the Mueller report, while Mueller's team clung angrily to their 448-page dramatized version.[39] But whichever way you cut it, there was no evidence of "collusion," no evidence of obstruction of justice, no case against the President.

Should I have fired Mueller once I realized the Special Counsel's office was sitting on its findings long after its determinations had been made? Doing so might have been legally justifiable, but it would have been politically catastrophic for the White House, and, I reasoned, a replacement for Mueller would perhaps even extend the investigation in order to justify his appointment. The President never asked me to fire Mueller, but if he had, I would have advised against it. Would I have liked to rein in the Mueller investigation and save the country millions of wasted taxpayer dollars? Of course, but I doubted it could be done without an even greater uproar and possibly even greater damage to our country. The President and the American people deserved to have this behind them.

■ ■ ■

Some of the double standards applied to President Trump's White House staff and political appointees were beyond parody. For example, when in March 2017 Attorney General Sessions called for the resignation of the remaining forty-six U.S. Attorneys appointed by President Obama,

Vanity Fair was breathless ("Trump's Firing of U.S. Attorneys Raises Eyebrows, Prompts Conflicts"[40]), and the *New York Times* reported it like a Fox News collusion scandal:

> The abrupt order came after two weeks of increasing calls from Mr. Trump's allies outside the government to oust appointees from President Barack Obama's administration. But the calls from the Acting Deputy Attorney General arose a day after Sean Hannity, the Fox News commentator who is a strong supporter of President Trump, said on his evening show that Mr. Trump needed to "purge" Obama holdovers from the federal government.

Neither the *Times* nor *Vanity Fair* recalled this exchange between Attorney General Eric Holder and Democratic California Congresswoman Maxine Waters in May 2009:

Waters: "The protocol has been that U.S. attorneys would hand in their resignations and would give the new administration an opportunity to make new appointments; we don't see that happening quite fast enough." *Politico* quoted her complaining to Holder during a congressional oversight hearing, "There is a danger with some of them being left there.... So whatever you can do to move them we appreciate it."[41]

Eric Holder assured her, "Elections matter—it is our intention to have the U.S. Attorneys that are selected by President Obama in place as quickly as they can."[42] Interestingly, there were only two Bush-appointed U.S. Attorneys who did not quit or get fired under Obama: Rod Rosenstein and Patrick Fitzgerald. (Fitzgerald became Comey's personal lawyer the same month Trump fired Comey.[43])

Invoking the Hatch Act, which puts limits on the political activities of federal government employees while they're on the job, a United States Office of Special Counsel (OSC) report recommended the White House fire Kellyanne Conway, President Trump's advisor, for disparaging Democratic political candidates on social media and on television.[44] "Let me know when the jail sentence starts," Conway laughed.[45] Given that her job is, in part, defending the President and his policies, the lines can certainly become blurred between what is policy-driven and what is politically driven. Two members of President Obama's cabinet violated the Hatch Act (Kathleen Sebelius and Julian Castro), and they weren't fired. In fact, George Washington University law professor Jonathan Turley cannot recall anyone being fired for violating the Hatch Act.[46] Former FBI Acting Director Andrew McCabe has already been fired for lying, but he has yet to be held accountable under the Hatch Act, as Iowa Senator Chuck Grassley suggested he should be, for allegedly using his FBI email to campaign for his wife, who received nearly half a million dollars in donations from a Hillary Clinton–related PAC.[47]

Washington's double standards go beyond hypocrisy; they can corrupt the rule of law, with Republicans sent to jail, and Democrats let off scot-free with media providing their cover. President Trump's incoming National Security Adviser Michael Flynn allegedly lied when he told the FBI he had had no contact with Russian Ambassador Kislyak during the transition between administrations. Incoming President Trump expressed his hope that then-FBI director Jim Comey could "let this go," and the Department of Justice investigated the President's request as an attempt to obstruct justice. Flynn pleaded guilty and as of this writing, could still face incarceration.[48] It is concerning that Andrew McCabe won't be charged for lying to the FBI and Jim Comey won't be punished for leaking.

Representatives of Hillary Clinton's presidential campaign paid middlemen for Russian rumors about candidate Trump which became the "Steele dossier," yet only she, not he, is considered a victim of Russian interference in the 2016 election.[49] Candidate Trump said he'd be willing to listen to rumors from Russians, and he wound up a target of a federal investigation into alleged collusion between his campaign and the Russians. But the Clinton campaign actually sought and used Russian disinformation in an attempt to smear Trump and has suffered no legal consequences for it.

To be fair, Hillary Clinton was also the victim of Justice Department double standards: when the Department of Justice declined to press charges against Jim Comey for violating its policies and his FBI employment agreement for mishandling classified documents, he did an exoneration victory lap on Twitter—even though the Department's Inspector General report chastised him for putting his own personal interests and desires ahead of the Department of Justice and the FBI. Comey tweeted:

> DOJ IG "found no evidence that Comey or his attorneys released any of the classified information contained in any of the memos to members of the media." I don't need a public apology from those who defamed me, but a quick message with a "sorry we lied about you" would be nice.[50]

One wonders who owes whom an apology. When the Department of Justice declined to prosecute Hillary Clinton for essentially the same offense in 2016—because, testified Lisa Page, President Obama's Justice Department instructed the FBI to not even consider it—Comey held an extraordinary press conference shaming Clinton for her "extreme carelessness."[51] Comey could have resigned in protest at Obama administration interference in his investigation. Instead, he accepted that the Justice Department would not prosecute Clinton but felt it was his job to let the American public know that while she wasn't charged with any crime, she wasn't innocent either. This above-the-law "non-exoneration" maneuver would be copied by Comey's so called "brother-in-arms," Robert Mueller in his report.

CHAPTER TWO

PRESUMPTION OF GUILT

In an October 2019 PBS interview, Hillary Clinton said, "So maybe there does need to be a [Clinton versus Trump presidential campaign] rematch. Obviously, I can beat him again."[1] Her crack spoke volumes. To Hillary Clinton and the Democratic "Resistance," President Trump's election was illegitimate. Though Hillary Clinton was trounced 306 to 232 in the Electoral College, she won the popular vote (thanks to deep blue California cities tipping the balance in her favor, her roughly four million popular vote majority in California exceeded, and thus entirely accounted for, her roughly three million popular vote majority nation-wide). Trump's resounding Electoral College victory absent a popular mandate has convinced the self-styled Resistance that Midwestern rubes who cling to their Bibles and guns in states like Iowa, Wisconsin, Michigan, Ohio, and Pennsylvania, hoarders of white privilege and antiquated Electoral College votes, were tricked by Russian internet trolls operating in collusion with the Trump campaign into flipping blue states to red in 2016.

Nearly four years have passed, and no one has demonstrated that the Russians' efforts had any greater impact on the 2016 presidential

election than they did on any other American presidential election, however much more sophisticated their attempts have grown. The two-year
Mueller investigation recommended indicting thirty-four individuals
(twelve of them Russian citizens involved in hacking the DNC). Most of
the recommended indictments involved financial crimes and false statements. But no one affiliated with the Trump campaign has been charged
with colluding with the Russians, despite nonstop media scrutiny and
investigation by the Justice Department.

I am proud to have voted for Donald Trump in the general election
as an Iowa resident. Barack Obama won Iowa in 2012, but Donald
Trump beat Hillary Clinton by 9.4 points—Trump's biggest victory in a
previously blue state. Iowans had very good reasons for making that
choice, and Hillary's "beat him again" talk invalidates all of us, our
votes, and the wisdom of the Electoral College established by the U.S.
Constitution.

When I moved in October 2017 from Iowa to Washington, D.C., I
entered a Justice Department that included Trump Resisters. With Sessions recused and Rod Rosenstein overseeing the Mueller investigation,
Andrew McCabe had opened a full-blown investigation of the President
of the United States. The allegation of collusion between the Russians
and President Trump had the thinnest of predicates (I would argue no
predicate), and the investigation was bending and breaking Justice
Department rules in the hopes of finding any evidence that could harm
the President politically.

"Viva la résistance," texted Kevin Clinesmith, the FBI's lead attorney
on the Hillary Clinton email probe, shortly after Trump was elected in
November 2016.[2] Clinesmith reportedly faces criminal charges for allegedly altering a CIA document to make the case for spying on Carter Page,
a Naval Academy graduate who had worked in Moscow, reported to the
CIA until 2013, and in 2016 was an obscure advisor to the Trump
campaign.[3]

"In the meantime, the FISA court has ordered the Justice Department
and FBI to provide information about any other surveillance applications

in which that same lawyer, Kevin Clinesmith, was involved. A lawyer for Clinesmith did not respond to a request for comment," the *Washington Post* reported in December 2019.[4] Clinesmith was the lawyer the FBI sent to interview another obscure Trump campaign adviser, George Papadopoulos, in February 2017.[5] Papadopoulos was arrested that July, pressured for a guilty plea in a secret October hearing, and sentenced for making a false statement to the FBI, which withheld exculpatory evidence it procured from him in September 2016. According to Inspector General Horowitz's December 2019 report: "Papadopoulos stated, among other things, that to his knowledge no one associated with the Trump campaign was collaborating with Russia or with outside groups like WikiLeaks in the release of emails."[6] Papadopoulos spent fourteen days in jail.

Although not identified by name in Horowitz's report, Clinesmith is believed to be "the primary FBI attorney assigned to (the Russia) investigation." He reported to fellow Trump-hater Peter Strzok. Strzok was protected by Deputy FBI Director Andrew McCabe, whose Democratic candidate wife was accepting money from a PAC of Democratic Virginia Governor Terry McAuliffe, a long-time friend and supporter of Hillary Clinton.[7]

According to Inspector General Horowitz's 2019 report, the FBI's Assistant Director of Counterintelligence Bill Priestap and the FBI's Assistant Director of National Security Michael Steinbach were concerned about Strzok's "personal relationship" with FBI agent Lisa Page and the instances where the two of them "bypassed the chain of command to advise McCabe about case-related information that had not been provided to Priestap or Steinbach." Priestap and Steinbach "did not know why McCabe kept Strzok assigned to the investigation."[8]

Horowitz also found that immediately after the 2016 election—between November 16 and December 15—the Justice Department's Bruce Ohr attended several meetings that included the FBI's Lisa Page, Peter Strzok, and Andrew Weissmann, even though he had no departmental business working on the Russia investigation. The attendees decided to keep their meetings a secret from the Justice Department's

criminal division leadership so their agenda wouldn't become "politicized" during the presidential transition.[9]

Remarks Horowitz:

> We concluded that this decision, made in the absence of
> concerns of potential wrongdoing or misconduct, and for
> the purpose of avoiding the appearance that an investigation
> is "politicized," fundamentally misconstrued who is ulti-
> mately responsible and accountable for the Department's
> work.... Department leaders cannot fulfill their manage-
> ment responsibilities, and be held accountable for the
> Department's actions, if subordinates intentionally withhold
> information from them in such circumstances.

Did bias against Trump—from top to bottom in this chain—influence
the FBI's decision to open the Russia investigation; Bruce Ohr's decision
to backchannel the Steele dossier from his wife's employer to the FBI; and
Strzok, Page, and Weissmann's decision to keep their meetings with Ohr
secret from their bosses?

I believe it did. Inspector General Horowitz rightfully maintains the
presumption of innocence throughout his report, carefully explaining
that he found "no documentary or testimonial evidence" that bias influenced the opening of the Russia investigation.

An undergraduate philosophy major could explain why asserting that
an "investigation yielded no evidence of bias" is not logically equivalent to
asserting "there was no bias." But former FBI Director Comey, his allies in
the media, and congressional Democrats made the leap: to them, Horowitz's
report proved there was no "Deep State," or "witch hunt," or "cabal" inside
the Department of Justice. To his credit, in a piece titled "Trump Isn't Totally
Wrong about the Deep State," leftist Jeet Heer, national affairs correspon-
dent for *The Nation,* took issue with *New York Times* editorial board
member Michelle Cottle, "who penned a paean to the anonymous bureaucrats she sees leading a resistance to an autocratic president."[10]

Nine days later, Horowitz tried some gentle tutoring when pressed by the Senate Homeland Security Committee: "We could not prove it. We lay out here what we can." Modeling professional restraint, Horowitz did not ascribe motives to actions. Horowitz's report did not forsake the presumption of innocence for the presumption of guilt, as the Mueller report did, in these infamous lines:

> Because we determined not to make a traditional prosecutorial judgment, we did not draw ultimate conclusions about the President's conduct.... Accordingly, while this report does not conclude that the President committed a crime, it also does not exonerate him.[11]

In other words, Mueller's team did everything they could to cast a shadow of guilt over President Trump *though they had no evidence that he was guilty of anything.* It is not a prosecutor's job to "exonerate" anyone. It is a prosecutor's job to determine whether there is sufficient evidence of a crime to make a legal case and therefore pursue charges. The Mueller team found no evidence but maintained a presumption, shared by the Deep State and the Resistance, that Trump *had to be guilty of something* simply because they hated him and thought he shouldn't be President. The presumption of innocence is a bedrock Anglo-American legal principle dating back to the Middle Ages. But we can't take that legal principle for granted. It's not only totalitarian regimes that conduct investigations or hearings with a presumption of guilt. It can happen whenever partisan passions overwhelm respect for the rule of law. The confirmation hearings of Supreme Court Justice Brett Kavanaugh, which occurred when I was chief of staff, were just such an example of Democrats allowing their rage over losing a Supreme Court seat to overwhelm traditional standards of fairness and due process, including a presumption of innocence.

Inspector General Horowitz's narrowly focused investigation into aspects of the FBI's conduct during the Russian collusion probe laudably gave its subjects the benefit of the doubt, presuming them to be innocent, without compelling, direct, hard evidence to the contrary. The scope of Inspector General Horowitz's 2019 report was limited to investigating certain actions within a single federal department, which is one reason why Attorney General William Barr authorized John Durham, the U.S. Attorney for Connecticut, to look into the origins of the Russia investigation not just within the walls of the Justice Department, but within the CIA and NSA, as well as globally.

Durham issued the following caution the day Horowitz's report was released:

> Our investigation has included developing information from other persons and entities, both in the U.S. and outside of the U.S. Based on the evidence collected to date, and while our investigation is ongoing, last month we advised the Inspector General that we do not agree with some of the report's conclusions as to predication and how the FBI case was opened.[12]

Two days later, Horowitz explained Durham's comment to curious members of Congress at a Senate Intelligence Committee hearing: "He said he did not necessarily agree with our conclusion about the opening of a full counterintelligence investigation, which is what this was. But there are also investigative means by which the FBI can move forward with an investigation called a preliminary investigation."[13]

Had the FBI opened a preliminary investigation, it wouldn't have been allowed to wiretap Carter Page, the only member of the Trump campaign who had connections to Russians (he had done business in Russia). But given what Horowitz called the Obama Justice Department's "low threshold" for such investigations, the IG report concluded that the FBI had sufficient predication to open a full investigation, wiretapping and all.

Though the investigation began very quietly during the first half of 2016, it officially opened on July 31, 2016, after George Papadopoulos allegedly told an Australian diplomat in London that he had heard the Russians had "dirt" on Hillary Clinton. This rumor met the "low threshold" required by the FBI to open an investigation, Inspector General Horowitz found. Footnote 192 of Horowitz's December 2019 report reveals:

> Rosenstein told us that at some later point—most likely in 2018—FBI officials represented to him that the basis for opening Crossfire Hurricane [the investigation into alleged Russian collusion with the Trump campaign] was the FFG ["Friendly Foreign Government"] information concerning Papadopoulos, and nothing else. He told us that he did not receive any information from the FBI indicating otherwise. He also told us that he did not have an opinion about whether the FFG information provided a sufficient basis to open the case.[14]

In other words, the Deputy Attorney General never made a determination as to whether the Mueller investigation was properly predicated in the first place. McCabe, Strzok, Clinesmith, *et al.* were so convinced of Trump's guilt that they did something unforgivable and un-American to Carter Page. Despite being told by the FBI's Office of the General Counsel in August 2016 they didn't possess enough evidence to justify wiretapping Page and being told by the CIA that same month that Page had been their trusted source from 2008 to 2013, they ignored that relevant information.[15]

In October 2016, the FBI applied for wiretapping permission to the FISA court using the only bit of evidence it possessed: the Steele dossier, pushed by Bruce Ohr and funded by the DNC, which they received on September 19. The FBI didn't tell the court what it knew about Christopher Steele's reputation, who paid him, the doubtful value of the information in the dossier, or Page's work as a CIA informant. I would suggest this is presumption of guilt at work.

By the time the application to spy on Carter Page wound up on FBI General Counsel Trisha Anderson's desk—in an "unusual way," she testified—it was already signed by Sally Yates and Andrew McCabe. Though she usually vetted applications, she felt no need to "second guess" this one:

> In this particular case, I'm drawing a distinction because my boss and my boss's boss had already reviewed and approved this application. And, in fact, the Deputy Attorney General [Sally Yates, at the time], who had the authority to sign the application, to be the substantive approver on the FISA application itself, had approved the application....
>
> [I]t received very high-level review and approvals—informal, oral approvals—before it ever came to me for signature. And so, in this particular case, I wouldn't view it as my role to second-guess that substantive approval that had already been given by the deputy director and by the Deputy Attorney General in this particular instance.

The application was approved on October 21, 2016, and would be renewed again in January, April, and, with the help of a CIA email doctored by the FBI's Clinesmith, again in June 2017 for the third and final time, a few months before I arrived at the Department of Justice.[16]

On page XIII of his report, Inspector General Horowitz describes how Clinesmith (referenced as "OGC Attorney") corresponded with a CIA representative (referenced as a "liaison") to address his superior's ("SSA 2," short for supervising special agent #2) concern that Carter Page had actually been a source for the CIA (referenced as "the other agency"), which would undermine the FBI's justification for seeking its third wiretapping FISA application:

> However, when the OGC Attorney subsequently sent the liaison's email to SSA 2 the OGC Attorney altered the liaison's

email by inserting the words "not a source" into it, thus making it appear that the liaison had said that Page was "not a source" for the other agency. Relying upon this altered email, SSA 2 signed the third renewal application that again failed to disclose Page's past relationship with the other agency.[17]

What would motivate an FBI lawyer to fraudulently alter evidence against an investigative target? Did Clinesmith, like the people he worked under on the Crossfire Hurricane investigation, believe the end justified the means? Did he presume Trump and his campaign were guilty of colluding with the Russians? Did he believe that the investigation would turn up something on Trump and his campaign, and by whatever means necessary he would prolong the investigation until it netted evidence—or until public opinion about Trump's behavior overrode the public's concern about due process and made his political position unviable?

After the 2016 election, Clinesmith texted that he was "numb," echoing the shock felt by a lot of people in Washington, New York, and California. They likely knew very few people who voted against Hillary Clinton. And, as statistician Nate Silver explained on FiveThirtyEight.com in a piece titled "There Really Was a Liberal Media Bubble":

> Political experts aren't a very diverse group and tend to place a lot of faith in the opinions of other experts and other members of the political establishment. Once a consensus view is established, it tends to reinforce itself until and unless there's very compelling evidence for the contrary position.[18]

The Washington establishment was convinced that Trump had no chance of winning the presidential election. When he did, the reaction among the anti-Trumpers in the Department of Justice and the FBI was epitomized by a Clinesmith text to an FBI colleague, "I am so stressed about what I could have done differently."

But there was more to it than that. Clinesmith lamented, "Plus, my god damned named [*sic*] is all over the legal documents investigating his staff." He was apparently both fearful of being exposed but also unrepentant for opposing Donald Trump from within the Justice Department, writing in a November 22, 2016, text message, "Viva le Résistance!"[19]

■ ■ ■

"He's gone rogue," House Speaker Nancy Pelosi complained, not about Clinesmith, Strzok, Page, McCabe, Weissmann, Mueller, Yates, Comey, or all the rest of the Justice Department anti-Trump Resistance, but about Attorney General William Barr, six months into his tenure.[20] His rogue action? When details about President Trump's July 25, 2019, telephone call with Ukraine's President reached the Department of Justice, the file was handled with the presumption of innocence. After years of Eric Holder, Loretta Lynch, Sally Yates, and then a recused Jeff Sessions followed by an Acting Attorney General (me), there was finally a new permanent sheriff in town with the standing, authority, and intent to enforce the time-honored rules of jurisprudence which a small group of rogue actors had ignored.

Barr's Justice Department received the whistleblower's complaint in August 2019 and declined to charge the President with a crime—because there was none. "Relying on established procedures set forth in the Justice Manual, the department's criminal division reviewed the official record of the call and determined, based on the facts and applicable law, that there was no campaign finance violation and that no further action was warranted," Barr's spokesperson told NBC.[21]

"President Trump engaged in this scheme or course of conduct for corrupt purposes, in pursuit of personal or political benefit," claims the article of impeachment on Abuse of Power that was passed without a single Republican vote, and even a few Democratic nays as well, in December 2019. Many Republicans were uncomfortable with the President's phone call where he asked the Ukrainian President to cooperate with two investigations involving

Ukraine, but every Republican in the House of Representatives agreed that the Democrats' charge of corruption lacked any corresponding proof. The presumption of innocence prevailed among Republicans, as it did in Inspector Horowitz's analysis.

The relevant excerpt of President Trump's phone call with Ukraine's President Volodymyr Zelensky leaves wide open the question of intent:

> I would like you to do us a favor though because our country has been through a lot and Ukraine knows a lot about it. I would like you to find out what happened with this whole situation with Ukraine, they say Crowdstrike... I guess you have one of your wealthy people... The server, they say Ukraine has it. There are a lot of things that went on, the whole situation. I think you're surrounding yourself with some of the same people. I would like to have the Attorney General call you or your people, and I would like you to get to the bottom of it. As you saw yesterday, that whole nonsense ended with a very poor performance by a man named Robert Mueller, an incompetent performance, but they say a lot of it started with Ukraine. Whatever you can do, it's very important that you do it if that's possible.[22]

The Resistance claims there is no other reason for Trump to have asked for this favor aside from seeking Ukrainian help to dig dirt on Democrats that he could use in the 2020 election. But there are plenty of other possible motivations behind this request, including simply getting answers about the role, if any, Ukraine played in the 2016 presidential election considering the exhaustive Russia investigation. Just as Horowitz didn't attempt to read the souls of Peter Strzok, Andrew McCabe, and Lisa Page when no documentary or testimonial evidence of bias resulted from his investigation, House Republicans similarly declined to assign a motive to the President's behavior.

The other thing—there's a lot of talk about Biden's son, that
Biden stopped the prosecution, and a lot of people want to
find out about that so whatever you can do with the Attorney
General would be great. Biden went around bragging that he
stopped the prosecution so if you can look into it.... It sounds
horrible to me.

Biden's comments at a Council on Foreign Relations event in Washington, D.C., where he bragged about getting Ukraine's Prosecutor
General fired, were already notorious. As BuzzFeed reported, "Even
those who worked closely with Joe Biden cringed when he said the
words." The story continued:

> Recounting a trip to Kyiv in late 2015, Biden described telling
> the then-president of Ukraine, Petro Poroshenko, that he had
> to fire the prosecutor general or the U.S. would not release $1
> billion in loan guarantees. "I looked at them and said, 'I'm
> leaving in six hours,'" Biden told the crowd, taking a long
> look at his watch for effect. "'If the prosecutor is not fired,
> you're not getting the money.' Well, son of a bitch." Here the
> audience laughed. "He got fired." [23]

Most U.S. media reports say that the idea that Ukraine meddled on
Hillary Clinton's behalf in the 2016 presidential election is "baseless"
and "discredited" and "debunked." They assert there was no connection
between Joe Biden's wanting the prosecutor fired and his son's
$50,000-a-month job as a board member of a Ukrainian gas company
named Burisma Holdings which was under investigation. Maybe there
is no there there.

But if you were Donald Trump, and the FBI had spied on your campaign, withheld briefings on potential Russian threats to your campaign,
and doctored emails to obtain court permission to wiretap your campaign advisor, and you discovered that the intelligence community had

been out to get you from day one, wouldn't you want your administration to review these things?

If the "Liberal Media Bubble" Nate Silver pointed to regurgitated untruths about you—such as "there was no spying on the Trump campaign" and "there was no bias in the Russia investigation" and "Special Counsel Mueller would have recommended charging the President were it not for Justice Department rules against indicting sitting Presidents"—would you not take the opportunity to check things out for yourself when told that Russia was the only foreign entity meddling in the 2016 election?

Reading the transcript between President Trump and President Zelensky, or the whistleblower's complaint, while presuming guilt, one leaps to the conclusion that President Trump asked Ukraine to investigate Hunter Biden because his father is a 2020 presidential candidate. The left assumes there would be no other reason to raise the investigation except for its value to a political campaign. But one obvious reason was to ensure there was no corruption.

If evidence existed showing President Trump's request was solely campaign-dependent, Attorney General Barr might have taken further action. If evidence existed proving President Trump intended to withhold aid and access to the White House unless Ukraine investigated the Bidens, Attorney General Barr might have taken further action. But under the presumption of innocence, law enforcement officials are not supposed to ascribe motives to people's behavior without evidence for those motives.

As Americans, we're entitled to believe whatever we want, no matter where the facts lead, as long as our actions don't impinge on the rights of others. American officers of the law, however, are empowered by the people to enforce the laws, potentially curtailing citizens' rights. Therefore, they are required to go only where the facts of a case lead them, consistent with the law. Until facts indicate otherwise, an officer of the law is required to treat a person, including Donald Trump, as innocent until proven guilty beyond a reasonable doubt.

Now that I am not employed by the Department of Justice, I am free to state that while I appreciate Inspector General Horowitz's statement that he found no testimonial or documentary evidence of bias, I *believe* on my reading of the evidence that anti-Trump bias *was* the reason the Russian collusion investigation was opened into the Trump campaign. Attorney General Barr and U.S. Attorney John Durham have suggested they have evidence that this may be the case, and I am confident that they will follow the facts and the law, as they should to determine if that is true.

When it comes to the Democrats and their assertion that President Trump's phone call with President Zelensky of Ukraine amounted to an impeachable offense, they had no actual evidence to back up their articles of impeachment. There is no evidence that he committed any crime, and his actions were certainly no more politically minded than the actions of Vice President Joe Biden in demanding the firing of a Ukrainian prosecutor who might have pursued an investigation into his son or the actions of three Democratic Senators who pressured Ukraine to help with the Mueller investigation into the Trump campaign.[24] (See Appendix C for their letter to the General Prosecutor of Ukraine.) The Democrats' hypocrisy and double standards are truly astounding—and infuriating.

■ ■ ■

Mar-a-Lago Club and Resort | Palm Beach, Florida
Via teleconference
November 22, 2018

MEMBER OF THE PRESS: Are you worried about Matt Whitaker's finances and his potential (inaudible)?

PRESIDENT TRUMP: No. Matt Whitaker is a highly respected person. And, you know, once I choose somebody, they always go through hell.

I had been Acting Attorney General for fifteen days at the time of that Thanksgiving Day press conference, and I had been presumed guilty—of bias against the Mueller investigation, of being a constitutional "nobody" (since acting cabinet heads don't require Senate confirmation under the 1998 Federal Vacancies Reform Act), and because I had provided very little legal advice to a company that no longer existed and that later had fallen afoul of the law (for reasons completely unrelated to my advice).[25]

Very quickly, I learned that if you are a political appointee in President Trump's administration, the media and congressional Democrats, among others, immediately presume you must be guilty of something and will stop at nothing to tear you down. If you are a "career official," on the other hand, with no evidence of support for the President, then you are regarded as someone free of malice, a modestly paid civil servant toiling with only the nation's best intentions at heart. In the press, "career official" is practically a synonym for "innocent," even, or especially, if that career official is revealed to be part of the "Resistance."

Leaking to the press was, unfortunately, endemic among the more politically minded officials of the Justice Department. I was far from the only victim. In fact, even anti-Trumpers could be the victims when other officials were trying to protect their own backs. For instance, FBI lawyer Lisa Page publicly complained about "my Justice Department betraying us" when her texts unrelated to the Inspector General's investigation were leaked by the Justice Department to the press.[26]

She described the machinations to The Daily Beast:

> A week or two later, Rod Rosenstein [then the deputy attorney general] was scheduled to testify on the Hill. And the night before his testimony, the Justice Department spokesperson, Sarah Flores, calls the beat reporters into the Justice Department. This is late at night on a weekday. Calls them in to provide a cherry-picked selection of my text messages to

review and report on in advance of Rod Rosenstein going to
the Hill the next morning.[27]

The day after Lisa Page's interview ran, Rod Rosenstein contacted The
Daily Beast. He responded that career officials (read: well-intentioned,
completely innocent public servants) were responsible: "To the best of my
knowledge, career Department of Justice officials determined in December
2017 that those text messages were NOT personal," he wrote. "They were
official government records related to FBI business, and there was no legal
basis to withhold them, so they should be released as requested by
Congress."[28]

In my own case, unidentified sources were more than happy to leak
to the media and congressional Democrats that I had to be guilty of
something as I stepped into the Acting Attorney General role on November 7, 2018. On October 11, 2018, President Trump had told Fox News
that "I can tell you, Matt Whitaker's a great guy. I mean, I know Matt
Whitaker." But only two days after I was appointed, the half-truth
smears continued, and the media relentlessly pressed the President. "I
don't know Matt Whitaker," the President said. "He has a great reputation, and that's what I wanted."[29]

It was true that I wasn't a long-time member of his inner circle, and
that was what he was trying to convey. I had only met him after I joined
the administration. Since I had become chief of staff, I had worked closely
with him and others throughout the White House, and I knew I had
made a good impression on him, and that people he respected had spoken
well of me. Shortly after he made those comments, we had a conversation
where he expressed his respect for my work and confidence that I could
do the job well.

I should also mention that as days passed and more information
came out, the President appeared to feel more confident in defending me.
In fact, he defended me in his November 22 press conference, two weeks
after my appointment, and on every other occasion when he was questioned about me.

Still, I knew that under these specific circumstances it would be difficult to survive in this environment long term. Whatever case I'd make against any vulnerabilities associated with me would fall on deaf ears because Democrats and bureaucratic elites simply weren't going to accept me: I was too much an outsider and had been tarred as having been allegedly appointed only because I had, as a private citizen, opposed Special Counsel Robert Mueller's investigation.

Two weeks after President Trump's Thanksgiving Day press conference, he nominated William Barr as his permanent Attorney General. I could feel the tide turning that day as the smears grew quieter. I was no longer their target. General Barr was the right man for the hour. I was not naïve about the media and about congressional and bureaucratic politics in Washington. I was well aware of partisan politics and the ideological bias of the press, but I had no idea the extent to which they would go to damage this President, me, and anyone who supported him or was willing to serve in his administration. I still thought there were some fundamental rules of fairness that almost everyone in positions of power and responsibility followed. I freely confess now: I was wrong.

CHAPTER THREE

COASTAL ELITISM

"**W**ho are you? Where did you come from? And how the heck did you become the head of the Department of Justice? Hopefully you can help me work through this confusion!"

I leaned in to the microphone to respond, but Hakeem Jeffries—the congressman from gentrified Brooklyn and nephew of the infamous Professor Leonard Jeffries, whom the City University of New York fired for anti-Semitic and anti-white tirades in the 1990s—cut me off: "Mr. Whitaker, that was a statement, not a question. I assume you know the difference."[1]

It was like badly scripted reality television, as the website Mediaite described it: "rhetorical questions presumably meant to troll" and throw me "off guard" as I testified before the House Judiciary Committee oversight hearing as the Acting Attorney General.[2]

Jeffries was dog whistling for his intended audience, the coastal elites, defined by the *Cambridge Dictionary* as "the group of educated, professional people living mainly in cities on the western or northeastern coasts of the U.S. who have liberal political views and are often considered to have advantages that most ordinary Americans do not have."[3]

Hillary Clinton was the candidate of the coastal elites in the 2016 presidential election, and she and they were stunned to learn that so many Americans did not share their priorities.

The morning after the election, *Time* explained "How Donald Trump Shocked the World":

> [... W]orking-class whites—who for decades have been slowly but surely drifting away from a coastal Democratic Party elite they view as economically and culturally out of touch with their needs—found his populist, protectionist rhetoric spoke directly to them.
>
> Vast areas of the country that had previously voted for Obama, from northeast Pennsylvania to eastern Ohio, from rural Iowa to Wisconsin and Michigan, swung solidly into Donald Trump's column.[4]

The coastal elites' shock that Donald Trump had won because the "deplorables"—"working class whites"—had turned the Electoral College to Trump shifted quickly to suspicion that the Russians had helped him gain his otherwise inexplicable victory. Similarly, the "confusion" Congressman Jeffries claimed to experience about how I became the head of the Justice Department was really nothing more than naked suspicion: I must be a simple country lawyer, unqualified for such a lofty station. (A former football player, standing 6'4" tall, with a shaved head, I was frequently mistaken in Washington for part of Attorney General Sessions' security detail rather than his chief of staff.)

I don't look like one of the coastal elites, and I don't act like one of them because I'm not one of them. I didn't go to the same schools they went to, and I don't spend my time worrying about reputation and status. All I want is to be authentic. I am proud of being from the Midwest, and I worked hard to earn both a law degree and an MBA while playing college football. At thirty-four, I was one of the youngest U.S. Attorneys in the Bush administration. Jeffries and his colleagues knew full well that

I was a Senate-confirmed U.S. Attorney in the Bush administration and that I had just been Attorney General Jeff Session's chief of staff for the past year, which legally made me a vetted and valid Acting Attorney General under the Federal Vacancies Reform Act. Five years of experience as a U.S. Attorney and my recent management of the day-to-day operations of the Justice Department as chief of staff meant that I was both capable and qualified to manage the Department.

Naturally however, congressional Democrats were angry; they had been demanding that Rod Rosenstein replace Jeff Sessions as Attorney General for reasons that were obvious to anyone paying attention. Rosenstein had reportedly talked about wearing a wire and secretly recording presidential conversations, he had allowed Andrew McCabe to make President Trump an investigative target, and then he appointed a Special Counsel to investigate the Trump campaign. Moreover, he was reportedly angry at President Trump for revealing that he had written a memo criticizing James Comey. It was that memo Trump cited as a reason for firing Comey as FBI Director. Democrats regarded him as Special Counsel Robert Mueller's shield against President Trump. "How Much Longer Can Rod Rosenstein Protect Robert Mueller?" fretted Jeffrey Toobin in the *New Yorker*, voicing the fears of many Democrats.[5] The Democrats were hostile to me from the beginning.

Rod Rosenstein checks all the coastal elites' boxes: an urban Northeasterner, he went to the University of Pennsylvania and Harvard Law School. He interned for Robert Mueller when Mueller was the U.S. Attorney for Massachusetts. He was appointed to Justice Department positions by Presidents Clinton, Bush, Obama, and Trump and thrived under both Republican and Democratic administrations for twenty-nine years at the Justice Department. While he was able to maneuver the inevitable inconsistency of his positions—for and against Jim Comey, for and against President Trump, and so on—I can understand his reluctance to testify to Congress on the Russia investigation.

Rod graciously told the press I was a "superb" choice for Acting Attorney General.[6] When the Justice Department expanded the definition of banned weapons to include bump stocks, Rosenstein suggested to me privately in a small senior meeting that having my signature on the regulation could prove a problem. I considered his argument but decided to sign it as the Acting Attorney General. Somehow that private deliberation among a small group of department officials wound up in the *Washington Post*: "Senior Justice Dept. Officials Told Whitaker Signing Gun Regulation Might Prompt Successful Challenge to His Appointment."[7] I don't know who the confidential source for the *Post's* story was, but it's a prime example of the toxic leaking that tarnished the Department. We were all on the same team, working towards the same goal for the American people—banning bump stocks. Why leak that? Whom did that benefit? Not the Department and its best interests, which should have been our only goal.

The media sometimes recognized that Rosenstein was on both sides of an issue. "Former Top FBI Lawyer Says Rosenstein Was Serious about Taping Trump," announced the *New York Times* three weeks after Rosenstein had indignantly dismissed the allegations with unnamed sources telling the press that Rosenstein was only being "facetious" and "sarcastic" when he talked about recording the President.[8] I still have no idea what was in Rod's head when he talked about taping the President.

Rod was clearly suffering reputational damage by the time he exited the Justice Department. After he left the Justice Department in April 2019, Rosenstein addressed a Yale Club audience in New York City and compared himself to John Adams, who drew public criticism for defending the British soldiers in the Boston Massacre. "Adams endured harsh criticism in the court of public opinion," Mr. Rosenstein said. "But in the court of law, he secured the acquittal of the British captain and six soldiers."[9]

James Comey is another member of the coastal elite: another urban Northeasterner, he attended the College of William & Mary and the University of Chicago Law School. President George W. Bush appointed him as U.S. Attorney for the Southern District of New York and Deputy

Attorney General, and President Obama appointed him as the Director of the FBI. He was so offended by Hillary Clinton's keeping classified State Department documents on her home server that he had to tell the media how he felt about it, while also letting her off the hook by not recommending that she be prosecuted. But when the Justice Department's Inspector General called him out for the same behavior—keeping classified government documents in his home—he gloated on Twitter that he hadn't been charged with a crime. He also felt he was exonerated of charges that he'd leaked classified documents to the media. Was it so much purer that he asked Columbia law professor Daniel Richman, a fellow member of the coastal elite, to leak the documents for him, admittedly hoping to trigger a Special Counsel? Taking advantage of years of experience as a Washington insider to manipulate the system to one's own advantage was behavior that I found truly appalling.

I became a U.S. Attorney in 2004 and remember well Comey's stirring farewell speech in the Great Hall of the Justice Department as he retired as Deputy Attorney General. It's worth quoting extensively because of its tragic irony:

> I expect that you will appreciate and protect an amazing gift you have received as an employee of the Department of Justice. It is a gift you may not notice until the first time you stand up and identify yourself as an employee of the Department of Justice and say something—whether in a courtroom, a conference room, or a cocktail party—and find that total strangers believe what you say next. That gift—the gift that makes possible so much of the good we accomplish—is a reservoir of trust and credibility, a reservoir built for us, and filled for us, by those who went before—most of whom we never knew....
>
> The problem with reservoirs is that it takes tremendous time and effort to fill them, but one hole in a dam can drain them. The protection of that reservoir requires vigilance, an

unerring commitment to truth, and a recognition that the
actions of one may affect the priceless gift that benefits all.[10]

Comey, who was fired six months before I arrived in Washington
and could have no basis on which to judge my intellect, told a radio host
who asked him about my appointment as Acting Attorney General in
November 2018 that I "may not be the sharpest knife in our drawer."[11]
I agree with him that all that have served at DOJ filled (or in some cases
drained) the reservoir of trust. Attacking my intellect, a subject he knows
nothing about, does nothing to fix the hole that he helped create.

I wonder how Robert Mueller feels about being likened to Comey now,
as he was in this 2013 assessment by the magazine, *Washingtonian*:

> The two men are deeply alike, sharing a background and core
> principles. Both educated at Virginia universities with a strong
> public service tradition (Mueller at the University of Virginia;
> Comey at William & Mary). They both achieved early success
> in the Justice Department and found subsequent life at private
> law firms lucrative but unfulfilling. Just years apart in the
> 1990s, they both gave up their top-tier private law firm jobs to
> return to the trenches of prosecuting criminals—Mueller as a
> junior prosecutor in Washington, D.C., and Comey in Rich-
> mond, Virginia. Both men were rising stars mentored and
> guided by Eric Holder in the 1990s during Holder's time in the
> Justice Department under the Clinton administration.[12]

"Mentored and guided by Eric Holder," for the record.

Here's what I noticed during my time in Washington: The first thing
coastal elites want to know about you is where you went to school; the
second is what you do for a living. They perk up if your answer includes
an Ivy League school or a handful of others, like Stanford, Chicago,
Duke, Georgetown, William & Mary, or the University of Virginia. And

if you work for a big law firm or are the general counsel of a well-known company, you're a somebody.

Don't get me wrong: I have nothing against big law firms and earning a "lucrative" salary, and I respect the intelligence and hard work required to be admitted to these top-ranking schools. It's fair to assume that graduates of these institutions in high profile positions in Boston, New York, Washington, D.C., San Francisco, and Los Angeles are extremely smart. It's not fair to assume the opposite. But it is also true that there is talent everywhere across America. Some high-ranking Justice Department officials in Washington and their coastal elite kin in the national media are, however, too snobbish or too insulated in their big city bubbles to concede this. In my opinion, those that serve in our government should be representative of the best and the brightest from across America, not just the coasts.

August 26, 2016:

STRZOK: Just went to a southern Virginia Walmart. I could SMELL the Trump support...

PAGE: Yep. Out to lunch with (redacted) We both hate everyone and everything.

PAGE: Just riffing on the hot mess that is our country.

STRZOK: Yeah...it's scary real down here....[13]

■ ■ ■

In September 2016, Hillary Clinton addressed a fundraiser full of coastal elites in New York City:

> "You know, to just be grossly generalistic, you could put half of Trump's supporters into what I call the basket of deplorables. Right?" Clinton said. "The racist, sexist, homophobic,

xenophobic, Islamaphobic—you name it. And unfortunately there are people like that. And he has lifted them up."[14]

Those of us who went to a state college or an agricultural school or practice a trade or started our own small business and live out in fly-over country or in the affordable cities and towns across America are nobodies to the coastal elite. Who are we? "Ignorant hillbillys" [sic], as Peter Strzok referred to residents of Virginia's Loudon Country who had voted for a Republican candidate for State Senator over then–FBI Deputy Director Andrew McCabe's wife, who ran as a Democrat.[15]

It was similar "ignorant hillbillies" who elected President Trump, and the coastal elites have felt the need ever since to intervene and invalidate that choice. They know better than the electorate, or so they tell themselves. They would protect the Constitution by undoing it. They see nothing wrong with trying to undo the results of the 2016 election, by whatever means necessary.

■ ■ ■

About 500,000 new businesses are created each year in America, and my father's business, an advertising agency, was once one of them. Like many new small businesses, his didn't last; I was eleven or twelve years old when I helped him move the furniture out of his rented office space. I learned early that without risk taking, there is no reward, and that to be an American entrepreneur you need to accept that sometimes your attempts will fail. My father went to work at a local company that sold scoreboards, and my mother taught school. We spent my whole childhood outside Des Moines, in Ankeny, a small city with a coal mining history and a John Deere plant that manufactures crop equipment.

My mom and dad are originally from Keokuk, Iowa's southernmost city, located near a Mississippi riverbed famous for the geodes it produces. They attended Southwest Community College together. He then went to Drake University in Des Moines to play baseball, and she went to Northeastern Missouri State (now called Truman State). Though both my parents were college graduates, they never put any pressure on me to be academically successful, and there was no obsessing over which schools I might get into or which career path I might take. More important was being involved in the community with family and friends.

Interestingly, Professor Kate Rousmaniere of Miami of Ohio University writes that Midwestern "education has been marked by an emphasis on building community—whether that be a collection of farm families, the residents of a newly formed village, or a mixed group of immigrants to cities. Central to the Midwestern vision of education has been the importance of civic education, work values, and community responsibility."[16]

That describes my experience growing up pretty well: a belief that the collective is stronger than the individual, and a desire all to row in the same direction. Community was important, and sports defined community. My dad played baseball in college; I started playing baseball when I was six. I played basketball and ran track, too, and then went to Coach Barry Switzer's football camp at the University of Oklahoma before high school started. At the time, Ankeny had a 4A high school, the biggest division in the state, and I have been told that I was the first sophomore to play the whole season on its varsity team. At the end of high school, I was as surprised as everyone else when the principal read the names of the kids whose GPAs represented the top tenth of the class, and mine was one of them.

During my senior year of high school, the University of Iowa's head coach Hayden Fry and his offensive coordinator Bill Snyder recruited me as a tight end for the Hawkeyes—full tuition, room, and board. In those days, scholarships could be offered on December 1 of your senior year of high school. I had a basketball game that day, so Snyder and Fry scheduled their visit for December 2. I remember their coming to my parents' house in Ankeny and offering me that scholarship. The next weekend was my official recruiting visit to the University of Iowa. It was a remarkable and exciting weekend for an eighteen-year-old kid. My player hosts were Marv Cook and Chuck Hartlieb who had just connected for the winning touchdown against Ohio State, a memorable play for all Hawkeye fans. (The following year, Coach Snyder left for Kansas State; both Fry and Snyder would later be inducted into the College Football Hall of Fame.) As soon as I arrived at Iowa, I saw that all my teammates were great players, and as this new level of competition proved, I wasn't going to be able to distinguish myself enough to pursue a professional football career. But the fact that I wasn't going to ascend to the NFL didn't stop me from playing my heart out for the team. (I brought that same attitude to my work inside the Justice Department; I worked as hard as I could, even though I knew early on I wouldn't be the permanent Attorney General.) Under the tutelage of the great Coach Hayden Fry, I learned to play smart against opposing teams. I did that most memorably when I caught a pass on a fake field goal in a 1990 game that sent us to the 1991 Rose Bowl. Coach Fry was known for his occasional trick play that would help even the playing field for our sometimes physically outmatched Iowa team. "He's been known for surprises throughout his career," an announcer noted of Coach Fry.[17]

Playing in the Rose Bowl in 1991 was a fantastic experience. Two weeks in Southern California being treated like royalty has an impact on a young man. But what may have taught me the most happened right before kick-off. Coach Fry had a friend named D. Wayne Lucas, a famous racehorse trainer. He invited Mr. Lucas to speak to the team in the locker room before the game. Mr. Lucas took the opportunity to give a great speech about success, which under any other circumstances I would have paid money to hear. By the time he got around to the third of his four keys to success, the referees and network television producers had grown impatient for the Iowa football team to take the field. Five minutes later, the situation was desperate, and a referee forced us to leave the locker room, much to the dismay of Mr. Lucas. I don't remember everything D. Wayne Lucas talked about that day, but I did learn a valuable lesson: know your audience, and know when to conclude before you get the hook.

Figuring out big systems is one of my strengths, whether that big system is a federal government department or a Big Ten school. Football players had to keep every afternoon open for practice, so we were allowed to choose our classes before the general student body. Plenty of students take five years to finish college if they play football (some even if they don't), but I determined I'd make the most of my scholarship: I arranged my classes so that within five years, I'd earned my bachelor's and was working on a law degree and an MBA—while playing football and keeping my GPA above 3.0.

I won three academic All-Big Ten awards, and the 1993 University of Iowa football media guide and the *Des Moines Register* listed me as a "GTE District VII academic All-American." I had used the loose term "academic All-American" on my resume based solely on that, until someone doing opposition research on me a quarter century later told the *Wall Street Journal* that I'd never officially been crowned "academic All-American" by the College Sports Information Directors of America in the early 1990s. "[I]f there is confusion at all, part of it could be how we listed it in our media guide," Iowa's Assistant Athletic Director Steve Roe told the *Journal*.

Barb Kowal of the College Sports Information Directors of America explained to the *Journal*: "the correct term for Mr. Whitaker's honor is '1992 GTE District VII Academic All-District selection.' She said CoSIDA was less formally organized in the 1990s and 'we know that people over time use terms interchangeably and innocently.'" This non-story was just another attempt to discredit me and my rise up the political depth chart.[18]

It was the complimentary subscription to the *Wall Street Journal* I received as an MBA student that flipped on my political lights. Its op-eds made me think; its editorials resonated as articulate common sense to me. (Prior to discovering the *Journal*, I had never thought much about my political philosophy although I had been a Republican for as long as I could remember. I attended the Iowa caucuses in 1988 in support of George H. W. Bush, getting elected to the Polk County Republican convention as a delegate and receiving extra credit in my government class. But as an eighteen-year-old, I wasn't serious about considering opportunities in politics.) The ideas I started soaking up as an MBA student made me want to study law, and I was able to play for the Hawkeyes through my first year at Iowa's law school. Anything's possible if you do the work and say yes when opportunities arise.

After graduating and practicing law in Minneapolis for several years, I returned to Iowa. I invested in several small businesses and practiced law in the Des Moines area. I've proudly served thousands of clients over the years, earning a lot from some and a few hundred from others. The worst $10,000 I ever earned was for my service on the "advisory board" of a Miami-based company that the Federal Trade Commission would shut down in 2017 for defrauding customers by promising to market their inventions. I was not the only honest professional convinced to associate with this outfit: other members of its unofficial "advisory board," which never met, included a professor emeritus of physics at the University of Connecticut, an infectious disease doctor at Florida International University, a surgeon specializing in robotics, a retired Army Lieutenant General who was the head of counterterrorism at the U.S. State Department from 2007 to 2009, and a future member of Congress.

Together we comprised a board of advisors, not a board of directors with fiduciary responsibilities. I gave all my clients sound legal advice, but I didn't—and couldn't—make decisions for them as an outside counsel for hire. I had no knowledge of any fraud, and the court-appointed receiver liquidating the company confirmed that there was no evidence that I had any knowledge of the fraud committed by the company. I wish I had never agreed to represent this client, and I feel awful for everyone who was hurt by them (as I, in my own way, was).

Between my service at the Department of Justice, I was self-employed leading my own law firm and serving many different clients. As entrepreneurs or managers of small businesses, well-intentioned Americans take risks working with all kinds of clients and institutions. You take clients as they come, and you do your best for whomever pays you for your services. I worry that many intelligent, practical, civic-minded Americans are dissuaded from public service, either as elected or appointed officials, because of innocent mistakes they have made in the past and the abuse they see heaped on people whose lives haven't been perfectly curated.

Would Hakeem Jeffries have opened with "Who are you? Where did you come from? And how the heck?" if I, like him, had been from a notable family, held degrees from Georgetown and New York University, and worked for a white-shoe international law firm?

■ ■ ■

While preparing to write this book, I asked Greg Scott what he found different about the culture at the Justice Department in California's Eastern District, where he remains the U.S. Attorney, compared to the culture inside its Washington, D.C., headquarters, where he worked five days a week for three months. "In this office," he said, referring to his staff in Sacramento, Fresno, Yosemite, Bakersfield, and Redding, "it's all 'we' and 'us.'" I, too, felt that way about the U.S. Attorney's office in the Southern District of Iowa. My impression of Washington is that it's "all about me." There's no institutional loyalty, and it's catastrophic. I was appalled by how cozy Justice Department colleagues were with the media in Washington. They seemed to crave relationships with members of the press. Leaking is socialization in Washington; there's no such thing as a private conversation. It's very hard to trust that people are being honest and straightforward. Often someone would tell me something that I didn't need to know hoping that I would leak it (to their benefit). That's not how I operated, but they became so accustomed to these games that they assumed everyone played them.

The leaking culture was systemic; there were twenty-seven ongoing leak investigations while I was at the Justice Department, and it's now public record that the then–Acting Director of the FBI, Andrew McCabe, was one of the culprits. Worried about his professional reputation when a *Wall Street Journal* report detailed his wife's political ties to Hillary Clinton and his refusal to recuse himself from the investigation into her missing emails, McCabe authorized Lisa Page to feed a counternarrative to the *Journal* in which he stood up to the Obama Justice Department's efforts to squash the probe into the Clinton Foundation's alleged influence peddling:

> According to a person familiar with the probes...a senior Justice Department official called Mr. McCabe to voice his displeasure at finding that New York FBI agents were still openly pursuing the Clinton Foundation probe during the election season.... "Are you telling me that I need to shut down a validly predicated investigation?" Mr. McCabe asked, according to people familiar with the conversation. After a pause, the official replied, "Of course not," these people said....[19]

Not only was it illegal, unethical, and unhelpful to the Department for McCabe and Page to leak details of an investigation, the truth value of the leak was dubious. The *Journal's* Devlin Barrett pointed out:

> Others further down the FBI chain of command, however, said agents were given a much starker instruction on the case: "Stand down." When agents questioned why they weren't allowed to take more aggressive steps, they said they were told the order had come from the deputy director—Mr. McCabe.[20]

After leaking to the *Wall Street Journal* through Lisa Page, the 2018 Justice Department Inspector General's report revealed that McCabe called the New York field office several times and acted "angry" regarding "leaks and the *WSJ* article," warning there "will be consequence[s] and get to bottom of it post elect[ion]. Need leaks to stop. Damaging to org."[21] McCabe even lied to investigators several times, denying he authorized the leaking of details on the Clinton Foundation investigation.

McCabe admitted his charade to an internal FBI investigator on August 18, 2017, as The Daily Beast found in transcripts released in 2020:

> "I remember saying to him, at, I said, sir, you understand that we've put a lot of work into this based on what you told us," the agent said. "I mean, and I even said, long nights and weekends working on this, trying to find out who amongst your ranks of trusted people would, would do something like that. And he kind of just looked down, kind of nodded, and said yeah I'm sorry."[22]

I was chief of staff to Attorney General Jeff Sessions when he made the decision to fire McCabe for lying under oath. The decision was rich with irony, because McCabe was the one who had initiated the investigation into Sessions for allegedly lying under oath to Congress (about having had no discussions with Russians during the campaign). McCabe was also the one who was involved with President Trump's first National Security Advisor, General Michael Flynn, getting him to plead guilty for making false statements under oath (about speaking with Russian Ambassador Sergey Kislyak after Trump was elected but before he was inaugurated). McCabe was apparently so desperate to polish his reputation in the media that he thought it was worth breaking the law to do so.[23] It made me wonder how much time was wasted at the Department of Justice spinning national news media or trying to set traps for President Trump and his allies instead of doing the nation's work in supporting law enforcement and serving the American people.

The first time Greg Scott's name was mentioned in the press in connection with the Special Counsel investigation was February 8, 2019, when I testified before the House Judiciary Committee that he had been present at a briefing by Mueller's team. Greg had been spending many work weeks with me in Washington since November 11, but not a single person in the three California offices he oversees as U.S. Attorney thought to whisper it to the *Sacramento Bee* or any other media. What the boss was doing at headquarters in Washington, D.C., would have been a huge scoop for some enterprising Assistant U.S. Attorney to offer a California reporter, perhaps with the hope that some future prosecution might receive favorable play. But it never happened. No one leaked, including Greg himself. It's just not the jungle Washington is; neither was the U.S. Attorney's office in Iowa's Southern District where I tried to inculcate an appreciation for teamwork, working together to accomplish the mission.

"As part of the orientation I do for young lawyers who join this office, I ask them to raise their hands if they've ever been part of something bigger than themselves. Because that's what working for the Department of Justice is. The ones who raise their hands usually tell me they served in the military or played team sports," Greg says.

Greg's impressions of Washington remind him of the story in David Halberstam's book *The Best and the Brightest* about how Vice President Lyndon Johnson was dazzled by the intellects and resumes of President John F. Kennedy's newly appointed cabinet members, particularly by the bona fides of the new Defense Secretary Robert McNamara. Johnson gushed about them to Sam Rayburn, the House Speaker at the time. Rayburn, a Texan, replied, "Well, Lyndon, you may be right, and they may be every bit as intelligent as you say, but I'd feel a whole lot better about them if just one of them had run for sheriff once." Note that Greg was an elected county attorney, and I have run for public office twice.

Halberstam comments on the media's unquestioning adoration of the "glamourous" Kennedy administration: "Credit was given more readily for educational prowess and academic achievement than for accomplishment in governance."[24]

I sometimes felt the same way; the culture in Washington seemed to be one-part resume enhancement and self-promotion, to one-part maneuvering through leaks and smears, with less attention than there should have been on actually getting the people's business done.

Less than one month after becoming Acting Attorney General, I had the honor of attending the state funeral of President George Herbert Walker Bush at Washington's National Cathedral. Thirty years had passed since I had been a delegate for him in the Iowa caucuses. Here I sat surrounded by former Presidents, Supreme Court Justices, congressional leaders, and cabinet Secretaries, representing the Department of Justice in Washington's National Cathedral. Supreme Court Justice Brett Kavanaugh was among the attendees, and I couldn't help but think of the vile character assassination he and his family had endured just two months earlier during his confirmation hearings. Even though I wasn't a candidate for Senate confirmation, I was still weathering relentless smears myself.

Former Vice President Dick Cheney noticed me there, shot me his trademark smirk, and cracked, "Having fun yet?"

CHAPTER FOUR

THE SOVEREIGN DISTRICT OF NEW YORK

Exactly one month after I began serving as the Acting Attorney General, Justice Department employees in my chain of command unexpectedly and without notification or briefing accused President Trump of committing a crime. I was frustrated but not shocked by what they did. This break in protocol came from a U.S. Attorney's office a three-hour train ride away in Lower Manhattan: the Southern District of New York, long referred to as the "Sovereign" District of New York.

Without giving any of its executive branch superiors a heads-up, consistent with DOJ practice, the office essentially accused President Trump of committing a campaign finance crime in a publicly filed court briefing, a salacious accusation perfectly timed for maximum media coverage between Thanksgiving and Christmas 2018 as the Special Counsel's investigation was nearing its twentieth month of fruitlessness. Everyone familiar with Justice Department norms recognized the Southern District of New York's surprise as the dangerous sucker punch it was.

There is a time-honored process inside the Justice Department whereby U.S. Attorneys' offices around the country issue internal "Urgent Reports" to let their superiors in Washington know about important upcoming cases or case developments. (These reports are issued ad hoc by U.S. Attorneys' offices.) One would expect that if federal prosecutors were going to take the extraordinary step of suggesting that the President of the United States was a party to a crime, an "Urgent Report" to the Department of Justice in Washington, D.C., would be appropriate, or a phone call at the very least. Notoriously unaccountable to the executive branch Department empowering it, the Sovereign District was unwilling to consult with superiors.

In the December 7, 2018, sentencing memorandum filed in federal court, the Southern District of New York's Attorneys suggested that their boss, the President, was an unindicted co-conspirator with Michael Cohen, his former personal attorney who had pleaded guilty in court ten days earlier to charges of tax evasion, making false statements to financial institutions, and, as the Southern District of New York coyly revealed on its website, "to making unlawful, excessive contributions to the 2016 presidential campaign in the form of payments to two women to secure their silence regarding the then-presidential candidate in order to prevent those stories from influencing the election."[1]

I was incredulous. To show President Trump was guilty of a campaign finance violation, Southern District of New York prosecutors would have to prove a double negative: that had he not been a candidate for federal office, he wouldn't have paid the two women in question. In my view, the Southern District of New York was generating a legally specious charge to torment the President with worry that he could be indicted and to erode political support for him. Prosecutors don't reference someone in a sentencing memorandum if they don't intend to go after him.

Former Southern District of New York prosecutor-turned–*National Review* columnist Andrew McCarthy confirmed this prosecutorial norm and read this sentencing agreement as a telltale sign that the President would be charged with a crime when he left office. McCarthy noted that "when Cohen pleaded guilty in August, prosecutors induced him to make an extraordinary statement in open court: the payments to the women were made 'in coordination with and at the direction of' the candidate for federal office—Donald Trump. Prosecutors would not have done this if the President was not on their radar screen."[2]

This toxic narrative—that the Southern District of New York was ready to indict the President and would be investigating his family members and businesses—circulated in the media the entire winter. But not only were there no official charges to answer, there was no evidence for the President's personal lawyers to examine—because from February until July 2019, the Southern District of New York fought the public's First Amendment and common law rights to read the warrants used to search Michael Cohen's business and hotel. Finally, on July 17, U.S. District Court Judge William Pauley ordered the Southern District of New York to file a status report and release the requested documents on the public docket by the next day. The result of that court order: the whole world learned that the Southern District of New York had closed the case, and no charges against the President or anyone else would be forthcoming. What an extraordinary smear tactic—and what an extraordinary abuse of power: misusing the authority of the Justice Department in an attempt to cause political damage to the President of the United States.

■ ■ ■

A writer for the *New Yorker* penned this humorous description of the Attorneys for the Southern District of New York:

> If you're not a lawyer, and you meet a quiet, studious-seeming person and ask him what he does for a living, you may hear, "I'm an Assistant United States Attorney for the Southern District of New York." Sounds dull, like "I'm a tax preparer." But the answer is a little like the one you get when you ask someone where he went to college and he says, "Um, Yale?" What you were really meant to hear was: "I'm a member of

the Killer Elite, baby! I'm special ops. I'm strike force. Be very afraid!"[3]

But there is nothing humorous about the power entrusted to U.S. Attorneys, whose charges can result in serious jail time, as was the case for Cohen. As a great prosecutor once admitted, the power to investigate is the power to destroy. The ones who are heedless of the Justice Department's regular order are worse than frustrating—they're dangerous. They might start out as well-intentioned public servants, but many get hungry for media attention and fame. They take on cases—like those involving terrorism and fraud—that capture the attention of the press and turn these lawyers into media-darling crusaders. Prosecuting a major target can put one on the path to fame and political fortune. Indicting the President of the United States, even after he leaves office, would earn some ambitious prosecutor eternal stardom. A headline in the *New York Times* called the Southern District of New York "A Steppingstone for Law's Best and Brightest." The article went on to explain: "Most prosecutors are hired in their late twenties, drawn from elite law schools, firms, and clerkships. They spend at least several years in the office, gaining valuable trial experience."[4] Although the Southern District of New York has undeniable talent and an impressive alumni network, it is clubby at best, rogue at worst.

William Barr acknowledged that during his first appointment as Attorney General (from 1991 to 1993), then–U.S. Attorney for the Southern District of New York Otto Obermaier "wasn't that independent, but he basically ignored 50 percent of what I said." (He was contrasting Obermaier with his predecessor, Rudolph Giuliani, who had a reputation for ignoring Washington much more frequently.[5])

In the heat of post–September 11, 2001, terrorism prosecutions, Mary Jo White—the first and only female U.S. Attorney for the Southern District of New York, holding that position from June 1993 to January 2002—reportedly pushed back against efforts by the administration of President George W. Bush to move terrorist prosecution cases and the

FBI agents assigned to them to the Attorney General's office in Washington to improve coordination. "White gamely maintained, when I asked her about it, that this move 'was the right thing to do,' though she said that she had advised the administration to put the New York agents in Maryland or Virginia, so that they could avoid having to spend a lot of time in meetings," Nicholas Lemann reported in his profile of White.[6]

As Attorney General, Jeff Sessions tried to implement new guidelines for U.S. Attorneys across the country consulting with the Justice Department's National Security Division in Washington, D.C., to help coordinate terrorism investigations among multiple offices. But the Southern District of New York complained about having to report to a Deputy Assistant Attorney General who was based in Washington, and Sessions relented under pressure in 2017. The following year, Sessions was surprised by the Southern District of New York's plea deal with Michael Cohen: we learned about Cohen's guilty plea the same day the media did.

The U.S. Attorney at the Southern District of New York, as well as the ninety-two other U.S. Attorneys across the country, sets the tone for the Assistant U.S. Attorneys working under him or her. It's very important for a President to appoint someone strong enough to stand up for the rule of law and push back against the biases of some at the *Sovereign District of New York*. We referred to this as going native. When President Trump was elected, Preet Bharara, a former aide to Democratic senator Chuck Schumer of New York, was the U.S. Attorney at the Southern District of New York. Senator Schumer reportedly called Bharara after the November 2016 election and told him the new administration wanted him to remain U.S. Attorney.

President-elect Trump and Bharara spoke a few times by phone during the transition, but on March 9, Bharara refused to return the first official phone call he received from President Trump. The following day, President Trump fired him. "[H]ad I not been fired, and had Donald Trump continued to cultivate a direct personal relationship with me, it's my strong belief that at some point, given the history, the President of the United

States would have asked me to do something inappropriate," Bharara told his podcast listeners.[7] President Trump replaced Bharara with Geoffrey Berman, who then immediately recused himself from the Russia investigation (and the Michael Cohen probe) without explanation.

As the head of the executive branch, the President is entitled to U.S. Attorneys whom he selects. If necessary, they should resign rather than recuse themselves from the most pressing matters involving the administration and their office. I have faith in the way the Founding Fathers designed the three coequal branches of government. The President is in charge of the entire executive branch, and if Congress doesn't like the way the President supervises government employees under his charge, Congress can try to impeach and remove him. But in the meantime, I thought the President had every right to be unhappy with the Southern District of New York. If you were an executive (the President) and expected to deliver results to stakeholders (the voters), but instead found yourself contending with a serve-your-own-ends culture like the Southern District of New York's, wouldn't you be frustrated? I certainly was.

The *New York Times* reported, based on anonymous leaks from Justice Department employees, that "there is no evidence that [Whitaker] took any direct steps to intervene in the Manhattan investigation [of Michael Cohen]. He did, however, tell some associates at the Justice Department that the prosecutors in New York required 'adult supervision.'"[8]

The fact is, just as I took no steps—directly or indirectly—to end or alter the Special Counsel's investigation into alleged Russian collusion with the Trump campaign, I took no steps—directly or indirectly—to intervene in the Southern District of New York's case against Michael Cohen (and, by implication, the President). But wouldn't any reasonable leader suggest that "adult supervision" is warranted when President Trump's appointed U.S. Attorney recuses himself from the Russian collusion investigation, the Southern District of New York openly agitates against the President, and the Special Counsel investigating the Russia case (Robert Mueller) and the former FBI Director and opponent of the President (James Comey) are both Southern District of New York alumni? Comey in particular had

gone above the law to try to subvert a President he didn't like. In strategi-
cally releasing documents to trigger Mueller's investigation, Comey's
behavior set a "dangerous example," according to the Inspector General's
August 2019 report.[9] And to whom did he leak these documents? Daniel
Richman, Columbia University professor and (yet another) alumnus of the
Southern District of New York. Richman in turn leaked Comey's FBI
memos to the *New York Times*.

Here is Richman talking to the *New Yorker* in 2013, sanctimo-
niously defending the Southern District of New York's revolving door
career climbers, and, ironically, talking about "playing by the rules":

> Daniel Richman, a Southern District alumnus who teaches
> at Columbia Law School, told me, "When you hear about a
> former Assistant U.S. Attorney coming back to the office to
> talk about an investigation, one could say, 'It's the old-boy
> network.' But those who are closer to the situation see that
> it's a much more beneficent system. The company chose a
> former Assistant U.S. Attorney. That shows it's committed to
> playing by the rules. And that's rewarded."[10]

Incidentally, when Berman recused himself, leadership of the Southern
District of New York investigation into Michael Cohen first fell to Assistant U.S. Attorney Robert Khuzami, formerly President Obama's Chief of
Enforcement at the Securities and Exchange Commission. Unlike Berman,
Khuzami was a career official who couldn't be fired because of civil service
protections. Yet even as a "career" official, "Khuzami has spent his entire
career walking back and forth through the revolving door between government and Wall Street," one media profile reports.[11]

■ ■ ■

Two months after I became the Acting Attorney General, Democrats
took control of the House of Representatives. Exactly three months to

the day, I testified before Congress. By this point, William Barr had already been nominated as the next Attorney General, had cleared the Senate Judiciary Committee, and was on his way to a full Senate confirmation vote. I could have avoided the Judiciary Committee's requests to appear, and let the responsibility fall to Barr once he was confirmed. But if political theater had to happen, better it drew oxygen from the end of my tenure than the beginning of Barr's.

There was no doubt theater was what the Democrats wanted. Immediately after the 2018 midterm election, the Democrats came for me with torches burning. Without so much as a handshake introduction, incoming House Judiciary Chairman Jerry Nadler and incoming House Government Reform and Oversight Chairman Elijah Cummings (who passed away in late 2019) phoned my office together, put me on speaker, and started jamming me: *We want you to testify! First thing! Are you exerting executive privilege? We have the power to subpoena you!*

Time out. *Executive privilege? Subpoena?* I was ready and willing to appear before Congress because I believe in its authority to conduct oversight of the executive branch of government. That is an appropriate function of the legislative branch. I would appear voluntarily on Friday, February 8, 2019.

Regardless of my willingness, and unable to resist political showmanship, Nadler's committee voted on February 7 to authorize subpoena power over me even though subpoenas are a last resort used on witnesses who resist testifying. "This subpoena is nothing short of political theater," complained Doug Collins of Georgia, the House Judiciary Committee's highest-ranking Republican.[12] (Collins grew accustomed to Nadler's games. One of Nadler's tricks was putting time-sensitive DOJ email correspondence that Collins was cc'd on in the snail mail so Collins would receive the message days after the fact.)

The *New York Times's* unnamed sources also claimed I had told Justice Department colleagues that I felt my job was to "jump on a grenade" for the President. This subpoena authorization vote was one of those grenades. The specter of President Trump's Attorney General appearing before Jerry Nadler's committee in the same sentence as "subpoena" was a nonstarter for me.

"Such unprecedented action breaches our prior agreement and circumvents the constitutionally required accommodation process," I said in a prepared statement to the media. "Based upon today's action, it is apparent that the Committee's true intention is not to discuss the great work of the Department of Justice, but to create a public spectacle." I would be "forced to decline to participate in the hearing" the next day, a Justice Department official wrote to Nadler. "When we start subpoenaing witnesses who come in voluntarily, we're setting a dangerous precedent," said ranking member Doug Collins at the time.

Fortunately that evening, Nadler relented: "If you appear before the Committee tomorrow morning, and if you are prepared to respond to questions from our Members, then I assure you that there will be no need for the Committee to issue a subpoena on or before February 8...."[13]

This was still not enough assurance that Chairman Nadler wouldn't serve a subpoena to create a public spectacle while I sat in the chair testifying. Late that night, the Justice Department received written assurances that no subpoena would be served on the day of the hearing.

"The fact Chairman Nadler would try to force the public disclosure of private conversations that he knows are protected by law proves he only wants to play politics," White House Secretary Sarah Sanders said. "The Chairman should focus on helping the American people rather than wasting time playing pointless political games."

On February 8, I was the first Trump cabinet official to testify before the new Democrat-controlled House, and I testified unequivocally in my opening statement: "At no time has the White House asked for, nor have I provided, any promises or commitments concerning the Special Counsel's investigation or any other investigation." That included the Southern District of New York's investigation.

But House Democrats were determined to show that President Trump tried to obstruct justice (and this seems almost too ludicrous to type) by allegedly yelling at me.

This is the exchange between me and Rhode Island Democrat Jim Cicilline that raised Democrats' hopes I had perjured myself trying to hide the President's alleged attempts at obstruction:

CICILLINE: Sir, answer the question yes or no, did the President lash out to you about Mr. Cohen's guilty plea?
WHITAKER: No, he did not.
CICILLINE: And did anyone from the White House or anyone on the President's behalf lash out at you?
WHITAKER: No.
CICILLINE: Mr. Whitaker, did the President lash out to you on or about December 8, 2018, to discuss a case before the Southern District of New York where he was identified as Individual-1?
WHITAKER: No, Congressman.
CICILLINE: Did anyone on the President's behalf either out—inside the White House or outside the White House contact you to lash out or to express dissatisfaction?
WHITAKER: Did they contact me to lash out?
CICILLINE: Yes, did they reach out to you in some way to express dissatisfaction?
WHITAKER: No.

This interlude, among others, convinced me beyond doubt that the House is not a serious deliberative body in its current composition. The Democrats have been so excited to impeach President Trump for so long, no matter the facts, that they can barely string two sentences together. Even Aaron Blake of the *Washington Post* had to marvel: "Also complicating this is the jumbled exchange. Cicilline asks both about 'lashing out' and expressing dissatisfaction in one question, and Whitaker asks him to clarify that the question is about lashing out. Cicilline says 'yes,' but then invokes expressing dissatisfaction again in his question."[14]

Still, "Democrats say that Whitaker's responses to the committee may have been perjury. [Democratic Congressman] Hakeem Jeffries [of

New York], a Judiciary Committee member, told *Mother Jones*...that Whitaker had been an 'erratic and potentially untruthful witness.'"[15]

Five days after I testified, Nadler sent me a letter on House Judiciary Committee letterhead:

> Your testimony on this topic [the Southern District of New York investigation] is directly contradicted by several media reports. The President's personal attorney responded to those reports with an acknowledgment that "[t]he President and his lawyers are upset about the professional prosecutors in the Southern District of New York.... Moreover, the Committee has identified several individuals with direct knowledge of the phone calls you denied receiving from the White House. As a result, we require your clarification on this point without delay.[16]

Congress's duty to perform oversight of the executive branch is one I take very seriously as I believe the three branches of government are responsible for policing each other. I was struck that Congressman Nadler had spent five days constructing a three-page letter obsessing over whether President Trump had expressed an *emotion* to me about the Southern District of New York investigation—and that sadly, that letter included only two sentences about "several policy matters as well" pertaining to the Justice Department on which Nadler wanted clarification: "asylum seekers," "gay, lesbian, and transgender individuals," and "members of the Jewish community (and other religious minorities)." Nothing else.

William Barr was confirmed as the Attorney General the very next day, on February 14. I had served in the acting position, been threatened with perjury charges, and didn't know what was in store for my future. And I still didn't know whose (if anyone's) accusations I was defending myself against.

Nadler's letter to me referenced only one media report I had allegedly "contradicted": a CNN report based on anonymous sources. Who were these "several individuals with direct knowledge" of the phone calls I received from the White House? I would spend another three weeks at the Justice Department, but with no end to the leaking on the horizon.

On February 19, 2018, a *New York Times* "exposé" on page A1 merely rehashed the claims of the unnamed "individuals" who reached out to CNN: "Mr. Trump called Matthew G. Whitaker, his newly installed Attorney General, with a question. He asked whether Geoffrey S. Berman, the United States Attorney for the Southern District of New York and a Trump ally, could be put in charge of the widening investigation, *according to several American officials with direct knowledge of the call* [emphasis added]." Again, no names, no accountability, and no way for readers to assess the credibility or motives of the leakers.

Later in the story, the *Times* again quoted "people with knowledge of the discussions."[17]

I left the Department of Justice on March 4, 2019, and returned as a private citizen to answer Chairman Nadler's letter in a closed door session of the House Judiciary Committee a little over a week later. Chairman Nadler told the press that I "did not deny that the President called him to discuss Michael Cohen, the Michael Cohen case, and personnel decisions in the Southern District." Nadler didn't even ask me about the "several policy matters" he had mentioned in his letter the previous week. Again, more theater.

Republican staffers present during my testimony told the press I "did not remember" any conversations with Trump about Cohen, but "couldn't say with certainty one way or the other."[18]

What I can say with certainty is that no matter what the facts were, Chairman Nadler was never going to decide President Trump didn't need to be impeached. Nine days later, Attorney General Barr would receive the Special Counsel's report that had taken twenty-two months to compose and cost taxpayers nearly $32 million.[19] Nadler and his allies would shift their hopes for impeachment from the fruitless Southern District of New York investigation to the fruitless Mueller report.

CHAPTER FIVE

HOW THE SPECIAL COUNSEL UNDERMINES THE CONSTITUTION

Think about this for a moment: James Comey leaked memos of his Oval Office conversations with the President to an intermediary (his friend Daniel Richman) in the knowledge that the intermediary would leak the memos to the *New York Times*—a serious violation that put the former FBI Director in legal jeopardy—because he wanted a Special Counsel appointed to investigate the President and, we can reasonably assume, harry him out of office. Were criminal charges and jail time (which Comey avoided) and the unavoidable loss of credibility suffered by the FBI as a result of Comey's unprofessional behavior, all worth it to him if a Special Counsel were appointed who would ultimately deprive President Trump of due process? When asked by Senator Susan Collins during his Congressional testimony if he showed the memos to anyone outside the Justice Department, Comey admitted his violation and that triggering a Special Counsel was his goal:

> I asked—the President tweeted on Friday after I got fired that
> I better hope there's not tapes. I woke up in the middle of the
> night on Monday night because it didn't dawn on me

originally that there might be corroboration for our conversation. There might be a tape. My judgment was, I need to get
that out into the public square. I asked a friend of mine to
share the content of the memo with a reporter. Didn't do it
myself for a variety of reasons. I asked him to because I
thought that might prompt the appointment of a Special
Counsel. I asked a close friend to do it.[1]

Comey's desire to move an investigation into the "public square"
and "prompt the appointment of a Special Counsel" perfectly exemplifies
former Attorney General Griffin Bell's concern about due process in
Special Counsel investigations: the target is publicly identified, regardless
of whether prosecutors ever find evidence warranting criminal charges.
Comey's unique understanding of Washington's inside baseball enabled
him to wield this weapon.

In a regular Justice Department investigation, the target's identity
remains private unless charges are filed. Of course in President Trump's
case, no charges were filed because no evidence of criminality was discovered, but his name was dragged through the mud for two years by
the Special Counsel investigation. Being the target of a Special Counsel
investigation is a lose-lose proposition, which is why Comey wanted to
trigger one so badly. By leaking his memos about the President, Comey
was intent on forcing the hand of Rod Rosenstein, the only one with
statutory power to appoint a Special Counsel while Jeff Sessions was
recused from matters Russian. Reportedly by this point, Rosenstein was
unhappy that his memo recommending Comey's firing became public,
and he thought that he himself could be fired. Meanwhile McCabe put
the President's name into the soon-to-be Special Counsel investigation
without any apparent justification.

Rosenstein appointed Mueller days later.

"I was very concerned that I was able to put the Russia case on
absolutely solid ground in an indelible fashion, that were I removed
quickly and reassigned or fired that the case could not be closed or vanish

in the night without a trace," McCabe told CBS.[2] McCabe and Comey were united in their common desire to subject a boss they despised to an investigation without due process. Remember, the power to investigate is the power to destroy financially and politically.

Robert Mueller, Rosenstein's pick as Special Counsel, had a cleaner reputation. A highly decorated U.S. Marine Corps officer and Vietnam War veteran, Mueller's career as a U.S. Attorney, and FBI Director (from 2001 to 2013) was bipartisan and interspersed with private sector experience. When President Trump noted that Mueller had resigned his membership from the Trump National Golf Club in Sterling, Virginia, and had asked for a refund for a portion of his initiation fee in 2011, the President's White House advisors assured him these were not "true conflicts" that would disqualify him from being impartial.[3] I know that while this was not a true conflict, it may have stoked negative feelings on both sides.

But as this twenty-two-month investigation dragged on, it became increasingly difficult to trust that Mueller was paying any attention to the investigators he hired, or to their agenda. Andrew McCabe claims he (strangely, not Mueller) acted quickly to remove Peter Strzok from the Special Counsel's investigation when the anti-Trump texts Strzok and Lisa Page exchanged were revealed.[4] The majority of the investigators Mueller hired had donated to either Hillary Clinton, Barack Obama, or the Democratic National Committee—their constitutional right, just as Strzok and Page had (they claim) a constitutional right to text their political opinions of President Trump to each other on government-issued phones. But really, were these hiring decisions wise? Is donating to candidates and using government phones for political speech wise behavior for career government lawyers? "Career" is not a synonym for "impartial or non-partisan," though lazy minds may equate the two.

Mueller's investigators claim their bias against Trump didn't affect their investigation, but how else to understand the blow-by-blow details selectively leaked despite the prosecutorial ethos against trying any case in the media? Even if Robert Mueller wasn't the one leaking to the press himself, his case was a daily, public evidentiary briefing against the President because of what appeared to many to be his team's leaking. And many times the leaks were tactical *disinformation*, one of the most egregious being that the Special Counsel investigation was expanding to include the President's family members and businesses.

Two months before I returned to the Justice Department as Jeff Sessions's chief of staff, I wrote an op-ed for CNN. Because this op-ed caused so much controversy when I became the Acting Attorney General, it is worth reprinting in its entirety. (Even in retrospect, I'd still call it *perfect*.)

> Last month, when President Donald Trump was asked by the *New York Times* if Special Counsel Robert Mueller would be crossing a line if he started investigating the finances of Trump and his family, the President said, "I think that's a violation. Look, this is about Russia."
>
> The President is absolutely correct. Mueller has come up to a red line in the Russia 2016 election-meddling investigation that he is dangerously close to crossing.
>
> According to a CNN article, Mueller's investigators could be looking into financial records relating to the Trump Organization that are unrelated to the 2016 election. According to these reports, "sources described an investigation that has widened to focus on possible financial crimes, some unconnected to the 2016 election." The piece goes on to cite law enforcement sources who say non-Russia-related leads that "involve Trump associates" are being referred to the Special Counsel "to encourage subjects of the investigation to cooperate."
>
> This information is deeply concerning to me. It does not take a lawyer or even a former federal prosecutor like myself to conclude that investigating Donald Trump's finances or his family's finances falls completely outside of the realm of

his 2016 campaign and allegations that the campaign coordinated with the Russian government or anyone else. That goes beyond the scope of the appointment of the Special Counsel.

In fact, Deputy Attorney General Rod Rosenstein's letter appointing Special Counsel Robert Mueller does not give Mueller broad, far-reaching powers in this investigation. He is only authorized to investigate matters that involved any potential links to and coordination between two entities— the Trump campaign and the Russian government. People are wrongly pointing to, and taking out of context, the phrase "any matters that arose or may arise directly from the investigation" to characterize Special Counsel's authority as broad.

The word "investigation" is clearly defined directly preceding it in the same sentence specifically as coordination between individuals associated with the campaign of Donald Trump and Russia. The Trump Organization's business dealings are plainly not within the scope of the investigation, nor should they be.

Indeed, Sunday on Fox News, Rod Rosenstein acknowledged Mueller had limited authority and would need to seek his permission to expand the investigation.

Beyond the legal reading, the broad authority argument defies plain logic: If the Special Counsel could investigate anything he wants, why would there even need to be a letter spelling out the specific limits of the investigation?

One of the dynamics at play here is that people are conflating this investigation and Kenneth Starr's 1994 investigation into President Bill Clinton. While partly understandable at first glance, the two investigations are not comparable — not only have more than two decades passed since then, but a completely new law and legal framework governing

separate investigations has also passed. Starr was an independent counsel and Mueller is a Special Counsel, the two
words are different for a reason.

Any investigation into President Trump's finances or the
finances of his family would require Mueller to return to Rod
Rosenstein for additional authority under Mueller's appointment as Special Counsel.

If he were to continue to investigate the financial relationships
without a broadened scope in his appointment, then this would
raise serious concerns that the Special Counsel's investigation was
a mere witch hunt. If Mueller is indeed going down this path,
Rosenstein should act to ensure the investigation is within its
jurisdiction and within the authority of the original directive.

I've prosecuted several financial crimes at the federal level
and I've also defended plenty in my private practice. From this
unique vantage point, I can understand how a motivated prosecutor, in a broad investigation into the financial affairs of
high-profile individuals, can become overzealous toward the
targets of such probes—with calamitous results. While no one
is above the law, in situations such as this, any seasoned prosecutor must use discretion both judiciously and expertly.

It is time for Rosenstein, who is the acting attorney general
for the purposes of this investigation, to order Mueller to limit
the scope of his investigation to the four corners of the order
appointing him Special Counsel.

If he doesn't, then Mueller's investigation will eventually
start to look like a political fishing expedition. This would not
only be out of character for a respected figure like Mueller, but
also could be damaging to the President of the United States
and his family—and by extension, to the country.[5]

Note well that I didn't argue that the Special Counsel regulation was
unconstitutional; I didn't argue Robert Mueller was biased. I argued only

that Rod Rosenstein should hold Mueller's investigation to a well-defined scope: just the 2016 Trump campaign and its alleged collusion with the Russians. There was no justification for investigating the President's family members and business associates in an attempt to find some-thing—*anything*—out of order that could be used to undermine the President politically, but this is exactly what Democrats in Congress and their media allies wanted.

To me, this was a statement of the obvious—but the ire it drew from those out to impeach the President proved it needed to be made; the President's opponents wanted an utterly unconstrained Special Counsel with a blank check to investigate anything and everything.

The apparent duplicitous leaks from the Special Counsel's office, like all the other leaks, served no purpose other than to fuel congressional Democrats' impeachment plans, and perhaps to goad President Trump. Robert Mueller should have been accountable to someone for the behavior of his investigators. But aside from Congress's withholding money from the Special Counsel as part of its oversight duty, there was no way to regu-late the Special Counsel. All authority resides in the Justice Department regulation that gives the Attorney General little supervisory power, except for firing the Special Counsel himself (for cause).

The way the Justice Department regulation reads, the Attorney General can fire the Special Counsel for "misconduct, dereliction of duty, incapacity, conflict of interest, or for other good cause, including viola-tion of Departmental policies." The President, however, is the head of the executive branch in which the Special Counsel and Attorney General serve, and they derive their authority from the President's Article II powers.

Disputing the *New York Times's* characterization of his conversations with White House Counsel Don McGahn about the Special Counsel, President Trump tweeted, "I never told then–White House Counsel Don McGahn to fire Robert Mueller, even though I had the legal right to do so. If I wanted to fire Mueller, I didn't need McGahn to do it, I could have done it myself." I would have to agree. The Special Counsel role is an appointed role masquerading as a civil service position, with extraordinary job protections.

Still: post-Watergate, and to the press, firing a Special Counsel would be seen as tantamount to a cover-up. If the President had ordered me to fire Mueller, I would have told him it would only worsen his political situation. This was a very different fact pattern from when Nixon fired Special Prosecutor Archibald Cox, but that wouldn't have mattered to the media. When Cox subpoenaed President Nixon's Oval Office tapes, which revealed that the President knew about the burglary of the Democratic National Committee's offices at the Watergate complex, Nixon ordered Attorney General Elliot Richardson to fire Cox. Richardson resigned rather than fire Cox, as did his Deputy, William Ruckelshaus. Finally, third-in-command Robert Bork agreed to fire Cox. The so-called Saturday Night Massacre was a public relations disaster for Nixon. And years later, the U.S. Senate refused to confirm Bork for a seat on the U.S. Supreme Court.

By the time I was appointed Acting Attorney General, the investigation had concluded that there was no "collusion" as would later be explained in the Mueller report. Limiting or stopping the Special Counsel investigation was unnecessary at this point. It was November 2018, and the investigation was wrapping up without charges against the President. All information flowing from the Special Counsel's office to me daily via Greg Scott and the Deputy Attorney General's office (following DOJ regular order) was that it was over, and that it was a goose egg. From November through February, I waited for the report. It turns out that during this period, the investigation's under-supervised investigators were writing "Part II" of the Mueller report, which was essentially a piece of political journalism meant to appease those disappointed by the lack of any evidence of wrong-doing by the Trump campaign.

■ ■ ■

After spending $32 million in taxpayer money on this two-year investigation, Robert Mueller appeared before the House Judiciary and

Intelligence Committees on July 24, 2019, four months after delivering a 448-page report that alleged no crimes. The most surprising revelation from Mueller was that he had asked Congress to allow Aaron Zebley, his former law partner turned chief of staff to the Special Counsel, to sit next to him at the table while he testified. This was unheard of—I never would have thought to ask Greg to sit next to me at the witness table when I testified before the Judiciary Committee— and perhaps a tacit admission that Mueller was not adequately familiar with his own report.

Congressional Democrats allowed Mueller's request; they were depending on a colorfully damning performance from Mueller to raise public support for impeachment which the 448-page report had failed to generate on its own. At age seventy-four, Mueller appeared healthy, and indeed he had rejoined his law firm WilmerHale in October 2019 as a partner conducting white-collar investigations.[6] But his testimony left the impression that he had entirely outsourced the investigation he was appointed to oversee. He failed to recall important details, incidents, and facts. Democrats strove to create made-for-television highlights by questioning Mueller. The highlights, however, only caused greater confusion—the most important confusion coming when California Democrat Ted Lieu asked Mueller, "The reason you did not indict Donald Trump…is because of the OLC decision. Is that correct?" Lieu was referring to an October 16, 2000, opinion issued by the Justice Department's Office of Legal Counsel which argued, "The indictment or criminal prosecution of a sitting President would unconstitutionally undermine the capacity of the executive branch to perform its constitutionally assigned functions."[7]

This OLC opinion is controversial, because prosecutors—Special Counsel prosecutors included—are members of the executive branch, and they can't fire their own boss. This does not mean the President can break laws with impunity: the onus is on the legislative branch to impeach and convict a sitting President if he engages in criminal activity. If that were done, *then* the executive branch could prosecute him. But nothing the Special Counsel discovered tested this OLC theory's practical application.

When he met with Greg Scott in January, Aaron Zebley had confirmed that the OLC opinion was *not* a factor in the Special Counsel's declination to charge President Trump with crimes. James Quarles had communicated the same message to Attorney General Barr and Rod Rosenstein at their March 5, 2019, meeting.[8] Despite these repeated professions, Mueller replied to Lieu: "That is correct." The response was totally stunning, and patently incorrect. But the President's opponents held their breaths, hoping it was the bombshell revelation they needed.

"This is very, very close to Mueller saying that but for the OLC memo, Trump would have been indicted," breathlessly tweeted Preet Bharara, the former U.S. Attorney for the Southern District of New York whom President Trump had fired.[9] Mueller's 448-page report was written ambiguously enough to confirm Bharara's impression, and that ambiguity cannot have been unintentional. In drafting Part II of the report, the so-called "non-exoneration" section, the Special Counsel went above the law to imply President Trump deserved impeachment. At this moment in time, only verbally and in private, had the Special Counsel's office admitted that the OLC memo was not the reason for their declination to charge the President. But I knew their failure to find any criminal evidence was the reason they didn't charge him.

Then, upon returning from a break between committee hearings, the highly respected former Director of the FBI initiated a bizarre 180-degree reversal as the House Intelligence Committee readied itself to question him:

> Now before we go to questions, I want to add one correction to my testimony this morning. I want to go back to one thing that was said this morning by Mr. Lieu who said, and I quote, "You didn't charge the President because of the OLC opinion." That is not the correct way to say it. As we say in the report, and as I said at the opening, we did not reach a determination

as to whether the President committed a crime. With that, Mr. Chairman, I'm ready to answer questions.[10]

Aaron Zebley deserves credit if he pulled Mueller aside and counseled him to realign his testimony with what his top staff had already communicated to the Department of Justice. But this episode should give every American reason to pause and reflect on how well, pursuant to a broad regulation, Special Counsels are managed, or more accurately, are not managed.

How familiar with the report's contents was Robert Mueller, the man given responsibility for investigating a duly elected President who was enormously unpopular in Washington, D.C.? How familiar was he with the machinations of his staff? "His talent was leading a group where it already wanted to go," Greg was advised by legal professionals who had worked with Mueller in the recent past.

"Always be the last one in the group to speak," Mueller reportedly advised an attorney who asked for career advice as she took a new job. If Mueller wasn't the driver of this taxpayer-financed two-year-long expedition that resulted in nothing but a salacious dramatization of an innocent President's torment at the hands of an angry bureaucracy, who was?

■ ■ ■

Aaron Zebley was not Mueller's puppet-master, but he was Mueller's longtime lieutenant, both in the public and private sectors. It was ironic that while in private practice with Mueller in 2016, he had represented Bill and Hillary Clinton's information technology aide, Justin Cooper.[11] Cooper had helped Secretary of State Clinton set up her private home email server where she kept classified State Department documents. Cooper also helped her avoid turning over to the authorities her personal mobile devices that had classified messages on them—by smashing them with a hammer.

When Greg met with Aaron Zebley in late January, he felt certain Zebley was a straight shooter, and his presentation was clear: there would be no charges against the President, the OLC memo was *not* the justification for that decision, and the investigation would be over by mid-February. "Right now the investigation is—I think—close to being completed.... I hope we can get the report from Director Mueller as soon as possible," I told the press on January 28, 2019.[12]

But mid-February came and went with no Special Counsel report. William Barr began his term as Attorney General on February 14, 2018; I left the Department of Justice shortly thereafter. On March 5, Barr and Rosenstein met with James Quarles from the Special Counsel's office who reaffirmed that the OLC memo was inconsequential to the decision not to charge the President. It was then that the reason for the delay became clear: the Special Counsel was taking the extraordinary liberty of drafting a "non-exoneration" explanation: Part II of the Mueller Report.

Part II upended the presumption of innocence that every American is entitled to when confronted by a prosecutor or an investigation, but it was pure political theater, not law. I suspected that Andrew Weissmann was behind it; others thought they saw the fingerprints of Deputy Solicitor General Michael Dreeben. When "top criminal law expert" Dreeben was hired by Mueller in June 2017, the *National Law Journal* commented: "The move signals that Mueller may be seeking advice on complex areas of criminal law, including what constitutes obstruction of justice."[13]

Perhaps Dreeben is also an expert in the new legal standard of "non-exoneration," created when Jim Comey held the October 2016 press conference explaining why Hillary Clinton would not be indicted. Comey should have been fired on the spot for that bit of above-the-law punditry. The Justice Department is not supposed to explain why it's *not* indicting someone. Part II was an act of the "Resistance," voluminous material produced for Jerry Nadler and Adam Schiff's impeachment campaign.

When Barr learned on March 5—only three weeks into the job— what the Special Counsel's office had in store, he came up with the perfect strategy. On March 24, Barr sent to Congress his four-page summary of the 448-page report's "principal conclusions" (See Appendix B for Barr's full summary). It contained essentially what Zebley had told Greg Scott: the Special Counsel had found no evidence of criminal activity by President Trump or his campaign. Barr brought the Special Counsel investigation back to the legal facts.

Mueller's response to Barr verges on the hysterical:

> As we stated in our meeting of March 5 and reiterated to the Department early in the afternoon of March 24, the introductions and executive summaries of our two-volume report accurately summarize this Office's work and conclusions. The summary letter the Department sent to Congress and released to the public late in the afternoon of March 24 did not fully capture the context, nature, and substance of this Office's work and conclusions. We communicated that concern to the Department on the morning of March 25. There is now public confusion about critical aspects of the results of our investigation. This threatens to undermine a central purpose for which the Department appointed a Special Counsel: to assure full public confidence in the outcome of the investigations. See Department of Justice, Press Release (May 17, 2017.)[14]

In fact, this letter was an attempt by Robert Mueller and his team to spin their own report—the legal substance of which Attorney General Barr had accurately summarized in four pages. What Barr hadn't done— and what the Mueller team wanted to do—was go beyond the law and assert that even though they had no evidence of criminal activity, they could not exonerate the President of wrong-doing (as if it is a prosecutor's job to exonerate anyone). The report (and Mueller's letter) exposed the whole of the Special Counsel investigation: it was a *political* act against the President, not a disinterested *legal* investigation.

From the beginning, Russian interference in the 2016 election should have been investigated by a regular U.S. Attorney, with proper oversight from the Department of Justice, run by an un-recused Attorney General. Investigators like Strzok and Page would have been weeded out, those leaking to the media would have been held accountable, and once the investigation concluded that no crimes had been committed, the Attorney General could have demanded a concise report immediately. The appointment of a Special Counsel gave the President's enemies a safe haven and their own budget. The Special Counsel regulation, as it is currently written, must never be co-opted in this way again.

■ ■ ■

When President Trump appointed me Acting Attorney General, critics challenged the constitutionality of my appointment because Congress hadn't had the chance to vet me. In Article II, Section II, the Constitution says that the President "shall nominate, and by and with the Advice and Consent of the Senate, shall appoint high government officials."

Checks and balances are important to a proper, functioning government, but over the past several decades, Congress has abdicated more and more of its responsibilities to the other branches of government, making Deep State bureaucrats more powerful than voters. In passing the 1998 Federal Vacancy Reform Act, the courts pointed out to my challengers, Congress delegated some of its advice and consent power to the executive branch, allowing the President to appoint high-ranking employees to cabinet level positions on a temporary basis without congressional approval.

So my critics pivoted and instead focused their white-hot daily scrutiny on the questions of whether I managed the Special Counsel (another government employee who had not been confirmed by the Senate) and how.

My own appointment had been validated by an act of Congress, but Robert Mueller's appointment as a Special Counsel was a creation of the Justice Department. There is no law passed by Congress and signed by the President establishing a Special Counsel position. It was created by departmental fiat in 1999 by the late Attorney General Janet Reno and her advisors. The Justice Department simply declared that the Attorney General has the authority to appoint an outsider who can subpoena, charge, and jail American citizens. In my opinion, that's unconstitutional—not to mention crazy.

The 1999 Special Counsel regulation basically creates a Grand Inquisitor, someone who is judge, jury, and executioner. It is the embodiment of the runaway administrative state typical of countries like Russia and China, where due process is unknown.

I'm not the only one who thinks so. "Robert Mueller is . . . at best an employee, and, under *Buckley v. Valeo*, 424 U.S. 1 (1976), employees cannot deprive citizens of life, liberty, or property on their own, which makes Mueller's appointment as an inferior officer unconstitutional," Northwestern law professor Steven Calabresi explained in an op-ed for *The Hill* newspaper in 2018.[15]

Congress wasn't always so feckless. After Watergate, it reformed the "special prosecutor" position by passing an "independent counsel" law in 1977. Designed to expire (or "sunset") and prompt Congress to reconsider it every few years, it required a three-judge panel from the judicial branch to appoint someone, if asked by the Attorney General, who could be compelled by Congress. Congress or the Attorney General could fire the independent counsel, so all three branches of government were involved. This is the law that governed Ken Starr's investigation of President Bill Clinton, which led to Clinton's impeachment. But today, according to the Congressional Research Service, no *law* empowers Special Counsels. The Special Counsel regulation exists merely as a Justice Department regulation.

In 1999, Congress allowed the "independent counsel" provi-
sions of law to expire.... The Attorney General retains the
general authority to designate or name individuals as "Special
Counsels" to conduct investigations or prosecutions of particular matters or individuals on behalf of the United States.
Under regulations issued by the Attorney General in 1999,
the Attorney General may appoint a "Special Counsel" from
outside of the Department of Justice who acts as a special
employee of the Department of Justice under the direction of
the Attorney General.[16]

I agreed with Professor Calabresi intellectually then, but now that I
have experienced firsthand the bad faith, I believe that this role could be
handled by a sitting U.S. Attorney. Mark Penn, who worked as a political
advisor and pollster for both Bill and Hillary Clinton (and worked for
President Bill Clinton throughout the Ken Starr investigation and the
subsequent impeachment of the President), has proposed numerous
reforms to the Special Counsel regulation. Many of his reforms are common sense. He would amend the regulation so that "Special Counsels
are hereby classified as principal officers, requiring confirmation by the
Senate. Their terms will be for one year unless renewed by the Justice
Department and confirmed by the Senate. If the investigation involves
political campaigns or administration officials, the team will have
roughly equal numbers of prosecutors from the two parties...."[17]

As the independent counsel law was expiring in 1999, Griffin Bell
testified about its many inherent problems before the Senate Committee
on Government Affairs. He had served as President Jimmy Carter's
Attorney General in the post-Watergate era, during the law's creation.
Bell's analysis twenty years before the Mueller investigation concluded
was uncanny. Bell immediately called out the assault on due process that
results when in "isolation" a prosecutor can pursue a publicly named
target of an investigation:

One problem with the Special Counsel statute that probably cannot be repaired is the inherent absence of due process from the procedure itself. This is the isolation of the independent counsel from the Executive Branch and the isolation of the putative defendant from the safeguards afforded all other Federal investigatees. The inherent checks and balances the system supplies heightens the occupational hazards of a prosecutor taking in too narrow a focus, a possible loss of perspective and a single-minded pursuit of alleged suspects seeking evidence of some misconduct. This search for a crime to fit the publicly identified suspect is generally unknown or should be unknown to our criminal justice system.

Bell was exactly right: searching for a crime (Collusion? Obstruction of justice? Abuse of power? Bribery?) to fit the suspect is not American. Any Special Counsel reform ought to require a higher standard of predication than what was used to investigate President Trump.

Bell goes on to point out the "disparate treatment" the target of a Special Counsel receives, compared to targets of regular federal investigations: federal prosecutors don't publicly acknowledge they are investigating someone and prematurely damn their reputation in the court of public opinion. (The moment President Trump's critics learned he was a target of Robert Mueller's investigation, he was deemed guilty.)

The person being pursued publicly in the investigation is treated differently from other suspects being investigated by Federal prosecutors who are afforded the protection of no comment by the prosecution on a pending investigation, including not acknowledging the fact of the investigation. Such disparate treatment can hardly be justified on the ground that the Special Counsel treats with only those holding political office or their associates.

And as though Bell could see twenty years into the future and read
Mueller's 448 pages of unfair criminal insinuation, he condemned the
practice of a Special Counsel's "suggesting guilt although there was no
indictment" by drafting a final report.

> The final report by the Special Counsel can be another exam-
> ple of lack of due process by suggesting guilt although there
> was no indictment. An example is the report of Judge Walsh
> in the Iran-Contra investigation. This treatment would never
> be given by the Department of Justice to an ordinary person
> who was investigated but not indicted. The final report should
> be eliminated. It is quite enough to indict or close the
> investigation.[18]

But the "final report" that rightly concerned Bell remains in the
Justice Department code:

> § 600.8 Notification and reports by the Special Counsel. (c)
> Closing documentation. At the conclusion of the Special
> Counsel's work, he or she shall provide the Attorney General
> with a confidential report explaining the prosecution or dec-
> lination decisions reached by the Special Counsel.[19]

Note well, that the report is supposed to be "confidential" and provided solely to the Attorney General. But the Mueller team knew the
report would be made public—even President Trump wanted it out in
the open—and they, in my opinion, abused that privilege by going far
beyond any legal requirement, writing a book-length condemnation that
lacked any legal standing against the President. It was a grossly inflated
Washington Post opinion piece, perhaps meant to provide some sort of
emotional satisfaction to the President's opponents, once the Special
Counsel team finally officially conceded there was no evidence of criminal activity by the President or his campaign. In my mind, if there was

any abuse of power, it was committed not by the President but by his opponents who abused the power of the Justice Department to harass the President of the United States for no good reason. Remember, the power to investigate is the power to destroy.

CHAPTER SIX

CRIMINALIZING THE POLITICAL

N ever have I seen this many people—in government, in the media, in the opposition party, and among other political opponents—hunting for but failing to find criminal evidence against someone as has been the case with President Trump. Highly motivated investigators full of influence in the media, law, and politics have turned over every aspect of Donald Trump's life as a public figure and come up with no evidence of criminality at all.

Surely an outer-borough New York City real estate developer would be enmeshed in criminal activity too thick to escape by Election Day 2016? Republican primary candidates dug; the DNC dug; the media dug. But the "October surprise" of 2016 was a hot mike recording of jarringly offensive locker room bravado from a 2005 *Access Hollywood* taping. The comments were politically toxic, but they were not criminal.

Back in September 2015, the Fusion GPS opposition research team started a factually shady campaign "cataloguing Trump's [alleged] long history of lies, contradictions, dubious business deals, and ties to organized crime; *Village Voice* investigative reporter and longtime Trump chronicler Wayne Barrett gave them access to boxes of files on Trump collecting dust in his Brooklyn brownstone," James D. Walsh reported in *New York Magazine*.[1]

Trump was hardly the consensus candidate for the Republican nomination, so even the conservative *Washington Free Beacon* paid Fusion GPS for opposition research on Trump and "multiple candidates in the Republican presidential primary" until May 2016, though the *Free Beacon's* website states it "had no knowledge of or connection to the Steele dossier, did not pay for the dossier, and never had contact with, knowledge of, or [provide] payment for any work performed by Christopher Steele."[2]

"Ultimately, [Fusion GPS was] contracted by Marc Elias, an attorney representing the DNC and the Clinton campaign. 'The only way I could see working for HRC is if it is against Trump,' Simpson wrote in an email to his partners," *New York Magazine's* James Walsh reported. The Steele dossier, motivated by personal animus against Donald Trump, and funded by a combination of DNC and Clinton campaign dollars, was essentially the lone predication for investigating Donald Trump's alleged criminality. The Steele dossier's central and essential role in the investigation testifies to the lack of real criminal evidence existing against Donald Trump and his campaign.[3]

Reportedly, the U.S. intelligence community, led by John Brennan at the CIA and James Clapper at the National Security Agency, was also looking for crimes in Donald Trump's past but couldn't come up with anything more than the unverified and discredited rumors in the Steele dossier. Yet Comey's FBI and Brennan's CIA inexplicably professed "high confidence" in the Steele dossier, and Clapper's NSA expressed "moderate confidence." They presumed Donald Trump was guilty because of their overwhelming disdain and contempt for him, and the quality of their evidence was an afterthought.

The three of them approached President-elect Trump on January 6, 2017, to present evidence that the Russians had meddled in the 2016 elections to help Trump win. Comey, in a one-on-one with the President, relayed the "salacious" contents of the dossier, insinuating not only that the Russians had helped Trump win, but that Trump was now controlled by their implied extortion.

Their presumption of Trump's guilt wasn't subtle, and their accusatory posture wouldn't have been lost on an international real estate developer who had seen these tactics before on construction sites and in the behavior of corrupt politicians and strong-arming union leaders. "Top FBI officials were 'quite worried' Comey would appear to be blackmailing Trump," Michael Isikoff's Yahoo! News headline confirmed:

> "We were quite worried about the [J. Edgar] Hoover analogies, and we were determined not to have such a disaster happen on our watch," said Jim Baker, then the FBI's top lawyer in an interview with the Yahoo! News podcast *Skullduggery*. But he and Comey determined the bureau had an obligation to tell Trump of the uncorroborated allegations because "the press has it; it's about to come out. You should be alerted to that fact."[4]

BuzzFeed published the dossier on January 10, 2017. Who leaked the dossier, and why, is currently a matter under investigation by U.S. Attorney John Durham.[5] Given Comey, Clapper, and Brennan's sit-down with Trump during the presidential transition, the FBI's surveillance of the Trump campaign and transition team, and the potential crimes committed to wiretap Carter Page, it would make sense to me if President Trump was weary of the cast of characters he was inheriting from President Obama.

Here's my question, and I know it's shared by many honorable Justice Department employees and alumni: If Comey felt his new boss was crossing a line criminally, why didn't he advise him of that? Or quit? Who on earth would instead type an official FBI memo on the meeting and violate department policy to store it in a home safe?

When White House Counsel Don McGahn felt President Trump was asking him to do "crazy shit" (allegedly, according to the Mueller report,

to fire Special Counsel Robert Mueller and offer refutations of investigation leaks to the media), McGahn allegedly threatened to resign rather
than follow orders. Why didn't Comey do that?

One could empathize if, as Comey alleges, President Trump felt bad
that his pick for National Security Adviser Michael Flynn was facing jail
time for allegedly telling a lie to the FBI, claiming that he had no contact
with Russian officials during the presidential transition. I could understand if President Trump did in fact tell Comey, "I hope you can let this
go." Declining to prosecute someone is an Article II power, as is pardon-
ing criminals. But I can't understand why, instead of explaining his
position or taking his concerns to Acting Attorney General Sally Yates,
Comey deceptively agreed with Trump that Flynn was a good guy: "Yes,
he is a good guy."

Trump fired Comey on May 9, 2017. A few days before his firing,
Comey had refused to tell lawmakers what he had told President Trump
privately three times: *that the President himself was not under criminal
investigation.* The Associated Press reported on Comey's Capitol Hill
theater:

> But on May 3, 2017, when Comey was summoned to Capitol
> Hill to explain his handling of the Hillary Clinton email
> investigation, he denied the President the public vindication
> he'd sought.... Comey pointedly refused to say whether any
> members of the Trump campaign were or were not under
> criminal investigation—including the President himself. "The
> Department of Justice has authorized me to confirm" the
> existence of a broader investigation into potential collusion
> between Russia and the Trump campaign, Comey said.
> "We're not going to say another word about it until we're
> done."[6]

Having been face to face with Donald Trump many times myself and
having seen how good he is at reading people, I'm sure the President could

sense Comey's treachery from their first meeting. It was politically risky for the President to fire the FBI Director during an investigation of the 2016 campaign, but I admire Donald Trump for taking bold action because he thought it was the right thing to do. What's politically expedient isn't always the right decision, as history shows. Left in power, Jim Comey might have become the next J. Edgar Hoover, pursuing his own agenda and acting above the law, and the Deep State—the "permanent government" and the Washington establishment—would have felt even more empowered and entrenched than it already is.

There is nothing criminal about a President's exercising his Article II powers to fire an FBI Director. And if the President was not a party to a crime, then he couldn't be obstructing justice by firing someone in his chain of command. But Deputy FBI Director Andrew McCabe seized on Comey's firing as a justification for making President Trump himself an investigative target in a criminal investigation. I still can't figure out how Andrew McCabe took these two facts (the legitimate firing of James Comey and the ongoing investigation of the Trump campaign) and arrived at the conclusion that he should target the President in a criminal investigation. To do so assumes that the chief executive, exerting his constitutional authority, has committed a criminal act because you personally might disapprove of his action or his politics.

The appointment of Special Counsel Robert Mueller continued Comey and McCabe's criminalization of the legitimate political actions of the President. Despite finding no evidence of the President or his campaign's colluding with the Russians, Robert Mueller and his investigators could not let their report go without trying to use it to continue to cast a cloud over the President, making the report itself a political act under the guise of a legal investigation.[7]

"If we had had confidence that the President clearly did not commit a crime, we would have said so," Mueller declared when he resigned from the Justice Department two months after I did, in what CNN described as a "rare and remarkable" public statement.[8] "We did not, however, make a determination as to whether the President did commit a crime...."

The Constitution requires a process other than the criminal justice system to formally accuse a sitting President of wrongdoing."

"Mueller: Trump Is Not Not a Criminal," *New York Magazine's*
Jonathan Chait eagerly translated for his left-wing readership. "So Mueller can't *explicitly* say he would have charged Trump with a crime if he
could have, and he also can't *explicitly* tell Congress to impeach the
President. Instead he's heavily hinting at both points."[9] If he was hinting
at both points, he was doing so at odds with what his own staff had told
us about the lack of evidence.

House Judiciary Committee Chairman Jerrold Nadler didn't need
hints or even explicit instructions from Mueller. He was eager to
impeach President Trump regardless of whether there was criminal
evidence or not. "Given that Special Counsel Mueller was unable to
pursue criminal charges against the President, it falls to Congress to
respond to the crimes, lies, and other wrongdoing of President Trump—
and we will do so."

The impeachment of Donald J. Trump orchestrated by Jerrold
Nadler and Adam Schiff was a foregone conclusion from November 7,
2018, the day Democrats won control of the House. Right up until
December 2019, they considered mining the Mueller report for evidence
of criminality for which to impeach Trump.

Was Trump's alleged desire to fire Mueller evidence of obstruction
of justice? Were his alleged orders to White House Counsel Don
McGahn, which McGahn ignored, obstruction of justice? Were his
alleged attempts to limit the Mueller investigation by requesting that a
private citizen, Corey Lewandowski, ask Attorney General Jeff Sessions
to call the investigation "unfair" and put guardrails around future
expansions of it, an obstruction of justice? And what about what he said
to Paul Manafort about not "flipping" or "breaking"?

The fact is, none of these allegations, if true, amounts to obstruction
of justice; in no case was there evidence of criminality. Yet the Mueller
Report's second volume trotted out all these politically toxic, real or
alleged statements made by President Trump—all well within his Article

II powers as President—and insinuated they were criminal without recommending criminal charges. Mueller declined to make a "traditional prosecution decision," which only meant he most likely wanted to leave an impression of criminality even though he had no evidence to prove it. There was no *there* there, but he refused to admit it.

Because there was no legal weight in Mueller's bizarre essay on obstruction of justice, House Democrats finally opted not to impeach President Trump for "obstruction of justice," but for two other things: "obstruction of Congress" (a separation of powers argument for the judicial branch to decide, not sitting members of Congress), and, quite foolishly, "abuse of power." "Obstruction of Congress" is not a crime; the executive and legislative branches of government are, as every civics student used to know, separate and equal; the Constitution intentionally set them in tension and opposition to each other. And I hate to break it to the impeachment-happy Democrats, but "abuse of power" is not a crime either.

■ ■ ■

Abuse of power is not a crime.

When I first spoke those words on national television, Democrats and their media allies postured shamelessly, insinuating that Matthew Whitaker, President Trump's former Acting Attorney General, was condoning abuse of power. Any Justice Department line attorney can tell you that "abuse of power" is not a crime.

And if we're going to talk about those who abused their power, who held themselves above the law, we should be talking not about the President who has acted utterly within the law, but about the former Justice Department leaders who criminalized politics they didn't like, making Donald Trump a target of a Russian counterintelligence investigation without responsible predication. Or we could talk about the Special Counsel investigation, which was meant to provide evidence, or actually innuendo, for a totally partisan impeachment of President Donald Trump. Not a single

Republican in the House voted for either impeachment article because neither impeachment article is anywhere close to the standard of a "high crime or misdemeanor" that would justify impeachment.

That high-ranking administration officials aiding Nancy Pelosi, Jerrold Nadler, and Adam Schiff would entangle themselves in such banana republic capers, sickens and embarrasses me and many of my former colleagues.

The Constitution allows a Speaker like Nancy Pelosi to choose to impeach a President for almost anything, whether it's a crime (like bribery) or not (like abuse of power). A simple House majority could impeach a President for cursing, using a plastic straw, or authorizing Deferred Action for Childhood Arrivals (DACA) and call it "abuse of power." But previous House Speakers did not so lower the bar. As Alex Swoyer noted in the *Washington Times*, the House Democrats' votes for "impeaching Trump for abuse of power and obstruction of Congress...were unprecedented in that they were not based on a crime. The prior two impeachments, President Johnson in 1868 and President Clinton in 1998, both included criminal charges, violating a federal statute and perjury, respectively." Moreover: "Josh Blackman, a professor at South Texas College of Law, said he worried about the precedent set by the Trump impeachment. 'This vote could turn any political act the opposite political party disagrees with into an abuse of power,' he told the *Washington Times*."[10]

Pelosi's House Democrats essentially impeached President Trump for his hardball personality and politics, which some Republicans and Independents don't care for either. In 2016, voters gave Donald Trump a stunning Electoral College victory, and it seems extraordinary that so many Democrats appear to echo the words of Democratic Congressman Al Green who said, "I'm concerned that if we don't impeach this President, he will get re-elected."[11]

Perhaps hand-wringing bureaucrats wouldn't have had the same conversation with Ukraine's new President. But unelected federal employees, such as the so-called whistleblower who heard secondhand about the telephone call, don't get to determine America's foreign policy—the elected President does. In the case of Ukraine, Congress authorized spending, and President Trump's Defense Department and Office of Management and Budget disbursed it, as required by law, before the date it was due. As provided in the Constitution, the President has broad latitude to conduct America's foreign policy. His exercise of this broad power is not an abuse of power, not against the law, and not a violation of the Constitution.

I am gravely concerned that "the Resistance," including some high-ranking leaders at the Justice Department, have set a new standard of criminalizing political actions and beliefs with which they disagree. It troubles me that Justice Department resisters quietly slipped into the ranks of congressional impeachers. As *Politico* reported, former Department of Justice Russia-probe official Mary McCord and her "team that includes former National Security Council and DOJ attorneys first appeared earlier this fall on the legal docket as attorneys representing the Judiciary Committee in its fights for [former White House Counsel Donald] McGahn's testimony and [Robert] Mueller's grand jury evidence."[12] Mueller's "pit bull," Andrew Weissmann, went from the Justice Department's internal Russia investigation to the Special Counsel's office to MSNBC as a paid political analyst whose on-air debut was the first day of impeachment hearings.[13]

In his November 2019 address to the Federalist Society, Attorney General Barr aptly captured the criminalization of politics as a means of taking out President Trump:

> Immediately after President Trump won election, opponents inaugurated what they called the "Resistance," and they rallied around an explicit strategy of using every tool and maneuver available to sabotage the functioning of his administration. Now, "Resistance" is the language used to describe insurgency against rule imposed by an occupying military power. It obviously connotes that the government is not legitimate. This is a very dangerous—indeed incendiary—notion to

import into the politics of a democratic republic. What it means is that, instead of viewing themselves as the "loyal opposition," as opposing parties have done in the past, they essentially see themselves as engaged in a war to cripple, by any means necessary, a duly elected government.[14]

If the law writers in Congress and the law enforcers in the Justice Department are going to conspire against politicians they don't like, honest people offering themselves up for public service don't stand a chance. Only those approved by the Washington establishment and bureaucratic elites will govern us if impeachment becomes the new normal.

When Congress considered impeaching President Bill Clinton for abuse of power, it was because he had lied under oath, an actual federal crime. His proven perjury cost him his law license in Arkansas and a fine. President Richard Nixon resigned before Congress finished its articles of impeachment, but those articles would have accused him of conspiring to hide details of the Watergate burglary, an actual crime. Democrats feverishly wished Robert Mueller would recommend charging President Trump with actual crimes, but he could not. He could only perpetuate the presumption of guilt that the Resistance imposes on Donald Trump, regardless of the lack of legal evidence.

Scrambling to bolster their weak case for impeaching Trump in 2019, Nadler's staff hurriedly alleged that the President's "abuse of power" with respect to Ukraine *did* in fact include crimes, and tucked "bribery" and "multiple federal crimes" on page 127 of a 169-page supplemental report delivered to the House Rules Committee after midnight on December 16, 2019.[15] If Nancy Pelosi, Jerry Nadler, and Adam Schiff believed President Trump's July 25, 2019, telephone call with Ukraine's President and his ensuing actions were crimes, why didn't they lay it on the line in the light of day and allege crimes in their articles of impeachment? Why withhold constitutional due process from the accused and conduct impeachment inquiry hearings in a secret

"Sensitive Compartmented Information Facility" where the public and the President's lawyers couldn't scrutinize testimony?

The first time I audaciously reminded anyone who cared to listen that, in itself, abuse of power is not a crime, was on Laura Ingraham's Fox News Channel program, *The Ingraham Angle*, on October 22, 2019. The coastal elite went to DEFCON 1. *Vogue, Esquire, Vanity Fair, Salon,* and *New York Magazine* all rushed to join their fellow Resisters in the political media to school me on morality and the law. Harvard Law School's Lawrence Tribe, who traveled to Washington to advise the House Democrats on impeachment strategy, called my statement "the epitome of ignorance."[16] Two months later, when not a single Republican senator showed willingness to convict President Trump for abuse of power and obstruction of Congress, Professor Tribe advised Speaker Pelosi to withhold her lame impeachment articles from the U.S. Senate, denying the accused his constitutional right to a speedy trial.[17] (Apparently it's okay to pass impeachment articles along party lines, as the Democrat-controlled House did, but not to acquit the President along party lines in a Republican-controlled Senate. Maybe I am ignorant.)

Why isn't "abuse of power" a federal crime? According to the Legal Information Institute:

> In general, every crime involves three elements: first, the act or conduct ("*actus reus*"); second, the individual's mental state at the time of the act ("*mens rea*"); and third, the causation between the act and the effect (typically either "proximate causation" or "but-for causation"). In a criminal prosecution, the government has the burden of proof to establish every element of a crime beyond a reasonable doubt.[18]

Had Speaker Pelosi put actual crimes before the House for a vote, she would have failed. So House Democrats did what Robert Mueller's team did: they blurred the distinction between the criminal and the political.

What if a Republican-controlled House had voted to impeach President Obama's political conduct as "abuse of power"? President Obama blindsided the Justice Department in October 2015 when asked on CBS's *60 Minutes* about Hillary Clinton's use of a private email server when she was his Secretary of State. Though the Obama administration had prosecuted other federal employees for keeping classified information on their personal computers, Obama blithely assured Steve Kroft: "I can tell you that this is not a situation in which America's national security was endangered."

"[T]o me, anyone looking at this case would have seen a national security component to it. So I don't, I truly do not know where he got that from," Obama's Attorney General Loretta Lynch remarked in the Inspector General's June 2018 report, titled "A Review of Various Actions of the Federal Bureau of Investigation and Department of Justice in Advance of the 2016 Election."[19] "I don't know where it came from. And I don't know, I don't know why he would have thought that either, to be honest with you."

Waving off a national security threat to protect one's Secretary of State who is running for President would seem to rise to the impeachment standard that the Democrats have now set, and they should willingly agree that it meets Alexander Hamilton's criteria for impeachment in *Federalist 65*: "those offenses which proceed from the misconduct of public men, or, in other words, from the abuse or violation of some public trust."

Three months after President Obama's *60 Minutes* comments, his Press Secretary Josh Earnest told White House reporters that Department of Justice prosecutors would make the decision on whether to indict Clinton, but "it does not seem to be headed in that direction." Earnest also said Clinton was not a "target" of the FBI investigation.

The Inspector General report reveals: "Lynch's chief of staff stated that Department officials were 'very upset' about Earnest's statement, because 'as far as we knew, no one at Department of Justice had spoken to anyone in the White House about it.'"

How else to interpret this than President Obama's telegraphing the Justice Department to ignore a threat to national security? The Justice Department hadn't communicated anything to President Obama about the emails' contents, so how would he know they didn't threaten national security? "[Former White House senior advisor David] Axelrod similarly told the OIG [Office of the Inspector General] that Earnest's comments implied that the White House had received a briefing on the Midyear investigation, which he said 'never happened.'"

But President Obama still wasn't done laying down the law (so to speak). On April 10, 2016, he told *Fox News Sunday* that despite the belated discovery of classified and top-secret emails on Hillary Clinton's private server, "I continue to believe that she has not jeopardized America's national security. Now what I've also said is that—and she has acknowledged—that there's a *carelessness* [emphasis mine], in terms of managing emails, that she has owned, and she recognizes."[20]

President Obama politicized the criminal, making it excusable if it was done by a member of the administration. "Lisa Page confirmed to me under oath that the FBI was ordered by the Obama DOJ not to consider charging Hillary Clinton for gross negligence in the handling of classified information," tweeted Congressman John Ratcliffe, sharing the transcript on Twitter.[21]

And, reported CNN, "electronic records show Peter Strzok, who led the investigation of Hillary Clinton's private email server as the No. 2 official in the counterintelligence division, changed Comey's earlier draft language describing Clinton's actions as 'grossly negligent' to 'extremely careless....'"[22] Gross negligence is a chargeable crime. Carelessness, however extreme—like abuse of power—is not a crime. On July 5, 2016, FBI Director James Comey bizarrely announced, "Although there is evidence of potential violations of the statutes regarding the handling of classified information, our judgment is that no reasonable prosecutor would bring such a case."[23] CNN's Stephen Collinson and Tal Kopan captured the surrealism of that day:

In a stunning moment of Washington theater, Comey stepped
up to the microphone to deliver the FBI's findings just over
two hours before Clinton climbed aboard *Air Force One* to
travel to her first campaign event with President Barack
Obama. Adding to the tension, he made clear the White
House and the Justice Department "do not know what I am
about to say."[24]

That press conference was the beginning of the end of Jim Comey's
career inside the Justice Department. It revealed his poor judgment and
bias toward the Obama administration and willingness to let its officials
off with the equivalent of a warning and a rebuke, while in effect being
complicit in the administration's protection of its own.

THE CASE FOR A STRONG UNITARY EXECUTIVE

I nside a Justice Department fifth floor conference room—not the Attorney General's, with the oil paintings of *Justice Defeated* and *Justice Triumphant*, but the smaller one attached to the chief of staff's office—I sat at the table eating lunch with Christopher Wray one day during the 2018 federal government shutdown. Chris was Jim Comey's successor as FBI Director, and in many ways, Comey's opposite: his focus was on the internal workings of the Bureau, and his style was methodical. He didn't seem to obsess about his reputation in the media and outside the Bureau or history's memorialization of him.

I was Acting Attorney General during the shutdown, so Chris asked me, in my capacity as a cabinet member, to deliver a message to President Trump: "On behalf of all the people in federal law enforcement who are asked to put their lives on the line every day for the job, ask the President to end the shutdown. They haven't been paid in a month, and they're hurting. End it for them."

I agreed with Chris's deep concern for the well-being of the men and women who reported to him. He was normally so deliberative and could come across as a stoic, but this was something he was passionate about,

and something he thought needed to be done, and done now. I assured
Chris that on at least two separate occasions I had expressed to President
Trump the concerns that I had about the shutdown and its impact on
federal law enforcement officers.

The President understood that it is bad enough to do a job well and
not get paid for it. But it is another level of sacrifice to put your life on
the line and not get paid. For me, it was personal as well. As Acting
Attorney General, I had an FBI security detail assigned to me. I saw them
every day, and every day I knew they ran the risk of taking a bullet for
me. At this point, they hadn't been paid in a month. Inevitably, I worried
about them and their families.

Emotionally, I sympathized with the argument that law enforcement
shouldn't become ensnared in politics. People don't get into law enforcement, at least at the rank and file level, for political reasons. They do it to
protect and serve the people around them. When politicians get into argu-
ments that make it harder for these people to do their jobs, it's painful to
watch. But one of the things about public service is that our lives are not
entirely our own. We are beholden to the people. We are certainly beholden
to the legislative branch that writes our laws, and to the executive branch
that is charged with enforcing them. Having been at the table in the White
House Situation Room during the shutdown negotiations, I saw the President and the Vice President working hard to end the disagreement. But the
Democrats' hatred for this President would not allow them to give him
even a small victory despite the harm it was doing to law enforcement. I
concluded that Speaker Nancy Pelosi and Minority Leader Chuck Schumer
were unwilling to compromise at all costs, and their behavior was signifi-
cantly responsible for the pain inflicted on government employees and in
particular on the men and women of law enforcement.

During my time in the Justice Department, I'd often hear colleagues
assert our need for "independence" from the administration, and on one
level, I could understand. But in some instances, that made no sense to
me—perhaps because I only arrived in Washington in 2017 and hadn't
been schooled in its ways. But where is it written that the Department of

Justice should be absolutely independent from the administration, I asked my new colleagues? Nowhere.

Don't misunderstand: judicial independence is of course a core American tradition and an essential feature of stable governments around the world. But I think some people inside the Department of Justice forget that while the judicial branch represents the independent judiciary, the executive branch is in charge of the cabinet department in which they work; the fact that the department has "Justice" in its title doesn't change that fact.

Our Constitution's framers gave the President no authority over members of the judicial branch of government. The President appoints federal judges, and Supreme Court Justices, but once they're confirmed by the Senate, they're untouchable by the executive branch.

On the other hand, the Constitution gives the President total authority over his cabinet members and their employees, including at the Department of Justice. Article II, Section II reads:

> The President shall be Commander in Chief of the Army and Navy of the United States, and of the Militia of the several States, when called into the actual Service of the United States; he may require the Opinion, in writing, of the principal Officer in each of the executive Departments, upon any Subject relating to the Duties of their respective Offices, and he shall have Power to grant Reprieves and Pardons for Offences against the United States, except in Cases of Impeachment.
>
> He shall have Power, by and with the Advice and Consent of the Senate, to make Treaties, provided two thirds of the Senators present concur; and he shall nominate, and by and with the Advice and Consent of the Senate, shall appoint Ambassadors, other public Ministers and Consuls, Judges of the Supreme Court, and all other Officers of the United States, whose Appointments are not herein otherwise provided for, and which shall be established by Law: but the Congress may

by Law vest the Appointment of such inferior Officers, as they think proper, in the President alone, in the Courts of Law, or in the Heads of Departments.

The President shall have Power to fill up all Vacancies that may happen during the Recess of the Senate, by granting Commissions which shall expire at the End of their next Session.[1]

The way I read this section of the Constitution, it argues for a strong, unified executive branch embodied by one person at the top, the President. President Ronald Reagan's Attorney General Ed Meese has helped me appreciate the wisdom of "unitary executive theory," which allows Presidents to use their power as commander in chief quickly and effectively, a life-saving ability in an era of terrorism conducted by state-sponsored proxies or by criminals unaligned with governments. Eliana Johnson's analysis in *Politico* explains:

> Conservative heroes from Robert Bork to the late Justice Antonin Scalia have been advocates of this theory. Bork carried out President Richard M. Nixon's directive, in the midst of the Watergate scandal, to fire independent special prosecutor Archibald Cox because he determined the President had the right to do so. Scalia, in a 1988 dissenting opinion, argued that the President had the power to fire any executive branch official, including an independent counsel.[2]

Like it or not, the President can hire and fire any political appointee he wants, including those inside the Department of Justice. He has the legal power to order the Justice Department to conduct investigations. He can order its members not to testify before Congress. And he can order them to work without pay when Congress shuts off funding in a brutal negotiation with the executive branch. Article II gives the President a great deal of authority and power; the President is expected to use that power subject to the restraints—the checks and balances—that the

Constitution vests in the legislative and judicial branches of government. What the Constitution does not do is give the power of checking and balancing presidential authority to career civil servants or anyone else employed by the executive branch.

The argument over whether Article II allows President Trump to prevent current and former White House advisors such as White House General Counsel Don McGahn from testifying before congressional impeachment hearings is, as of this writing, still under consideration in the judicial branch, the appropriate venue for its adjudication. In December 2019, U.S. District Court Judge Kentanji Brown Jackson—appointed by President Obama—ruled against the President. Judge Jackson opined that "stated simply, the primary takeaway from the past 250 years of recorded American history is that Presidents are not kings.... This means that they do not have subjects, bound by loyalty or blood, whose destiny they are entitled to control."[3]

Then "Congress Is King," the *Wall Street Journal* editorial page smartly retorted.[4] How is it that the elected President of the United States can't issues orders to executive branch employees, but the president's opponents in Congress, like Jerry Nadler and Adam Schiff, can? Conflicts between our three branches of government were well anticipated by the Founding Fathers. Questions like this will likely go all the way to the U.S. Supreme Court. But it seems common—and constitutional— sense that the President controls the executive branch of government.

If the President didn't have authority over his Attorney General, or the FBI Director, or the thousands of people who report to them, who would those people be answerable to other than their own consciences? Can you imagine a Secretary of State or a Secretary of Defense who operated independently of the President because foreign policy and the nation's security shouldn't be subject to politics? This will sound counterintuitive, but an independent Department of Justice should concern every American. In practice that means a Department of Justice unconstrained by executive authority (which is itself constrained by elections, the Congress, and the judiciary) and entitled to do pretty much what it wants. Lord Acton's famous warning that power corrupts, and absolute power corrupts absolutely, certainly comes to mind.

But Eric Holder, President Obama's "wingman" and first Attorney General, doubled down on this vision of an independent (read: unaccountable) Justice Department in a *Washington Post* op-ed last year:

> When appropriate and justified, it is the Attorney General's duty to support Justice Department components, ensure their integrity, and insulate them from political pressures. His or her ultimate loyalty is not to the President personally, nor even to the executive branch, but to the people—and the Constitution—of the United States.[5]

What Holder is advocating for here is a government full of Jim Comeys: government officials determining on their own what the Constitution demands, deciding which laws to prosecute and which to ignore, selectively releasing information to the media about Americans under investigation, and held accountable neither to the chief executive nor to voters. Holder impugns Attorney General William Barr as "nakedly partisan" and "unfit to lead the Justice Department." Ironically, Barr is actually returning accountability and a respect for the law and the Constitution to the Justice Department (something no one would accuse Holder of doing).

■ ■ ■

I have not worked within the Department of State, or the Department of Defense, or the CIA, or the National Security Agency, but I fear the atmosphere in these institutions is little different from what I encountered inside the Department of Justice. Some government bureaucrats have a way of inflating their importance and presumed authority. Certainly anyone following the 2019 impeachment proceedings against President Trump saw unelected experts serving in government appear convinced that they, rather than the elected President of the United States with whom they happened to disagree, should determine the country's foreign or military policy. It seemed to me that their attitude was often that President Trump was a dangerous interloper in their business.

But when Americans elect a President, they're signing on for that President's policies. Those policies might be opposed to existing policies, they might conflict with long-standing practices and beliefs inside executive branch departments and agencies. But that's how the people effect change—by electing candidates who promise something different.

Longtime career civil servants can easily get it into their heads that they, the "experts," need to protect the American people from their populist ignorance and from the policies of a President whom the "experts" deem unsavory. I found remarkable the following analysis of Jonna Mendez, the CIA's retired Chief of Disguise, who was an agent in Moscow (among many other overseas assignments) and sits on the board of Washington D.C.'s Spy Museum. A 2019 *Wall Street Journal* interview with her reveals:

> Ms. Mendez worries about partisan politics interfering with the CIA's work, which "should never be political." Yet she is confident that the CIA's division chiefs won't stand for inappropriately politicized guidance, even if it comes from the very top. "Say that somebody said, 'Let's ease off the Russians.' I don't think they would," she says. "They don't know how to ease off the Russians. They only know one speed and one direction, and that's ahead."[6]

The mentality is that an executive branch agency's work "should never be political," coupled with admiration for bureaucrats who ignore their elected boss. Political is synonymous with accountability to the people, but defenders of the Deep State, like editorial writer Michelle Cottle, fail to realize that. Here is Cottle in the October 20, 2019, edition of the *New York Times*:

President Trump is right: the Deep State is alive and well. But it is not the sinister, antidemocratic cabal of his fever dreams. It is, rather, a collection of patriotic public servants—career diplomats, scientists, intelligence officers and others—who, from within the bowels of this corrupt and corrupting administration, have somehow remembered that their duty is to protect the interests not of a particular leader, but of the American people.[7]

How do these patriotic public servants determine what's in the interests of the American people? Do they call them up and ask them, "Did you really mean to vote for Donald Trump? Don't you realize his agenda is disagreeable to those of us who are 'experts' and know better? Do I have your permission to ignore him?" Or do they go about their business regardless of voters' choices, satisfied by their own intelligence and expertise, like Jonna Mendez described: one speed, and one direction, and that's ahead?

Inside the Justice Department, before I arrived and while my hands were tied by Jeff Sessions's recusal, the bureaucratic elites who thought of themselves as patriotic public servants were moving at one speed, and in one direction: against the will of voters like me in Iowa, Wisconsin, Michigan, Ohio, and Pennsylvania, people who knew what they were doing when they voted for Donald Trump over Hillary Clinton in 2016.

"I would rather be governed by the first two thousand people in the Boston phone book than by the Harvard University faculty," William F. Buckley famously quipped. The Deep State—half of which went to Harvard—just doesn't get it.

■ ■ ■

Even as a private citizen outside government again, it disturbs me on a personal level that congressional Democrats, aided by bureaucratic elites and egged on by a baying, partisan media, followed their worst instincts to their natural conclusion and impeached President Trump. I am, however, encouraged that this anti-democratic alliance picked on precisely the wrong President.

To me, he hasn't aged a day since I first met him in 2017, which is incredible considering the attacks he has withstood in Washington and in the media. Other Presidents have grown old prematurely from the daily hand-to-hand combat. But Donald Trump is wired differently than most: he thrives in this environment; he seems energized by it; and in the crazy partisan atmosphere that is Washington today, it requires an extraordinary person like him to take the constant flak—and return it with interest. The Democrats and the bureaucratic elites, protected by the media, have long believed they can bully Republicans, who, like Jeff Sessions, tend to be polite and respectful and mindful of the written and unwritten rules of honest and good behavior. Trump hasn't played their game. He won't be bullied. He intends to deliver on his campaign promises. When critics attack him and try to stop him from enacting his policies—the policies he promised to the voters who elected him—he takes it personally, in the best sense. He feels a responsibility to the people who elected him, and he is more than willing and capable of trading rhetorical blow for rhetorical blow.

To the frustration of the coastal elites who were certain Donald Trump would be a one term President, if even that, his willingness to be combative and controversial has yielded a list of accomplishments most Presidents would envy. President Trump fought for and won the confirmations of Supreme Court Justices Neil Gorsuch and Brett Kavanaugh, and he has made it a priority to appoint judges to the federal courts who respect the Constitution as it is written. He fought for and won permanent tax cuts on corporate profits, investment income, and inheritances—ripe targets for left-wing demagoguery. He has headed a hugely successful effort to repeal unnecessary government regulations, set the Keystone and XL pipelines in motion, and opened federal lands in Alaska for drilling. He has also successfully negotiated and signed the United States–Mexico–Canada Agreement and negotiated improved trade relations with China.

There is no disputing that President Trump has presided over a record economic expansion, with job growth and wage gains that have especially helped the low-income workers left behind during the Obama administration. Blacks, Latinos, and those without high school degrees have the lowest unemployment rates ever recorded in our history. The United States has become a net natural gas exporter for the first time since 1957, our coal exports have increased by 60 percent, and our oil production is at an all-time high.

President Trump has brought back America's confidence on the world stage, retaliating decisively against Iran's proxy terrorist attacks on U.S. personnel and property and withdrawing the United States from bad international deals struck by the previous administration, such as the Paris Climate Accord and the Iran nuclear deal.

President Trump has not been afraid to challenge anti-tariff economic orthodoxy and to use the threat of taxing imports as a bargaining chip against China in trade negotiations and against Mexico in immigration affairs. In late 2019, China agreed to honor American intellectual property rights and to stop making American producers share technology secrets to gain access to its markets (or face tariffs). Even the left-wing British newspaper *The Guardian* had to give a backhanded compliment to Trump's hardball diplomacy with its January 26, 2020, headline: "Mexico Has Become Trump's Wall."[8] The President's threat of tariffs has brought about the cooperation of Mexico's government in preventing Central American migrants from breaching our southern border.

More threatening to Donald Trump's opponents than his shocking electability is his efficacy. President Trump has done a lot since the 2016 election to make America a safer, freer, and more prosperous country. That's on the record. But his opponents have gone to dangerous and extreme lengths to prevent him from acting on his mandate and his agenda. Impeachment was the natural conclusion of the Democrats' and the Deep State's effort to delegitimize an election they never accepted. Now that the somber process of impeachment has been so cheapened by Jerry Nadler, Adam Schiff, and Chuck Schumer, will it be readily weaponized against

On February 8, 2019, I was the first Trump cabinet official to testify before the new Democrat-controlled House at a Judiciary Committee oversight hearing called by its new chairman, New York City's Jerrold Nadler. But House Democrats weren't interested in conducting serious oversight or hearing about the accomplishments of the men and women of the Department of Justice. They were out to delegitimize President Trump from their first day in power. *Reuters*

Watching President Trump lead effectively while under withering attacks from the media, Democrats in Congress, former government officials, and even members of his own Justice Department was like nothing else I've witnessed or even read about in American history. The traits that so upset his detractors are the very same traits that keep him pushing forward to accomplish his agenda for the American people. *Getty Images*

Under the tutelage of Hall of Fame Coach Hayden Fry at the University of Iowa, I learned to play smart against opposing teams. I did that most memorably when I caught a pass on a fake field goal in a 1990 game that sent us to the 1991 Rose Bowl and also during this catch in 1991 against our rival Iowa State. Cedar Rapids Gazette

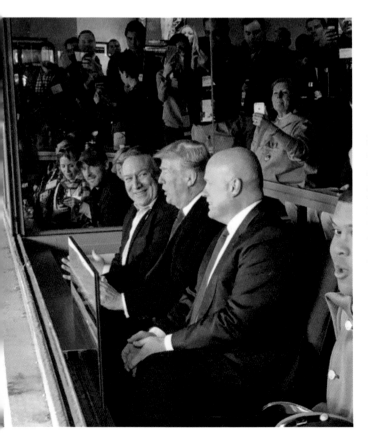

Seated with Secretary of State Mike Pompeo and President Trump at the 2018 Army–Navy football game. Like serving in the military or playing team sports, working in the Department of Justice is an opportunity to be part of something bigger than oneself. *Courtesy of the White House*

Despite all the resistance in the Department of Justice, we had so many important accomplishments between 2017 and 2019; they could fill an entire book. Here, I am briefing the President in the Roosevelt Room at the White House on this administration's School Safety initiative. *Courtesy of the White House*

While Acting Attorney General, I attended the 2018 Presidential Medal of Freedom ceremony in the White House's East Room. Left to right in this photo are Secretary of State Mike Pompeo, Treasury Secretary Steve Mnuchin, myself, and Commerce Secretary Wilbur Ross. It was a pleasure to serve with them. *Courtesy of the White House*

The one favor I ever directly asked President Trump for was his attendance at the Department of Justice's Project Safe Neighborhoods conference in Kansas City. I departed the White House via *Marine One* with Jared Kushner and the President. *Getty Images*

President Trump delivered spectacularly in Kansas City; he genuinely loves the men and women in law enforcement who put their lives on the line every day. *Courtesy of the Department of Justice*

House Judiciary Committee Chairman Jerrold Nadler (center) laughed in spite of himself when he started to break the prior agreement we had made about the terms of my testimony and I politely advised him that his "five minutes were up." (That statement also elicited some gasps from Congressional Democrats in attendance.) *Getty Images*

I could have deferred the Judiciary Committee's requests to appear and let the responsibility fall to Attorney General William Barr once he was confirmed. But if political theater had to happen, better it drew oxygen from the end of my tenure than the beginning of Barr's. *Reuters*

Having been at the table (far left) in the White House Situation Room during the 2018 federal government shutdown negotiations, I saw the President and the Vice President working hard to end the stalemate. But Democrats' hatred for this President would not allow them to give him even a small victory despite the harm it was doing to law enforcement. *Courtesy of the White House*

With members of the Memphis Police Department's SWAT team, getting ready to board after visiting the Western District of Tennessee U.S. Attorney's Office to discuss combatting violent crime in Memphis. For me, the shutdown felt personal. As Acting Attorney General with an FBI security detail, I looked members of federal law enforcement in the eye every day knowing they weren't getting paid while they risked their lives to keep me safe. *Courtesy of the Department of Justice*

Advising me during my time as Acting Attorney General was one of the most impressive public servants I have ever worked with: McGregor Scott, U.S. Attorney for California's Eastern District, former elected county attorney, and a twenty-three-year U.S. Army Reserve veteran who retired a Lieutenant Colonel. "Greg" and I met while we were both serving as U.S. Attorneys in President George W. Bush's administration. *Courtesy of the Department of Justice*

Exiting the Department of Justice the evening he resigned, Jeff Sessions wished me well. Having served honorably as a U.S. Senator for over twenty years, he understood Washington's bureaucratic ways much better than I did. Trying to reform the Justice Department would be difficult. *Copyright C-SPAN*

Justice Triumphant by Leon Kroll (1935). Inside the Attorney General's conference room are two oil paintings commissioned during the Great Depression. One is called *Justice Triumphant* and the other *Justice Defeated*. They are situated in opposition to each other, and the images were a daily reminder of what was a stake in the Department. *Courtesy of the Library of Congress*

Justice Defeated by Leon Kroll (1935). It would be the ultimate irony if the Justice Department were abused to defeat the principles of justice itself—due process and the supremacy of the Constitution—but I fear that some of the bureaucratic elite have few qualms about that as long as it serves their partisan interest. *Courtesy of the Library of Congress*

the next "unacceptable" administration by partisan opponents in Congress, fueled by Special Counsel investigations and a Justice Department whose leaders hold themselves above the law?

I pray that's not the case and that this never happens to another President. This *cannot* ever happen to another President. This *cannot* be the new normal. People of good faith should respect the outcome of lawfully certified elections, the Electoral College, and Article II of the U.S. Constitution. Realizing that it protects us from the tyranny of kings and unduly empowered bureaucracies, we need to appreciate the elegance of the Framers' architecture. Both monarchies and oligarchies are unresponsive to the will of voters. Americans should reject both.

My fervent wish as a battle-scarred veteran of the Justice Department who served two tours and reentered the private sector each time, is that people like myself, who have not carefully curated their entire professional lives for sainthood or stardom, but who care deeply about serving our country, get into politics despite the very real risks to our personal reputations.

Washington, unfortunately, is home to many careerists who have little private sector experience and little tolerance for those who think outside the box (and differently from them). Some have held elected office for so long that they can't remember how to earn a living any other way. Some are in civil servant positions, going with the flow for the promise of a pension one day and a good salary in the here and now. There is a frightening degree of groupthink in Washington, D.C., and frankly, bigotry against outsiders. We need a free-flowing exchange of ideas and policy experiments in this country, balanced and checked by the Constitution—not a permanent standing bureaucratic class.

America needs new blood in its governing institutions—people from all parts of the country and walks of life; people who are willing to help inculcate the values of accountability, transparency, broad-mindedness, plainspokenness, and fair play into our great nation's political discourse. The election of President Donald Trump marked a beginning of that—and I am proud to have been a part of it too.

ACTING ATTORNEY GENERAL AND SECRETARY OF HOMELAND SECURITY SUBMIT JOINT REPORT ON IMPACT OF FOREIGN INTERFERENCE ON ELECTION AND POLITICAL/CAMPAIGN INFRASTRUCTURE IN 2018 ELECTIONS

Department of Justice

Office of Public Affairs

FOR IMMEDIATE RELEASE

Tuesday, February 5, 2019

Acting Attorney General and Secretary of Homeland Security Submit Joint Report on Impact of Foreign Interference on Election and Political/Campaign Infrastructure in 2018 Elections

Report Concludes No Material Impact of Foreign Interference on Election or Political/Campaign Infrastructure in 2018 Elections

Acting Attorney General Matthew G. Whitaker and Secretary of Homeland Security Kirstjen M. Nielsen yesterday submitted a joint report to President Donald J. Trump evaluating the impact of any foreign interference on election infrastructure or the infrastructure of political organizations, including campaigns and candidates in the 2018–midterm elections.

The classified report was prepared pursuant to section 1(b) of Executive Order 13848, *Imposing Certain Sanctions in the Event of Foreign Influence in a United States Election,* which the President issued on Sept. 12, 2018.

Throughout the 2018 midterm election cycle, the Departments of Justice and Homeland Security worked closely with federal, state, local, and private sector partners, including all 50 states and more than 1400 local jurisdictions, to support efforts to secure election infrastructure and limit risk posed by foreign interference. Efforts to safeguard the 2020 elections are already underway.

Although the specific conclusions within the joint report must remain classified, the Departments have concluded there is no evidence to date that any identified activities of a foreign government or foreign agent had a material impact on the integrity or security of election infrastructure or political/campaign infrastructure used in the 2018 midterm elections for the United States Congress. This finding was informed by a report prepared by the Office of the Director of National Intelligence (ODNI) pursuant to the same Executive Order and is consistent with what was indicated by the U.S. government after the 2018 elections.

While the report remains classified, its findings will help drive future efforts to protect election and political/campaign infrastructure from foreign interference.

ATTORNEY GENERAL WILLIAM BARR'S SUMMARY OF THE MUELLER REPORT

The Attorney General
Washington, D.C.

March 24, 2019

The Honorable Lindsey Graham
Chairman, Committee on the Judiciary
United States Senate
290 Russell Senate Office Building
Washington, D.C. 20510

The Honorable Jerrold Nadler
Chairman, Committee on the Judiciary
United States House of Representatives
2132 Rayburn House Office Building
Washington, D.C. 20515

The Honorable Dianne Feinstein
Ranking Member, Committee on the Judiciary
United States Senate
331 Hart Senate Office Building
Washington, D.C. 20510

The Honorable Doug Collins
Ranking Member, Committee on the Judiciary
United States House of Representatives
1504 Longworth House Office Building
Washington, D.C. 20515

Dear Chairman Graham, Chairman Nadler, Ranking Member Feinstein, and Ranking Member Collins:

As a supplement to the notification provided on Friday, March 22, 2019, I am writing today to advise you of the principal conclusions reached by Special Counsel Robert S. Mueller III and to inform you about the status of my initial review of the report he has prepared.

The Special Counsel's Report

On Friday, the Special Counsel submitted to me a "confidential report explaining the prosecution or declination decisions" he has reached, as required by 28 C.F.R. § 600.8(c). This report is entitled "Report on the Investigation into Russian Interference in the 2016 Presidential Election." Although my review is ongoing, I believe that it is in the public interest to describe the report and to summarize the principal conclusions reached by the Special Counsel and the results of his investigation.

The report explains that the Special Counsel and his staff thoroughly investigated allegations that members of the presidential campaign of Donald J. Trump, and others associated with it, conspired with the Russian government in its efforts to interfere in the 2016 U.S. presidential election, or sought to obstruct the related federal investigations. In the report, the Special Counsel noted that, in completing his investigation, he employed 19 lawyers who were assisted by a team of approximately 40 FBI agents, intelligence analysts, forensic accountants, and other professional staff. The Special Counsel issued more than 2,800 subpoenas, executed nearly 500 search warrants, obtained more than 230 orders for communication records, issued almost 50 orders authorizing use of pen registers, made 13 requests to foreign governments for evidence, and interviewed approximately 500 witnesses.

The Special Counsel obtained a number of indictments and convictions of individuals and entities in connection with his investigation, all of which have been publicly disclosed. During the course of his investigation, the Special Counsel also referred several matters to other offices for further action. The report does not recommend any further indictments, nor did the Special Counsel obtain any sealed indictments that have yet to be made public. Below, I summarize the principal conclusions set out in the Special Counsel's report.

Russian Interference in the 2016 U.S. Presidential Election. The Special Counsel's report is divided into two parts. The first describes the results of the Special Counsel's investigation into Russia's interference in the 2016 U.S. presidential election. The report outlines the Russian effort to influence the election and documents crimes committed by persons associated with the Russian government in connection with those efforts. The report further explains that a primary consideration for the Special Counsel's investigation was whether any Americans – including individuals associated with the Trump campaign – joined the Russian conspiracies to influence the election, which would be a federal crime. The Special Counsel's investigation did not find that the Trump campaign or anyone associated with it conspired or coordinated with Russia in its efforts to influence the 2016 U.S. presidential election. As the report states: "[T]he investigation did not establish that members of the Trump Campaign conspired or coordinated with the Russian government in its election interference activities."[1]

The Special Counsel's investigation determined that there were two main Russian efforts to influence the 2016 election. The first involved attempts by a Russian organization, the Internet Research Agency (IRA), to conduct disinformation and social media operations in the United States designed to sow social discord, eventually with the aim of interfering with the election. As noted above, the Special Counsel did not find that any U.S. person or Trump campaign official or associate conspired or knowingly coordinated with the IRA in its efforts, although the Special Counsel brought criminal charges against a number of Russian nationals and entities in connection with these activities.

The second element involved the Russian government's efforts to conduct computer hacking operations designed to gather and disseminate information to influence the election. The Special Counsel found that Russian government actors successfully hacked into computers and obtained emails from persons affiliated with the Clinton campaign and Democratic Party organizations, and publicly disseminated those materials through various intermediaries, including WikiLeaks. Based on these activities, the Special Counsel brought criminal charges against a number of Russian military officers for conspiring to hack into computers in the United States for purposes of influencing the election. But as noted above, the Special Counsel did not find that the Trump campaign, or anyone associated with it, conspired or coordinated with the Russian government in these efforts, despite multiple offers from Russian-affiliated individuals to assist the Trump campaign.

---

[1]   In assessing potential conspiracy charges, the Special Counsel also considered whether members of the Trump campaign "coordinated" with Russian election interference activities. The Special Counsel defined "coordination" as an "agreement—tacit or express—between the Trump Campaign and the Russian government on election interference."

Obstruction of Justice. The report's second part addresses a number of actions by the President – most of which have been the subject of public reporting – that the Special Counsel investigated as potentially raising obstruction-of-justice concerns. After making a "thorough factual investigation" into these matters, the Special Counsel considered whether to evaluate the conduct under Department standards governing prosecution and declination decisions but ultimately determined not to make a traditional prosecutorial judgment. The Special Counsel therefore did not draw a conclusion – one way or the other – as to whether the examined conduct constituted obstruction. Instead, for each of the relevant actions investigated, the report sets out evidence on both sides of the question and leaves unresolved what the Special Counsel views as "difficult issues" of law and fact concerning whether the President's actions and intent could be viewed as obstruction. The Special Counsel states that "while this report does not conclude that the President committed a crime, it also does not exonerate him."

The Special Counsel's decision to describe the facts of his obstruction investigation without reaching any legal conclusions leaves it to the Attorney General to determine whether the conduct described in the report constitutes a crime. Over the course of the investigation, the Special Counsel's office engaged in discussions with certain Department officials regarding many of the legal and factual matters at issue in the Special Counsel's obstruction investigation. After reviewing the Special Counsel's final report on these issues; consulting with Department officials, including the Office of Legal Counsel; and applying the principles of federal prosecution that guide our charging decisions, Deputy Attorney General Rod Rosenstein and I have concluded that the evidence developed during the Special Counsel's investigation is not sufficient to establish that the President committed an obstruction-of-justice offense. Our determination was made without regard to, and is not based on, the constitutional considerations that surround the indictment and criminal prosecution of a sitting president.[2]

In making this determination, we noted that the Special Counsel recognized that "the evidence does not establish that the President was involved in an underlying crime related to Russian election interference," and that, while not determinative, the absence of such evidence bears upon the President's intent with respect to obstruction. Generally speaking, to obtain and sustain an obstruction conviction, the government would need to prove beyond a reasonable doubt that a person, acting with corrupt intent, engaged in obstructive conduct with a sufficient nexus to a pending or contemplated proceeding. In cataloguing the President's actions, many of which took place in public view, the report identifies no actions that, in our judgment, constitute obstructive conduct, had a nexus to a pending or contemplated proceeding, and were done with corrupt intent, each of which, under the Department's principles of federal prosecution guiding charging decisions, would need to be proven beyond a reasonable doubt to establish an obstruction-of-justice offense.

Status of the Department's Review

The relevant regulations contemplate that the Special Counsel's report will be a "confidential report" to the Attorney General. *See* Office of Special Counsel, 64 Fed. Reg. 37,038,

---

[2] *See A Sitting President's Amenability to Indictment and Criminal Prosecution*, 24 Op. O.L.C. 222 (2000).

37,040-41 (July 9, 1999). As I have previously stated, however, I am mindful of the public interest in this matter. For that reason, my goal and intent is to release as much of the Special Counsel's report as I can consistent with applicable law, regulations, and Departmental policies.

Based on my discussions with the Special Counsel and my initial review, it is apparent that the report contains material that is or could be subject to Federal Rule of Criminal Procedure 6(e), which imposes restrictions on the use and disclosure of information relating to "matter[s] occurring before [a] grand jury." Fed. R. Crim. P. 6(e)(2)(B). Rule 6(e) generally limits disclosure of certain grand jury information in a criminal investigation and prosecution. *Id.* Disclosure of 6(e) material beyond the strict limits set forth in the rule is a crime in certain circumstances. *See, e.g.*, 18 U.S.C. § 401(3). This restriction protects the integrity of grand jury proceedings and ensures that the unique and invaluable investigative powers of a grand jury are used strictly for their intended criminal justice function.

Given these restrictions, the schedule for processing the report depends in part on how quickly the Department can identify the 6(e) material that by law cannot be made public. I have requested the assistance of the Special Counsel in identifying all 6(e) information contained in the report as quickly as possible. Separately, I also must identify any information that could impact other ongoing matters, including those that the Special Counsel has referred to other offices. As soon as that process is complete, I will be in a position to move forward expeditiously in determining what can be released in light of applicable law, regulations, and Departmental policies.

*   *   *

As I observed in my initial notification, the Special Counsel regulations provide that "the Attorney General may determine that public release of" notifications to your respective Committees "would be in the public interest." 28 C.F.R. § 600.9(c). I have so determined, and I will disclose this letter to the public after delivering it to you.

Sincerely,

William P. Barr

William P. Barr
Attorney General

MAY 4, 2018, MENENDEZ JOINT LETTER TO GENERAL PROSECUTOR OF UKRAINE ON MUELLER INVESTIGATION

United States Senate
WASHINGTON, DC 20510

May 4, 2018

Mr. Yuriy Lutsenko
General Prosecutor
Office of the Prosecutor General of Ukraine
13/15 Riznytska St.
Kyiv, 01011
Ukraine

Dear Mr. Prosecutor General:

We are writing to express great concern about reports that your office has taken steps to impede cooperation with the investigation of United States Special Counsel Robert Mueller. As strong advocates for a robust and close relationship with Ukraine, we believe that our cooperation should extend to such legal matters, regardless of politics. Ours is a relationship built on a foundation of respect for the rule of law and accountable democratic institutions. In four short years, Ukraine has made significant progress in building these institutions despite ongoing military, economic and political pressure from Moscow. We have supported that capacity-building process and are disappointed that some in Kyiv appear to have cast aside these principles in order to avoid the ire of President Trump. If these reports are true, we strongly encourage you to reverse course and halt any efforts to impede cooperation with this important investigation.

On May 2, the New York Times reported that your office effectively froze investigations into four open cases in Ukraine in April, thereby eliminating scope for cooperation with the Mueller probe into related issues. The article notes that your office considered these cases as too politically sensitive and potentially jeopardizing U.S. financial and military aid to Ukraine. The article indicates specifically that your office prohibited special prosecutor Serhiy Horbatyuk from issuing subpoenas for evidence or interviewing witnesses in four open cases in Ukraine related to consulting work performed by Paul Manafort for former Ukrainian president Viktor Yanukovich and his political party.

This investigation not only has implications for the Mueller probe, but also speaks to critically important investigations into the corrupt practices of the Yanukovich administration, which stole millions of dollars from the people of Ukraine. Blocking cooperation with the Mueller probe potentially cuts off a significant opportunity for Ukrainian law enforcement to conduct a more thorough inquiry into possible crimes committed during the Yanukovich era. This reported refusal to cooperate with the Mueller probe also sends a worrying signal—to the Ukrainian people as well as the international community—about your government's commitment more broadly to support justice and the rule of law.

We respectfully request that you reply to this letter answering the following questions:
1. Has your office taken any steps to restrict cooperation with the investigation by Special Counsel Robert Mueller? If so, why?

2. Did any individual from the Trump Administration, or anyone acting on its behalf, encourage Ukrainian government or law enforcement officials not to cooperate with the investigation by Special Counsel Robert Mueller?
3. Was the Mueller probe raised in any way during discussions between your government and U.S. officials, including around the meeting of Presidents Trump and Poroshenko in New York in 2017?

Sincerely,

Robert Menendez
United States Senator

Richard J. Durbin
United States Senator

Patrick Leahy
United States Senator

SELECTED SPEECHES
BY MATTHEW WHITAKER

During my tenure as Acting Attorney General I worked hard to advance the President's priorities for the Department of Justice including reducing crime in America, "backing the blue," and dismantling transnational criminal organizations. What follows is a selection of speeches I gave, in chronological order, which afforded me the privilege of meeting and working with thousands of Americans across the country.

Acting Attorney General Matthew Whitaker Delivers Remarks at the Department of Justice's Veterans Appreciation Day Ceremony

Washington, D.C.

■ ■ ■

Thursday, November 15, 2018

Remarks as prepared for delivery

Thank you, Lee for that kind introduction and thank you for your 36 years of service to the Department of Justice and your 12 years of stewardship of the Department's finances.

I also want to thank the Joint Armed Forces Color Guard for the Presentation of the Colors and Girale Wilson-Takahashi from our COPS office for that beautiful rendition of the National Anthem.

Thank you all for being here for the Department's eighth Veterans' Appreciation Day.

Above all, thank you to the 150 veterans who have joined us today.

Thank you for your service in our Armed Forces—and thank you for your service in this Department.

At this Department of Justice, we recognize that public safety is government's first and most important priority.

The men and women of our Armed Forces—Army, Navy, Marines, Air Force, Coast Guard—risk their lives for that mission every day, and each of us owes them a debt of gratitude.

This Department also works for public safety by enforcing our laws—but we know that our work depends upon the bravery and sacrifice of our troops.

We are proud of each one of the 27,000 veterans who serve in this Department.

Your skills, your patriotism, and above all your selfless character make you the kind of employees that any employer would want. But you've chosen to continue to serve your country—you've chosen to work in the Department of Justice. I commend you for that.

We are well aware that heroes walk these hallways.

Outside of my office is a memorial with the names of colleagues who during World War II made the ultimate sacrifice in the defense of our grateful country.

I also know firsthand of the heroes we have in department, because I am now literally surrounded by them each and every day. Most of the FBI agents in my security detail are veterans.

That includes Special Agent Damon Flores, who is a former Navy rescue swimmer in the Mediterranean and in the Persian Gulf. After his service in the Navy, he went to college on the GI Bill and got an accounting and finance degree. He quickly realized that accounting was not as exciting as being a rescue swimmer. He wanted a little more adventure, and so he signed up with the FBI. He marked his fourteenth anniversary with the Bureau just yesterday. Damon, congratulations.

We're also proud to be the home of Maura Quinn of DEA.

Maura graduated from the Naval Academy, and then in flight school she chose to fly helicopters so she could pilot a combat aircraft. After graduation she deployed twice—first with a carrier battle group to the Indian Ocean and then in support of Operation Desert Shield.

She served as an instructor pilot for two years and went to law school at night. As if she weren't busy enough, she gave birth to two children before graduation.

After law school, she joined the United States Attorney's Office in the Southern District of California and then the FBI's Office of General Counsel. he then served for eight years in the Chief Counsel's office at DEA. Over that time she became an expert in technology law—and today she serves as DEA's Deputy Assistant Administrator for Information Systems. Maura, thank you for your service.

I could go on and on. There are roughly 26,998 more examples that I could talk about.

But this is the caliber of people that we are so grateful to have in this Department.

Through our Veterans Employment Office in the Justice Management Division, we have made hiring veterans a priority and helped them make the transition into careers with the Department.

We want more exemplary employees like Damon Flores and Maura Quinn.

We will continue to invest in our heroes—because you're a good investment. You are, in the words of General John Kelly, "the very best this country produces."

Now I have the honor of introducing someone who knows that as well as anyone.

Our keynote speaker is the Director of Military Force Management Policy for the Air Force, Major General Robert LaBrutta. You might think of him as the Air Force's head of human resources.

Major General LaBrutta has served in the Air Force for the last thirty-seven years.

Today he is responsible for setting force management policy that affects more than half a million Air Force personnel—issues like assignments, evaluation, readiness, and transitioning back to civilian life.

Before this assignment he served as Commander of the Second Air Force at Keesler Air Force Base in Biloxi, Mississippi.

He has earned a number of distinguished awards including the Defense Superior Service Medal, the Legion of Merit, the Meritorious Service Medal, the Air Force Commendation Medal, the Air Force Achievement Medal, and many others.

Please join me in welcoming Major General Robert LaBrutta.

Acting Attorney General Matthew Whitaker Delivers Remarks Announcing a New Memphis Crime Gun Strike Force

Memphis, Tennessee

■ ■ ■

Wednesday, November 28, 2018

Remarks as prepared for delivery

Thank you, Mike for that kind introduction. More importantly, thank you for your eleven years of service as a District Attorney General and now as United States Attorney.

Thank you also to:

- Marcus Watson of ATF,
- Jim Catalano and Brett Pritts of DEA,
- Mo Myers of the FBI,
- U.S. Marshal Jeffrey Holt,
- Channing Irvin with the Secret Service,
- Postal Inspector Dwight Jones,
- John Condon of HSI,
- Sheriff Guy Buck,
- Sheriff Floyd Bonner,
- Sheriff John Mehr,
- Chief Julian Wiser of Jackson Police,
- Chief Buddy Lewis of Covington,
- Chief Richard Hall of Germantown,
- Chief Mark Dunbar of Millington,
- Chief Steve Isbell of Dyersburg,
- Larry Laurenzi, former U.S. Attorney, WDTN,
- Eddie Walker, Tipton County Sheriff's Office,
- District Attorneys General Amy Weirich, Jody Pickens, and Mark Davidson, and

- Captain Roy Brown, Captain Jimmie Johnson, and Captain Curtis Mansfield of the Tennessee Highway Patrol.

I am grateful for the contribution that each one of you makes toward our shared mission of protecting this community.

Every day our officers go into dangerous situations so that the rest of us don't have to.

And your work has a real impact on our communities. We don't just prosecute crime—we prevent crime.

After all, most people are not criminals. Most of the crime in this country is committed by relatively few criminals. If we can take those few criminals off of our streets, then we can keep them from committing a lot more crimes in the future.

Over the last few decades, the law enforcement community has developed new technologies and new strategies that have made us better able than ever to do just that.

This office, for example, submits all of the shell casings you find at crime scenes to the National Integrated Ballistic Information Network, or NIBIN, which can trace them back to the gun that fired them. That helps us find shooters and connect the dots between cases.

This is great work—and the Department of Justice is investing in it. Two months ago, we awarded $1.1 million for technology and for personnel to operate an ATF Crime Gun Intelligence Center—or CGIC—here in Memphis.

This is a model that was pioneered in recent years in Denver. Now we're bringing it to Memphis.

CGICs help reduce violent crime by using forensic science and data analysis to identify, investigate, and prosecute shooters and their sources for the guns they use for crime. Relying on intelligence from NIBIN, crime gun tracing, and good old fashioned police work, CGICs provide law enforcement leads in real time to identify serial shooters, disrupt criminal activity, and prevent future gun violence.

This Department is proud to invest in this important work.

I believe that we have a real mandate from the American people to keep them safe.

When President Trump came into office, violent crime had risen sharply. After two decades of historic decreases in crime, the trends had suddenly reversed.

From 2014 to 2016, the violent crime rate went up by nearly seven percent nationwide. Robberies went up. Assaults went up by over 8 percent. Rape went up by nearly 13 percent. Murder went up by 21 percent.

Here in Memphis murder went up by 40 percent.

In 2016, there were nearly 200 homicides in Memphis. That means that nearly 40 percent of all homicides in Tennessee happened right here in Memphis.

Unfortunately, violent crime in Memphis went up by another 10 percent in 2017. Last year the murder rate, the assault rate, and the robbery rate in Memphis were each five times the national average.

Obviously these are deeply concerning trends—and we've got to stop them. We've got to get back on track. We've got to get back to reducing crime like we did for twenty years, including over my five years as a United States Attorney.

And, of course, we recognize that every district is different. Here in Memphis, there is a great deal of concern about gun crimes.

Our local partners here in Memphis have told me that in the first ten months of this year, there were 283 reported armed car-jacking incidents within the city, which represents a 63 percent increase compared to the same period last year.

There has also been a dramatic increase in thefts from gun stores. I'm told that in 2018 there has been about a 66 percent increase in burglaries and robberies of gun stores.

That means more illegal guns on the streets—and more illegal guns in the hands of criminals. That usually means more shootings and more robberies.

That's why I am so impressed with what Mike and his team have been doing in this office. Under the local Project Safe Neighborhoods

initiative, they have made prosecuting the most violent offenders a priority, and it shows. Over the past three years, ATF has steadily increased
gun recoveries from more than 4,200 to more than 4,500 per year now.

Mike also seeks maximum penalties for gun crimes. As this office
has been telling the criminals: "gun crime means max time."

I think that is appropriate, because every year that a firearm offender
is behind bars is another year that he isn't shooting or robbing anybody
in Memphis.

That approach has led to a lot of successes here in Memphis.

This past January, you secured a thirty-year sentence for the highest
ranking Gangster Disciple gang member in Tennessee. This case involved
cooperation between FBI, ATF, TBI, Memphis police, and two sheriffs'
offices. That is an example of what law enforcement cooperation can
accomplish. AUSA Beth Boswell worked on that case. Great job.

In September, you secured another thirty-year sentence for a member
of the Gangster Disciples. This defendant had attempted murder with a
firearm in order to enhance his position with the gang. He also served
on a so-called "blackout squad" as a kind of enforcer. The FBI, ATF, the
TBI, three sheriffs' offices, Memphis police, and many other partners
worked on this case. Congratulations once again to AUSA Beth Boswell
for her work on that case.

And just two weeks ago, prosecutors in this office put an armed
robber behind bars for thirty years. That case was investigated by the
FBI's Safe Streets Task Force and prosecuted by AUSA Reagan Taylor. Reagan, congratulations.

There are a lot of other cases that we could talk about. You're doing
great work—and it's having an impact.

You have taken seriously your charge to identify and prosecute the
most violent offenders. But as Mike noted in his recent opinion piece,
"that focus is only meaningful if it results in better outcomes—reduction
in violent crime rates." And it is there that your work has truly proven
successful.

Here in Memphis, gun crimes went down by 17 percent through the
first nine months of this year. Murders went down 17 percent, robberies

went down 12 percent, rapes went down 18 percent, and domestic violence incidents went down 11 percent.

We are seeing these results all across the country where our United States Attorneys are reinvigorating their efforts against violent criminals under Project Safe Neighborhoods. Just like in Memphis, in cities and towns where US Attorneys and their local partners are identifying the most violent offenders in their communities, and ensuring they are held accountable in the federal, state, or local system.

Those efforts have helped us achieve our goals as a Department nationwide. In fiscal year 2018, the Department of Justice charged more defendants with gun crimes than in any year in Department history. In fact, we broke the record by a margin of 17 percent.

More importantly, violent crime and homicide went down nationwide in 2017. For 2018, one estimate projects that the murder rate in our twenty-nine biggest cities will decline by 7.6 percent.

We should celebrate these achievements.

But I'm here to say that we are just getting started.

Today I am announcing a new Memphis Crime Gun Strike Force, led by the ATF.

The Strike Force will initially be composed of highly experienced ATF agents and officers from the Memphis Police Department. To launch the Strike Force, ATF is realigning five agents and one senior supervisor. Over the long-term, we plan to add more ATF agents and expand participation to additional law enforcement partners.

For now it will be housed at ATF, but we hope to give the strike force its own dedicated space in the future.

The Strike Force will allow us to increase the focus of our investigations on those actively engaged in gun violence—the "trigger-pullers" and gun traffickers who supply them. That will enhance our capacity to investigate the criminals and organizations who operate across districts and state borders. The Strike Force will work closely with this office and Shelby County District Attorney Amy Weirich to ensure violent firearm offenders are identified, investigated and prosecuted.

In short, it will help us build on what we have already achieved over these past two years.

.The Department of Justice is going to continue to work to keep communities safe. We're going to continue to support our state and local partners—and I believe that our partnerships are going to continue to deliver results.

And so I want to conclude with something a mentor of mine used to say every time he spoke to law enforcement, and I believe it too: we have your back, and you have our thanks.

Acting Attorney General Matthew Whitaker Delivers Remarks in Nashville on Efforts to Combat the Opioid Crisis

Nashville, Tennessee

■ ■ ■

Thursday, November 29, 2018

Remarks as prepared for delivery

Thank you, Don for that kind introduction and thank you for your nearly six years of service to the Department of Justice and for your service as a state prosecutor in Alabama. Thank you also for your nine years of service in the Army Rangers and Army Special Forces. That's probably the only kind of work that could make prosecuting criminals seem boring by comparison.

Thank you also to: U.S. Attorney Doug Overbey from the Eastern District of Tennessee, U.S. Attorney Mike Dunavant from the Western District of Tennessee, and the head of our Criminal Division, Brian Benczkowski, and Chris Evans of DEA Louisville.

I also want to recognize Criminal Chief Brent Hannafan, who is the proud son of an Iowan. Brent, thank you for your service to this Department.

As a former U.S. Attorney myself, I know how important our U.S. Attorneys and our AUSAs are to the overall efforts of the Department of Justice and to keeping our communities safe.

Thank you all for your hard work and sacrifice to reduce crime and to fight the opioid crisis.

That work is more important than ever—because today we are facing the deadliest drug crisis in American history. Last year 70,000 Americans lost their lives to drug overdoses. That is the highest drug death toll in American history—by far. It's the equivalent of the population of Jackson, Tennessee, dead in just one year from drug overdoses. More Americans died of drug overdoses last year than from car crashes.

Despite rising prosperity and better technology, life expectancy in the United States actually declined over the last three years—and largely because of this epidemic. The last time life expectancy in this country declined for three years in a row was a century ago. This is simply unacceptable.

And overdose deaths don't tell the whole story. Millions of people are living with the painful consequences of a family member's addiction or an addiction of their own. I personally know people whose families have been impacted by drug addiction. We all do.

Appalachia has been especially hard hit by addiction and by opioid fraud. Some of the first pill mills in America were started in Southern Ohio, Kentucky, and West Virginia. And to this day Appalachian communities still have tragically high rates of addiction and overdose.

Here in Tennessee, drug overdose deaths overall have gone up by about 50 percent since 2013 and reached record highs. Here in the Nashville-Davidson area, the increase has been even bigger: an 88 percent increase since 2013. In 2017, Davidson County was second in the state for overdose deaths.

The vast majority of those overdose deaths are from opioids. Heroin deaths have increased more than fivefold in the Nashville-Davidson region since 2013.

This is a daunting situation. Your work has never been more difficult—but it has never been more important.

The Trump administration has your back in these efforts. The President has laid out a comprehensive plan to end this crisis. The three parts of his plan are prevention, enforcement, and treatment.

President Trump has improved our prevention efforts by launching a coordinated national awareness campaign about the dangers of opioid abuse.

And he is a strong supporter of law enforcement.

Under his leadership, the Department has put a special focus on fighting the deadliest drugs today: synthetic opioids like fentanyl.

These drugs are so powerful that all it takes is the equivalent of a pinch of salt to be fatal.

Not only are they powerful—they're also too easy to get. You can even go online and have them shipped right to your door.

Over the past two years, synthetic opioids have killed more Americans than any other kind of drug. Last year these drugs killed more than 29,000 Americans.

And so we've placed a special focus on prosecuting fentanyl cases over these past two years.

And we've been getting results.

Last July, the Department announced the seizure of a website that was the largest dark net marketplace in history. It was called AlphaBay. It hosted more than 220,000 drug listings and was responsible for countless fentanyl overdoses, including the tragic death of a thirteen-year-old.

In August we announced charges against a married couple who sold fentanyl on Alpha Bay. We believe they were once the most prolific synthetic opioid traffickers on the darknet in North America. We also worked with our partners in Canada to help them indict a man we believe was the third most prolific darknet synthetic opioid dealer in North America as well.

In January we began J-CODE, a new team at the FBI that focuses specifically on the threat of online opioid sales. They have already begun carrying out enforcement actions nationwide, arresting dozens of people across the country.

We know that the vast majority of the fentanyl in this country is made in China. That is why the Trump administration has become the first administration to prosecute Chinese fentanyl traffickers.

Last year, we announced the first two indictments against Chinese nationals for trafficking synthetic drugs in the United States. And then in August, we announced our third case—a forty-three–count indictment against a drug trafficking organization based in Shanghai.

This summer I went to China and met with Chinese officials to discuss this problem. I made it clear to them that we want them to be our partners in these efforts—and that they've got to do more to stop these drugs from coming here.

Nevertheless, we are interdicting drugs coming into this country at higher and higher levels. In fiscal year 2018, the DEA seized six tons of heroin, more than 100,000 pounds of methamphetamine, and nearly two tons of fentanyl. That's 70 percent more fentanyl than the year before. And that's enough drugs to kill every man, woman, and child in the United States.

Those interdiction efforts are important and necessary. But we know that one of the major causes of the opioid crisis in the first place was overprescribing. We're told that three out of four heroin addicts in the United States first started on prescription opioids. Even if that is an overestimate, it is still too many.

That's why President Trump has set the goal of reducing the national opioid prescription rate by one-third in three years. It's an ambitious goal, but we are well on our way to achieving it.

According to the DEA's National Prescription Audit, in the first eight months of 2018, opioid prescriptions were down by nearly 12 percent compared to a year before. And that's in addition to a seven percent decline last year.

We now have the lowest opioid prescription rates in 18 years. And we're going to bring them a lot lower.

We are also lowering the legal limits on opioid production. For next year, the DEA is lowering them by an average of 10 percent. That will bring us to about a 44 percent decrease in opioid production since 2016.

We are making it harder to divert these pills for abuse—and we're going after the fraudsters who exploit people suffering from addiction.

Two years in a row the Department of Justice has set records for health care fraud enforcement. This July we charged 601 defendants with more than $2 billion in medical fraud. This was the most doctors, the most medical personnel, and the most fraud that the Department of Justice has ever taken on in any single law enforcement action. This is the most defendants we've ever charged with health care fraud and the most opioid-related fraud defendants we've ever charged in a single enforcement action.

So far under President Donald Trump, the Department of Justice has charged more than 220 doctors with opioid-related crimes and convicted more than eighty of them. Sixteen of those doctors prescribed more than 20.3 million pills illegally.

We have also charged another 221 other medical personnel for opioid-related crimes.

In fiscal year 2018 we charged six percent more drug defendants overall than in fiscal year 2017. We prosecuted 36 percent more opioid defendants than the previous four-year average. We increased heroin prosecutions by 14 percent and oxycontin prosecutions by 37 percent. We are prosecuting more fentanyl defendants than ever before.

More importantly, however, overdose deaths in this country may have finally stopped rising or even come down.

From 2012 to 2017, drug overdose deaths per year in this country increased a shocking 74 percent.

According to the CDC, drug overdose deaths increased on a month-by-month basis until last September. The rolling twelve-month total then decreased by two percent from September 2017 through April 2018, which is the most recent data we have.

These are preliminary numbers—and we want much bigger decreases—but this is good news.

And we're not going to stop there. We are continuing to support you and help you succeed.

Last month we announced our new Appalachian Regional Prescription Opioid Strike Force.

This new Strike Force will be composed of twelve additional opioid fraud prosecutors across our nine Appalachian districts and the surrounding area. Each one of these prosecutors will have their own team of federal investigators and law enforcement agents. They'll also be mobile—so if a small case turns into a bigger case, then they can prosecute it in any Appalachian district they need to.

The Northern Hub of the Strike Force will be based in Fort Mitchell, Kentucky. The Southern Hub will be based right here in Nashville.

We've already used this Strike Force model to combat health care fraud—and it has been very successful.

We want to replicate that success in the fight against the opioid epidemic.

This new Strike Force is going to build on the successes that we have already achieved over these past two years, and I believe that it can help provide some relief to Appalachia.

I especially want to thank Matt Miner and Joe Beemsterboer for their great work in setting up this ARPO Strike Force. I know that you spent countless hours on the road over the past couple of months. But I also know that your tireless efforts, in conjunction with the work of the Strike Force prosecutors and the AUSAs in the United States Attorneys' Offices, will pay countless dividends.

This is our latest step—but it is not our last step. We are going to keep up this pace. We are going to keep supporting you, arming you with new resources and new weapons. We are going to keep coordinating with you and listening to you about how we can help.

And so I want to conclude with something a mentor of mine used to say every time he spoke to law enforcement, and I believe it too: we have your back, and you have our thanks.

Acting Attorney General Matthew Whitaker Delivers Remarks in Cincinnati on Efforts to Combat the Opioid Crisis, Announces $16 Million in Funding to Serve Las Vegas Mass Shooting Victims

Cincinnati, Ohio

■ ■ ■

Friday, November 30, 2018

Remarks as prepared for delivery

Thank you, Ben, for that kind introduction, and thank you for your thirteen years of service to the Department of Justice.

Thank you also to Kentucky U.S. Attorneys Rob Duncan of the Eastern District and Russell Coleman of the Western District, U.S. Attorney Mike Stuart of the Southern District of West Virginia, and the Assistant Attorney General in charge of our Criminal Division Brian Benczkowski.

Thank you all for your work to reduce crime in this community and across America.

As each one of you knows, this Department of Justice supports you, your prosecutors, and the state and local partners you work with.

We strongly support first responders and victims of crime.

And so—before I say anything else—I want to announce our next step to do just that.

Today, I am announcing that the Department of Justice will provide $16 million for the victims of last October's mass shooting in Las Vegas and for the first responders who came to the scene. These funds can be used to help pay for counseling, therapy, rehabilitation, trauma recovery, and legal aid. These new funds will build on the $3 million that we have already provided for law enforcement officers in the Las Vegas area.

We cannot undo the harm that was done that day, but we are doing what we can to help Las Vegas heal.

We are also working to reduce gun violence in this country. On Wednesday, I announced a new Memphis Crime Gun Strike Force, which will bring together the ATF and Memphis police to find, investigate, and prosecute firearms offenders.

But we have to acknowledge the hard truth that drugs are killing more Americans than guns—a lot more.

Nationwide in 2016, there were more than four times as many fatal drug overdoses as there were gun homicides.

Your work to fight the opioid epidemic is more important than ever—because today we are facing the deadliest drug crisis in American history. Last year 70,000 Americans lost their lives to drug overdoses. That is the highest drug death toll in American history—by far. That's roughly the size of the population of Canton, Ohio, dead in just one year from drug overdoses. More Americans died of drug overdoses last year than from car crashes.

Despite rising prosperity and better technology, life expectancy in the United States actually declined over the last three years—and largely because of this epidemic. The last time life expectancy in this country declined for three years in a row was a century ago. This is simply unacceptable.

And overdose deaths don't tell the whole story. Millions of people are living with the painful consequences of a family member's addiction or an addiction of their own. I personally know people whose families have been impacted by drug addiction. We all do.

Appalachia has been especially hard hit by addiction and by opioid fraud. Some of the first pill mills in America were started right here in Southern Ohio and Northern Kentucky. And to this day these communities still have tragically high rates of addiction and overdose.

The drug overdose death rate in Ohio more than doubled from 2013 to 2017. And here in Cincinnati, drug overdose deaths increased by 79 percent from 2014 to 2017.

The vast majority of those overdose deaths are from opioids. Statewide, 85 percent of overdose deaths in 2017 were from opioids.

This is a daunting situation. Your work to stop drug trafficking has never been more difficult—but it has also never been more important.

The Trump administration has your back in these efforts. The President has laid out a comprehensive plan to end this crisis. The three parts of his plan are prevention, enforcement, and treatment.

President Trump has improved our prevention efforts by launching a coordinated national awareness campaign about the dangers of opioid abuse.

And he is a strong supporter of law enforcement.

Under his leadership, the Department of Justice has put a special focus on fighting the deadliest drugs today: synthetic opioids like fentanyl.

These drugs are so powerful that all it takes is the equivalent of a pinch of salt to be fatal.

Not only are they powerful—they're also easy to get. You can go online and have them shipped right to your door.

Over the past two years, synthetic opioids have killed more Americans than any other kind of drug. Last year these drugs killed more than 28,000 Americans. Here in Ohio, 70 percent of overdoses deaths last year were fentanyl-related.

That's why we've placed a special focus on prosecuting fentanyl cases over these past two years.

And we've been getting results.

Last July, the Department announced the seizure of a website that was the largest dark net marketplace in history. It's called AlphaBay. It hosted more than 220,000 drug listings and was responsible for countless fentanyl overdoses, including the tragic death of a thirteen-year-old.

In August, we announced charges in the Northern District of Ohio against a married couple who sold fentanyl on Alpha Bay. In fact, we believe they were once the most prolific synthetic opioid traffickers on the darknet in North America. We also worked with our partners in Canada to help them indict a man we believe was the third most prolific darknet synthetic opioid dealer in North America.

In January, we began J-CODE, a new team at the FBI that focuses specifically on the threat of online opioid sales. They have already begun carrying out enforcement actions nationwide, arresting dozens of people across the country.

And in some of the districts where drug deaths are the highest, we are prosecuting every fentanyl trafficking case we can, even when the amount of drugs might be small.

We tried this strategy in Manatee County, Florida—just south of Tampa—and it worked. This past January, they had half the number of overdose deaths as the previous January. The Manatee County Sheriff's Office went from responding to eleven overdose calls a day to an average of one a day.

This summer, we expanded that effort to ten districts across America—including both Ohio districts, Southern West Virginia, and Eastern Kentucky. We call it Operation S. O. S.—and we're sending ten more AUSAs to help carry out this strategy.

But fentanyl isn't made in Ohio or any of these districts. The vast majority of the fentanyl in this country is made in China.

That is why the Trump administration has become the first administration to prosecute Chinese fentanyl traffickers.

A year ago, we announced the first two indictments against Chinese nationals for trafficking synthetic drugs in the United States. In August, we announced our third case—a forty-three–count indictment against a drug trafficking organization based in Shanghai.

This summer I went to China and met with Chinese officials to discuss this problem. I made it clear to them that we want them to be our partners in these efforts—and that they've got to do more to stop these drugs from coming here.

But I am thankful that some help is on the way. Last month, President Trump signed into law the STOP Act, which was authored by Senator Rob Portman of Cincinnati. This new law means that when packages come in from overseas, the Postal Service will have to tell Customs and Border Protection basic electronic information like where it's from, where it's going, and what's in it. That information will help law enforcement find dangerous packages and the criminals who are sending them. Just as importantly, the criminals will know that—and it will deter many of them shipping drugs in the future.

We are already interdicting drugs coming into this country at higher and higher levels. In fiscal year 2018, the DEA seized 70 percent more fentanyl than the year before. DEA seized enough drugs to kill every man, woman, and child in the United States.

Those interdiction efforts are important and necessary. But we know that one of the major causes of the opioid crisis in the first place was overprescribing. We're told that three out of four heroin addicts in the United States first started on prescription opioids. Even if that is an overestimate, that is still too many.

That's why President Trump has set the goal of reducing the national opioid prescription rate by one-third in three years. It's an ambitious goal, but we are well on our way to achieving it.

According to the DEA's National Prescription Audit, in the first eight months of 2018, opioid prescriptions were down by nearly 12 percent compared to a year before. And that's in addition to a seven percent decline last year.

We now have the lowest opioid prescription rates in eighteen years. And we're going to bring them a lot lower.

For next year, the DEA is lowering the legal limits on opioid production by an average of 10 percent.

That will bring us to about a 44 percent decrease in opioid production since 2016.

We are making it harder to divert these pills for abuse—and we're going after the fraudsters who exploit people suffering from addiction.

Two years in a row the Department of Justice has set records for health care fraud enforcement. This July we charged 601 defendants with more than $2 billion in medical fraud. This was the most doctors, the most medical personnel, and the most fraud that the Department of Justice has ever taken on in any single law enforcement action. This is the most defendants we've ever charged with health care fraud and the most opioid-related fraud defendants we've ever charged in a single enforcement action.

So far under President Donald Trump, the Department of Justice has charged more than 220 doctors with opioid-related crimes and convicted more than 80 of them. Sixteen of those doctors prescribed more than 20.3 million pills illegally. We have also charged another 221 other medical personnel for opioid-related crimes.

In fiscal year 2018, the Department of Justice charged six percent more drug defendants than in fiscal year 2017. We prosecuted 36 percent more opioid defendants than the previous four-year average. We increased heroin prosecutions by 15 percent and oxycontin prosecutions by 35 percent. We have dramatically increased the number of fentanyl prosecutions at the federal level two years in a row.

Those numbers are important—but what is more important is that overdose deaths in Ohio and across this country may have finally stopped rising.

From 2012 to 2017, drug overdose deaths per year in this country increased by 74 percent.

According to the CDC, drug overdose deaths increased on a month-by-month basis until September 2017. The rolling twelve-month total then decreased by 2 percent from September 2017 through April 2018, which is the most recent data we have.

Here in Ohio, the second half of 2017 saw 23 percent fewer overdose deaths than the first half of 2017. From September to the end of the year, overdose deaths dropped by 17 percent.

Of course, we want much bigger decreases, but this is very encouraging news.

And we're not going to stop there. We are continuing to support you and help you succeed.

Last month we announced our new Appalachian Regional Prescription Opioid Strike Force.

This new Strike Force combines the investigation, prosecution, and data analytics resources of the Criminal Division, nine U.S. Attorneys' offices, and the FBI, DEA, and the Department of Health and Human Service's Inspector General.

This new strike force will be composed of twelve additional opioid fraud prosecutors across our nine Appalachian districts and the surrounding areas. That includes the districts represented by each of the U.S. Attorneys who are here today.

Each one of these new AUSAs will have their own team of federal investigators and law enforcement agents. They'll also be mobile—so if a small case turns into a bigger case, then they can prosecute it any Appalachian district they need to.

The Southern Hub will be based in Nashville, where I visited yesterday.

And the Northern Hub of the Strike Force will be based just across the river from here in Fort Mitchell.

We've already used this Strike Force model to combat health care fraud—and it has been very successful. In Detroit and Miami—which were the first two cities where we deployed our Health Care Fraud Strike Force— Medicare Parts A and B billings have dropped by a total of more than $2 billion since 2010.

We want to replicate that kind of success in the fight against the opioid epidemic.

This new Strike Force is going to build on the successes that we have already achieved over these past two years, and I believe that it can help provide some relief to Appalachia and to Southern Ohio.

I especially want to thank Matt Miner and Joe Beemsterboer for their great work in setting up this ARPO Strike Force. I know that you spent countless hours on the road over the past couple of months. But I also know that your tireless efforts, in conjunction with the work of the Strike Force prosecutors as well as the AUSAs in the United States Attorneys' Offices, will pay countless dividends.

This is our latest step—but it is not our last step. We are going to keep up this pace. We are going to keep supporting you, arming you with new resources and new weapons. We are going to keep coordinating with you and listening to you about how we can help.

And so I want to conclude with something a mentor of mine used to say every time he spoke to law enforcement, and I believe it too: we have your back, and you have our thanks.

Acting Attorney General Matthew Whitaker Delivers Remarks at the 2018 Project Safe Neighborhoods Conference Awards Ceremony

Kansas City, Missouri

■ ■ ■

Thursday, December 6, 2018

Thank you, Jim for that generous introduction and thank you for your outstanding record of service in the military as a prosecutor, at Main Justice, and now at EOUSA. You're doing great work.

Thank you also to:

- Kansas City U.S. Attorneys Tim Garrison and Stephen McAllister,
- Kansas City Police Chief Rick Smith for the Midwest hospitality,
- Acting Associate Attorney General Jesse Panuccio,
- Deputy Director Tom Brandon of ATF
- Acting Administrator Uttam Dhillon of DEA
- Assistant Attorney General Stephen Boyd,
- My good friend Matt Dummermuth, the head of our Office of Justice Programs,
- Acting Director Katie Sullivan of our Office on Violence Against Women,
- The head of our COPS office, Phil Keith,
- Associate Deputy Attorney General, Robyn Thiemann
- The dozens of U.S. Attorneys who are here with their teams, and

- Each of you, who made the commitment to be here at the
  Conference this week, and who have partnered with the
  Department of Justice to make the PSN program work in
  your home cities.

I also want to thank President Donald Trump for joining us tomorrow. I think that his attendance at this conference says a lot about his commitment to supporting law enforcement and keeping the people of this country safe.

I want to thank him for honoring President George H. W. Bush by declaring yesterday a National Day of Mourning. I know the law enforcement community is especially mourning his loss. President Bush was a strong supporter of law enforcement and he helped lay the foundation for twenty-two years of declining crime in America.

So thank you to President Trump for honoring President Bush and for honoring us with his presence tomorrow.

Above all, I want to thank our sixteen award winners.

We received dozens of worthy nominations this year. But even with tough competition, each one of you stood out for recognition.

Each one of you has helped this Department reach new levels of effectiveness and productivity by implementing and supporting Project Safe Neighborhoods (PSN), which is our flagship violent crime reduction plan.

After all, PSN is about empowering our people out in the field. Rather than having Washington, D.C., dictate a uniform approach, PSN directs our U.S. Attorneys to work with their communities to develop a customized crime reduction plan to target the most violent criminals in the most violent areas, and to prevent and deter violent crimes before they happen.

I ran this program for five years as a United States Attorney in Southern Iowa and I know that it works. I've seen it firsthand. I've personally prosecuted PSN cases. So have my friends AUSAs Melisa Zaehringer and Kevin VanderSchel, who are here with us. Kevin became my First Assistant in 2009, and then later served as Acting U.S. Attorney. Kevin and Melisa, thanks for being here.

When I was U.S. Attorney, PSN helped us put away two gunmen who held a seventy-six-year old woman at gunpoint for an hour while they ransacked her farmhouse. The two men cut her phone line, destroyed her cell phone, and stole her car. A few weeks later, one of the defendants—who was a felon—bought two guns from an undercover ATF agent. He was arrested and the ATF agent found some of the stolen valuables in his car. He called the police in Iowa and asked if there had been any robberies in the area recently. That led to an investigation that put the robbers behind bars and achieved justice for that elderly woman.

For another example, Davenport Police responded to a call after a man allegedly threatened a woman, shot a gun into the air, and then stole a car and drove away. A week later, police across the river in East Moline responded to another call of a man making threats with a gun and then speeding off. The man was then pulled over for speeding back in Davenport. The officer recognized the vehicle, searched it, and found a gun. That was enough to put him behind bars so he couldn't threaten anybody with a gun anymore.

In Clinton, Iowa, a convicted felon beat up another man behind a convenience store with a shotgun. He was caught with the shotgun and we put him behind bars for nearly five years as a felon in possession of a firearm.

I could go on and on. We had many other successes because of PSN.

And those successes continue today in Iowa and across America.

The Southern District of Mississippi started Project EJECT—which brings together federal and local officers and prosecutors, the Mississippi state crime lab, nonprofit organizations, faith leaders, and community leaders. This team then works together to prosecute crime, deter crime, and help former prisoners make the transition back to society. They hold town meetings and speak at local schools to keep kids away from criminal activity.

In other words, they're hitting violent crime from every angle—and it shows. As of October, violent crime is down 16 percent in Jackson.

Our PSN Task Force in Dallas is Texas-sized: it brings together sixty people, including law enforcement officers, local government officials, local school personnel, and fifteen community organizations.

Collaboration between officers at the federal, state, and local levels in Dallas has already led to more than one hundred arrests of violent criminals in just the past eight months. And task force members have already strengthened the bonds between the community and our police officers through more than forty community meetings and events. Once a month, they meet with former prisoners returning home. They've already met with 300 former offenders and worked to help them get their lives back.

In Tampa, Captain Paul Lusczynski came up with the Violent Impact Player program—or VIP. Using criminal records and gang membership, Paul determined who the most violent criminals in Tampa are—and now he's helping to put them behind bars. One study credits VIP with a 7.9 percent drop in violent crime.

Of course, there are about ninety-one other districts that are achieving PSN successes, too—including right here in Kansas City.

Tim and his team recently conducted a PSN operation called Operation Washout, which led to the arrest of fifty-six known gang members or repeat violent offenders. Officers also seized methamphetamine, ecstasy, cocaine, and thirteen guns as part of this operation.

We are building on this success here in Kansas City with the brand-new Midwest Crime Gun Intelligence Center, which just became fully operational in September.

Here and across America, PSN is making us better at investigating crime, targeting prosecutions, and preventing and deterring crime. It's making our lawyers and our officers more effective.

And the numbers bear that out.

In fiscal year 2017, the Department of Justice prosecuted more violent criminals than in any year on record to that point. And then, in fiscal year 2018—after Attorney General Sessions announced that PSN was a priority again—we broke that record by a margin of 15 percent.

In fiscal year 2018, we also charged the highest number of federal firearm defendants in Department history. We broke that record by a margin of 17 percent. We charged nearly 20 percent more firearm defendants than we did in 2017 and 30 percent more than we charged in 2016.

Meanwhile we have also broken records for prosecuting illegal entry by illegal aliens, increased the number of white-collar defendants, the number of drug defendants, and increased the number of illegal aliens prosecuted for felony re-entry by 38 percent.

These numbers speak for themselves. But our goal as a Department is not to fill up the jails or the courts: our goal is to reduce crime. PSN is helping us do that by ensuring we are prosecuting the right people and maximizing our impact.

Violent crime and homicide were up in 2015 and 2016—but they were down in 2017. And for 2018, they will probably be down even lower. One estimate projects that the murder rate in our twenty-nine biggest cities will decline by 7.6 percent this year. That means fewer victims, fewer grieving families, and more peace of mind for the people we serve.

Drug overdose deaths were up in 2015 and 2016—but they were down in the last six months for which we have data, and opioid prescriptions are down nearly 20 percent since 2016.

These are important achievements that affect people's lives.

And they're your achievements. Each one of you played a key role in making them possible.

It is right that we celebrate that this week. But our work is not finished. We are going to continue to support our state and local partners—and I am confident that those partnerships are going to continue to deliver results.

And so, to all of our award winners, thank you for your outstanding service. And to all of you who are working side by side with us to improve safety and reduce crime—whether you are an officer, a prosecutor, a researcher, a faith leader, or a community partner—let me conclude with something a mentor of mine used to say: we have your back, and you have our thanks.

Acting Attorney General Matthew Whitaker Delivers Remarks at the Dallas Police Department on Project Safe Neighborhoods Efforts

Dallas, Texas

■ ■ ■

Wednesday, December 12, 2018

Remarks as prepared for delivery

Thank you, Erin for that generous introduction, for your outstanding leadership over your team of more than one hundred prosecutors serving 8 million Texans. Thank you for your decade of exemplary service to this Department.

Thank you also to Jeff Boshek of ATF, Eric Jackson of FBI, U.S. Marshal Rick Taylor, Dallas Police Department Executive Assistant Chief of Police David Pughes, and Deputy Chief Avery Moore, commander of DPD's Northeast Patrol Division.

Thank you all for being here.

It is great to be back in Texas.

Yesterday, I visited Austin.

Later today, I'll be visiting the George W. Bush Presidential Library.

I was honored to serve in the Bush Administration as a United States Attorney for five and a half years. It was extremely rewarding to help take illegal guns, drugs, and criminals out of the community where I grew up and where I'm raising my family. I am deeply grateful to President Bush for nominating me and for putting so much trust in me.

I am also deeply grateful to be here with you to say thank you.

Law enforcement officers in Dallas are important to this community—and you're important to law enforcement across the country.

It was not long ago that a political radical targeted Dallas police officers for assassination. He killed five officers and wounded seven.

We will never forget those officers.

Sadly, this was not the only case of targeted violence against police officers in recent years. But these attacks in Dallas were especially calculated and malicious.

They reminded us once again of the dangers that you face every single day.

This weekend we got yet another reminder when an FBI agent in Brooklyn was shot in the shoulder in the line of duty. He is expected to recover—but he has made a major sacrifice.

We are praying for him and his family. We are grateful to him and to all officers like you who put your lives on the line for us.

And so it is an honor to be here with you—and especially to be with officers who are doing such impressive work.

In fact, it is award-winning work.

Last week, Erin and I were in Kansas City for the first national Project Safe Neighborhoods Conference of the Trump Administration.

As this group knows, Project Safe Neighborhoods (PSN) is the centerpiece of our crime reduction strategy.

Under President Bush, it was a big success. One study showed that, in its first six years, PSN reduced violent crime overall by 4.1 percent, with case studies showing reductions in certain areas of up to 42 percent.

Under President Trump, we're going to make it an even bigger success.

Last October, former Attorney General Sessions made PSN our top crime-fighting priority once again. He deserves a lot of credit for that.

PSN works because it empowers our people out in the field. Rather than having Washington, D.C., dictate a top-down, uniform approach, PSN directs Erin and our other U.S. Attorneys to work with their communities to develop a customized crime reduction plan to target the most violent criminals in the most violent areas.

I ran this program for five years as a U.S. Attorney in Southern Iowa, and I know firsthand that it works.

I've prosecuted PSN cases personally—and I know a good PSN program when I see one. Last week I was pleased to award Erin and the

Northern District of Texas with one of our two Outstanding Overall Partnership awards.

Dallas's PSN Task Force is named for Officer Rogelio Santander of the Dallas Police Department, who was killed in the line of duty this past April.

The Task Force has been honoring his memory by continuing his work of putting away criminals and reducing crime in Dallas.

I want to congratulate P. J. Meitl, who serves as PSN coordinator here in Northern Texas.

P.J. is coming up on six years with the Department and he has already prosecuted more than 500 defendants and participated in more than fifteen jury trials, including the largest criminal prosecution of a single physician for healthcare fraud in Department history. He has also helped prosecute eighty-five alleged white supremacists. This is outstanding work. Let's hear it for P. J.

Last week's award shows that law enforcement in Dallas is setting an example of collaboration that other districts can follow.

Your PSN Task Force brings together more than sixty people, including law enforcement officers, local government officials, school personnel, and fifteen different community organizations.

It's a big group. And this group has hit the ground running.

Over the last eight months, you've held more than sixty community meetings and events. You're building trust and encouraging crime victims and witnesses to come forward and help us find the criminals.

At one event—the Community Unity Festival—you had more than 1,000 guests. Even for Texas, that's a lot of people.

These community engagement efforts have been led by Sergent Leroy Quigg. Great job, Sergent Quigg.

The Task Force has also been meeting with former prisoners once a month and helping them make the transition back to civilian life. I'm told that you're meeting with more than 300 former offenders monthly. In total, more than 2,400 have attended these "re-entry nights," where you offer job placement, counseling, and some straight talk about the consequences of reoffending.

All of this hard work is leading to tangible results. In just eight months, Dallas's PSN Task Force has led to more than 120 arrests of alleged violent criminals.

I'm told that Dallas Detective Calvin Scudder is leading the team in arrests. Great work, Detective.

PSN helped us indict two gang members who allegedly got into a shootout in front of a dollar store. One is a felon and one was under indictment when it happened—and it was caught on surveillance video.

PSN helped us indict two women for allegedly making a straw purchase of a Glock pistol. That gun was later used to kill the witness to a robbery. P. J. is prosecuting this case.

PSN helped us indict an alleged carjacker as a felon in possession of a firearm. In total, he is now facing up to forty-five years in prison.

And PSN helped shut down a convenience store that was a magnet for illegal activity.

These are important cases—but PSN is not about filling up the courts or the jails. Our goal is to reduce violent crime.

Thanks in large part to people in this room, we are achieving that goal. Violent crime is down in our target areas in Dallas by about 20 percent since the PSN Task Force got started.

Those are exactly the results that we want to see.

That is why the Department of Justice is proud to invest in you.

We have pledged to invest more than $700,000 in Dallas's PSN Task Force.

Your work is not just important to Dallas. It is important to the entire Department of Justice.

You're helping us achieve our goals as a Department nationwide.

In fiscal year 2017, the Department of Justice prosecuted more violent criminals than in any year on record to that point.

And then, in fiscal year 2018—after Attorney General Sessions announced that PSN was a priority again—we broke that record by a margin of 15 percent.

In fiscal year 2018, we charged the highest number of federal firearm defendants in Department history. We broke the previous record by a margin of 17 percent. We charged 30 percent more firearm defendants than we charged in 2016.

At the same time, we have also broken records for prosecuting illegal entry by illegal aliens, increased the number of white-collar defendants, the number of drug defendants, and increased the number of illegal aliens prosecuted for felony re-entry by 38 percent.

Violent crime and homicide were up in 2015 and 2016—but they were down in 2017. And for 2018, they will probably be down even lower. One estimate projects that the murder rate in our twenty-nine biggest cities will decline by 7.6 percent this year. That means fewer victims, fewer grieving families, and more peace of mind for the people we serve.

Drug overdose deaths were up in 2015 and 2016—but they were down in the last six months we have data. And opioid prescriptions are down nearly 20 percent since 2016.

These are important achievements that affect people's lives. And the people in this room are helping us achieve them.

Simply put, we could not have done it without our state and local partners.

And so, I want to conclude with something a mentor of mine used to say every time he spoke to law enforcement, and I believe it too: we have your back, and you have our thanks.

Acting Attorney General Matthew G. Whitaker Delivers Remarks at the Heritage Foundation to Commemorate 25th Anniversary of the Religious Freedom Restoration Act

Washington, D.C.

■ ■ ■

Wednesday, January 16, 2019

Thank you, Tom for that kind introduction and thank you for your leadership at the Ed Meese Center. Ed Meese is a personal hero of mine and you are helping to carry on his legacy of upholding the Constitution and defending the rule of law.

Thank you also to Jennifer Marshall, John Malcolm, and especially to our panelists. Each one of you brings a unique perspective to today's discussion—but we are all united in our shared values of tolerance and mutual respect.

I want to start by wishing everyone a happy Religious Freedom Day.

Two-hundred thirty-three years ago, the Virginia Senate passed the Statute for Religious Freedom, which remains one of the most eloquent defenses of religious freedom ever written.

It states that "truth is great and will prevail if left to herself ... [Truth] has nothing to fear ... unless ... disarmed of her natural weapons: free argument and debate."

The statute protected Virginians from being compelled to attend or support any religious service or ministry or from being punished because of their beliefs.

The statute did not claim that these were privileges or gifts to the people. It says, "we declare that the rights hereby asserted are of the natural rights of mankind."

The author of the bill—Thomas Jefferson—considered it one of his greatest achievements. In fact, on his tombstone, it does not say that he served as President. It says three things: that he authored the Declaration of Independence, founded the University of Virginia, and that he authored the Virginia Statute for Religious Freedom.

When the bill passed, Jefferson was in France as a diplomat. The legislator who championed the bill was a thirty-four-year old delegate named James Madison.

Within just a few years, Madison became the Father of the Constitution and authored the First Amendment.

Jefferson, Madison, and the rest of our Founders took great care to protect the rights of religious people in this country.

As we look back now, we can see why: because religious freedom has made this country stronger.

Every day in America religious charities feed the hungry, care for the sick and the elderly, and give our children a good education.

People of faith can be found in every walk of life and in every corner of this land. Good citizens of every creed have made contributions that have enriched this nation. That benefits all of us, whether we share their beliefs or not.

Religious freedom makes our country stronger. And that is why threats to religious freedom are also threats to our national strength.

For more than two centuries, the American people have recognized that.

In November we celebrated a much more recent statute than the Virginia Statute for Religious Freedom. We marked the twenty-fifth anniversary of the Religious Freedom Restoration Act, or RFRA.

RFRA codified in statute the strict scrutiny test that the Supreme Court had famously used in *Sherbert v. Verner* and *Yoder v. Wisconsin.*

Under RFRA, the government cannot burden someone's religious exercise unless it is seeking to further a compelling interest—and doing so by the least restrictive means it can.

Under RFRA, religious freedom is not absolute, but it is protected by one of the highest standards in constitutional law.

Government is still able to fulfill its purposes—but without infringing on people's rights.

It is a remarkable thing for any government to impose such restraints on itself.

It would have been much easier for a government to disregard the costs on individual liberty and conscience. And in all too many countries in this world, that's exactly what governments do.

But the enactment of RFRA was a bold affirmation that religious freedom and freedom of conscience are precious and deserving of protection, even when it makes things a little harder for the government.

This affirmation is even more striking because it was the result of a consensus. RFRA's enactment was completely bipartisan.

RFRA was authored by then-Congressman Chuck Schumer. It passed the House unanimously and was approved 97 to 3 in the Senate.

When he signed it into law, President Clinton said, "it is interesting to note ... what a broad coalition of Americans came together ... to protect perhaps the most precious of all American liberties, religious freedom."

Vice President Al Gore remarked that "when you have the National Association of Evangelicals and the ACLU ... the Traditional Values Coalition and People for the American Way [on the same side], we're doing something right."

What a difference twenty-five years makes.

Today many of RFRA's original supporters, including the ACLU, have changed their minds.

In recent years, when some states have attempted to pass their own versions of RFRA, they have been met with bitterness and hostility.

Meanwhile others have disregarded both the spirit and the letter of RFRA. They have tried to use the power of the state to make people choose between following their core beliefs and being good citizens—even when it is not remotely necessary.

For example, we've seen nuns ordered to pay for contraceptives.

We've seen a United States Senator refer to an evangelical Christian nominated by President Trump as "not someone ... this country is supposed to be about."

We've witnessed the ordeal of Jack Phillips in Colorado. That ordeal is still going on today.

We've seen groups that defend religious freedom—including one that is undefeated at the Supreme Court over the last seven years—labeled as "hate groups."

Sadly, there are many other examples.

But I'm proud to say that this administration is doing something about it. We have a President who is standing up for the First Amendment.

Soon after he took office, President Trump ordered the Department of Justice to issue legal guidance to the Executive Branch on legal protections for religious liberty. In October 2017, we issued that guidance, which explains the fundamental religious liberty principles in the Constitution and in federal statutes like RFRA.

We've been putting that guidance into action by defending the rights of the American people in both criminal and civil cases.

Under President Trump, we have obtained fourteen indictments and ten convictions in cases involving attacks or threats against houses of worship and against individuals because of their religion.

Under this administration, we have indicted fifty hate crime defendants. And in just the last fiscal year, we obtained thirty hate crime convictions.

With regard to civil cases, we have gone to court all across America to protect people of a wide variety of faiths.

We defended parents in Montana who claim that the state barred their children from a private school scholarship program just because they attend a religious school.

Under President Trump the Department has filed five amicus briefs in cases alleging discrimination in zoning laws. We have done so on behalf of a Hindu temple, a Catholic church, and we've filed a lawsuit of our own on behalf of an Orthodox Jewish congregation. We have also settled four cases involving mosques.

We got involved in a First Amendment lawsuit filed by Alliance Defending Freedom against Georgia Gwinnett College, a taxpayer-funded school that allegedly punished a student for sharing his faith outside of a designated "free speech zone."

And most recently, the Department filed an amicus brief defending a memorial honoring soldiers killed in World War I. The memorial is a large cross, built using private funds, that stood for nearly ninety years without any complaint.

But now, the plaintiffs say that it endorses one religion over another. They want it to be destroyed—but we believe that it should stand and continue to honor the memory of the fallen.

In July, we announced our Religious Liberty Task Force, which is responsible for making sure that we respect the conscience rights of the 115,000 Department of Justice employees.

It is also responsible for reviewing if there are instances in which the federal government is discriminating against religious institutions simply because they are religious—which is illegal under the Supreme Court's *Trinity Lutheran* decision.

That review will help us stay aggressive in defending the right of free exercise in court.

We are proud of our efforts in the courtroom. But not everything needs to be decided before a judge.

In the long run, perhaps it is more important to uphold RFRA in spirit, not just in the letter of the law.

RFRA promotes authentic tolerance—because RFRA makes a solemn promise to the people of this nation that we can find a place for them, regardless of who they are, and regardless of their beliefs.

RFRA affirms that good citizenship is open to every American, whether they're religious or not.

And above all, it underscores the fact that government's primary task is to protect the rights of its citizens.

That is why I am hopeful that we can recover the consensus in support of religious freedom that came together 25 years ago. If we do that, then we can create a culture that promotes true tolerance and respect.

And so, as we continue to carry out RFRA, I am grateful that we still have a broad coalition of supporters like all of you.

Opening Statement of Acting Attorney General Matthew G. Whitaker Before the House Judiciary Committee

Washington, D.C.

■ ■ ■

Friday, February 8, 2019

Thank you, Mr. Chairman and Ranking Member Collins for the opportunity to testify before the Committee today. I am looking forward to discussing with you some of the accomplishments and priorities of the Department of Justice. Before I start, I would also like to acknowledge the passing of Chairman Dingell. He was a statesman and a leader, and it is a sad day in this committee, I am sure.

First of all, let me say that it is an honor to represent the 115,000 men and women of the Department of Justice. The Department is blessed with extremely talented, highly principled public servants who are dedicated to upholding our great Constitution and the laws of the United States.

I saw that up close during my five and a half years as United States Attorney for the Southern District of Iowa. Our office put criminals behind bars, and we kept the people of Iowa safe.

I personally prosecuted several important criminal cases and worked with men and women from the ATF, DEA, FBI, the U.S. Marshals Service, and our state and local partners. It was a privilege.

In 2017, I returned to the Department and served for thirteen months as chief of staff to former Attorney General Jeff Sessions—a man for whom I have the greatest respect. He led the Department with integrity, with dedication to the rule of law, and with a commitment to carrying out the policies of the President. I am deeply honored that the President selected me to continue this work at the Department.

The Senate will soon consider the President's nomination for our next Attorney General. And let me just say this: no one is more qualified than Bill Barr. I am working to ensure that he will inherit a strong, confident, and effective Department of Justice. And I believe that he will.

For the last three months, I have had the privilege of serving as Acting Attorney General, and I am impressed every single day by the dedication and the hard work of our agents, attorneys, and support staff. Over this time, I have visited a number of our offices and met with federal prosecutors from across America. For example, in December, we held our Project Safe Neighborhoods conference—where employees from nearly every U.S. Attorney's office and hundreds of state and local partners celebrated our successes and reductions in violent crime.

Our hard work is paying off. I firmly believe that your constituents are safer because of the work that we have done over these past two years.

Under this Administration, crime is down—and police morale is up.

In Fiscal Year 2017, the Justice Department charged the largest number of violent crime defendants since we started to track this category back when Bill Barr was Attorney General. And then, in Fiscal Year 2018, we broke that record again—by a margin of nearly 15 percent. We also charged more defendants with gun crimes than ever before. In fact, we broke that record by a margin of 17 percent. The Department has also banned bump stocks, improved the background check system, and prosecuted those who lied to get a gun.

Our work is having an impact. In 2017—after two years of increases under the previous Administration—violent crime and homicide rates went down nationwide. We do not have official numbers yet for 2018, but one estimate projected that the murder rate in our twenty-nine biggest cities would drop by 7.6 percent. Those are real lives being saved.

Much of the crime in this country is related to drug abuse. But under this Administration, prescriptions for the seven most frequently abused prescription drugs are down more than 21 percent, to the lowest level in at least a decade. At the same time, the DEA has lowered the legal limits on production of the active ingredients in these prescription opioids by 47 percent since 2016.

But there is no doubt in the law enforcement community that the vast majority of the illegal drugs in this country are coming over our Southern border.

There is also no doubt that criminals and cartels seek to exploit weaknesses in our southern border for their own profits and purposes—including by subjecting women and children to dangerous and unspeakable conditions in an attempt to smuggle them into the United States. And of course, the dangers of our porous southern border become all the more apparent every time an illegal alien causes harm or death to innocent Americans across this country—such as what happened to an outstanding young woman from my home state of Iowa, Sarah Root.

For this reason and others, we continue our efforts to restore the rule of law at the border and in our immigration system. In Fiscal Year 2018, we charged more defendants with illegal entry than in any year in American history. In fact, we charged 85 percent more defendants with illegally entering America than we did in the previous year. At the same time, we increased the number of felony illegal re-entry prosecutions by more than 38 percent. Whatever our views on immigration policy, we should all be opposed to illegal immigration, and we should support these efforts.

The Department is also taking decisive action against human trafficking, both domestically and internationally. Human traffickers, like other criminal enterprises, take advantage of our porous Southern Border to smuggle women and children into the United States to exploit them. We are bringing prosecutions to dismantle transnational trafficking networks that lure victims across our borders and traffic them for profit. Last year, the Department of Justice secured a record of 526 human trafficking convictions—a 5 percent increase over the previous year.

The Department is also doing its part to aggressively prosecute hate crimes. Under this Administration, we indicted fifty hate crime defendants and obtained thirty hate crime convictions in Fiscal Year 2018.

In November, the Department provided election monitoring at polling places around the country. Our Civil Rights Division deployed personnel to thirty-five jurisdictions in nineteen states to monitor for compliance with federal voting rights laws. Our Public Integrity Section prosecutors served as subject matter experts for federal prosecutors and investigators nationwide, working with the FBI at the Strategic Information and Operations Center.

Over my time as Acting Attorney General, I have done everything in my power to continue regular order at the Department. The Department has continued to make its law enforcement decisions based upon the facts and law of each individual case, in accordance with established Department practices, and independent of any outside interference.

At no time has the White House asked for, nor have I provided, any promises or commitments concerning the Special Counsel's investigation, or any other investigation. Since becoming Acting Attorney General, I have run the Department with fidelity to the law and to the Constitution. During my time as the leader of the Department of Justice, the Department has complied with the Special Counsel regulations, and there has been no change in how the Department has worked with the Special Counsel's office.

Over the past day, the Department and the Committee have exchanged letters concerning the respective prerogatives of the Legislative and Executive Branches. I am pleased that we were able to reach an agreement that allows me to appear here voluntarily. I am pleased also that we agreed that each branch would seek to accommodate each other, and that if we have differences, we will try to work them out in good faith before resorting to subpoenas or other formal legal process.

I will answer the Committee's questions today as best as I can, but I will continue the long-standing Executive Branch practice of not disclosing information that may be subject to executive privilege, such as the contents of conversations with the President.

As the Supreme Court has recognized, this executive privilege is "fundamental to the operation of Government and inextricably rooted in the separation of powers under the Constitution."

I have spent nearly one third of my career in the Department of Justice, and I am personally committed to its success and its integrity. I hope that today's hearing will be constructive and help us to partner together to achieve the priorities of the American people. The men and women of this Department are proud of our accomplishments, but we know that Congress can help us achieve even more. And as our agents and our prosecutors have shown again and again: they deserve your support.

Thank you once again for the opportunity to testify today and for your attention to matters facing the Department of Justice.

Acting Attorney General Matthew G. Whitaker Delivers Remarks to the National Sheriffs' Association's Winter Conference

Washington, D.C.

■ ■ ■

Monday, February 11, 2019

Thank you, Sheriff Layton for that introduction and for your four decades of service to your fellow Hoosiers, including over these last eight years as Sheriff of Marion County.

I also want to thank:

- Secretary Nielsen for her remarks and for her partnership,
- Jonathan Thompson for his leadership and advocacy for our nation's 3,000 sheriffs,
- Former Wisconsin Badger Troy Vincent. Troy and I played against each other—and I am proud to say that my Hawkeyes won every time. I hope there are no hard feelings about that. But seriously, Troy, thank you for your strong support for law enforcement.

I especially want to thank my fellow Iowans who are here. Thank you to Sheriff Dan Altena of Sioux County—thank you for your three decades in law enforcement. And thank you to Sheriff Paul Fitzgerald of Story County—not far up the road from my hometown of Ankeny. Thank you for your four decades in law enforcement.

Thank you all for being here. On behalf of President Trump, I want to thank each of you for your service to our country.

Each one of you is continuing a proud and noble tradition.

America has changed a lot over the centuries—but sheriffs like you have always been there for us.

Sheriffs have kept the American people safe from the very beginning—and even before the beginning. The Father of our country, George Washington, was the son of a sheriff. The office of the sheriff was mentioned in Magna Carta 800 years ago and was already well-developed by that time.

This institution has endured through the centuries because it combines a broad jurisdiction with direct election by the people. It meets a permanent need for strength and accountability in law enforcement.

The people in your community have entrusted you with a great deal of power. But they know you—and you know them. Their priorities are your priorities.

In my time in law enforcement, I have seen that firsthand.

Over my five and a half years as U.S. Attorney for Southern Iowa, I saw how local cases could quickly turn into federal cases—and how sheriffs could play a key role in federal cases, too.

For example, the Dallas County Sheriff's office helped us pull off one of our most successful anti-drug operations over my time as U.S. Attorney. The DEA received a tip that a large quantity of cocaine and ecstasy was on its way to Des Moines.

When it got to Iowa, Deputy Sheriff Adam Infante—who is now Chief Deputy in Dallas County—went undercover and purchased 3,000 ecstasy pills and several ounces of cocaine and marijuana. That helped us put fifteen drug traffickers behind bars and it helped us find the route used by the traffickers. In total, we seized 22 pounds of cocaine, 4,400 pounds of marijuana, 7,000 grams of ecstasy, and $130,000 in cash. This operation could not have succeeded without this outstanding sheriff's deputy.

There are many other examples that I could talk about. As a prosecutor, I saw over and over again that law enforcement works best when we combine the resources and the training of our federal agents with the street-level intelligence of local officers like your deputies.

Since I came back to the Department as Chief of Staff and now as Acting Attorney General, my experience with Iowa's local law enforcement has informed my decisions and my priorities.

This Department of Justice recognizes that the vast majority of law enforcement officers in this country serve at the state and local levels. We know that we cannot succeed and accomplish our goals without you. And that recognition has guided everything that we do.

Above all, it has guided our efforts to reduce crime.

We've had our work cut out for us. When President Trump first took office, violent crime had been rising sharply for two years.

From 2014 to 2016, the violent crime rate went up by nearly seven percent nationwide. Robberies went up. Assaults went up by over 8 percent. Rape went up by nearly 13 percent. Murder went up by a shocking 21 percent.

But law enforcement has risen to the occasion. And under President Trump, the Department of Justice has taken steps to help you and your deputies to be more effective.

We have helped police departments hire more than 800 law enforcement officers across America, including more than a hundred sheriffs' deputies.

With your strong support, we strengthened asset-sharing and accelerated our review of adoption requests. In fact, our current policy is to review adoption requests twice as fast as is required by law.

But most importantly, we have worked to strengthen our relationships with sheriffs across America.

For example, back in December, Phil Keith of our COPS office and Jon Adler of our Bureau of Justice Assistance heard about a partnership between eight sheriffs near our Southern border. These sheriffs work together on drug interdiction: they tell each other what routes are being used by the smugglers, and they share intelligence in real time. It is working. I'm told that they've already seized a total of more than $20 million in drugs.

This team effort inspired us at the Department to ask how we could help you replicate that success elsewhere on our border. Phil and Jon have been working with you to create a Real-Time Intelligence Center that will empower Border sheriffs to share intelligence and interdict drug traffickers.

The Bureau of Justice Assistance is also providing resources, training, and technical assistance to local law enforcement along the border. I would encourage any of our border sheriffs who are here to take advantage of this opportunity.

Even if you're not a border sheriff, this training benefits you. What happens at the border does not stay at the border.

According to a new study from our Bureau of Justice Statistics, a majority of federal arrests in Fiscal Year 2016 took place in districts along the U.S.-Mexico border—and 36 percent of defendants in federal district courts were illegal aliens.

That is unacceptable.

This administration is determined to close the loopholes in our laws that are encouraging people to come here illegally—and we are enforcing the law effectively.

In category after category, the Department of Justice is more productive than ever.

In the last fiscal year, the Justice Department charged the greatest number of violent crime defendants since we started to track this category more than twenty-five years ago. We broke the previous record by nearly 15 percent.

We also charged more than 15,000 defendants with federal firearms offenses, which is a record. We broke that record by a margin of 17 percent.

Last year we charged more illegal aliens with illegal entry than ever before. In fact, we charged 85 percent more defendants with illegally entering America than we did in the previous year. And we increased the number of felony re-entry prosecutions by more than 38 percent.

All of these efforts that I've mentioned are adding up—and they're bringing down the crime rate in counties all across America.

In September, the FBI released final crime statistics for 2017. They showed that the violent crime rate and the homicide rate both went down after two years of increases under the previous administration.

For 2018, one estimate projects that the murder rate in our thirty largest cities declined by 7.6 percent. That is usually a good indicator of what is happening nationwide.

And as this crowd knows well: when you lock up gang members and violent criminals, you also have an impact on drug crime.

In fiscal year 2018, the Department of Justice charged six percent more drug defendants than in the year before. We prosecuted 36 percent more opioid defendants than the previous four-year average. We increased heroin prosecutions by 15 percent and oxycontin prosecutions by 35 percent. We have broken records for fentanyl prosecutions two years in a row.

More importantly, drug overdose deaths may have finally stopped rising.

According to preliminary data from the CDC, fatal overdoses stopped rising in September 2017—and then decreased by 2 percent through April 2018.

This is preliminary data, but it is still encouraging.

As our efforts have shown over these last two years, law enforcement works. And so, I want to thank each one of you for your hard work.

Thank you for your partnership in these efforts. We could not achieve these results without you.

This Department is going to keep working for a secure Southern border. We're going to keep enforcing the law aggressively. And we're going to keep supporting you in your important work.

And so, I want to conclude with something a mentor of mine used to say every time he spoke to law enforcement, and I believe it too: we have your back, and you have our thanks.

FOR READER REFERENCE: THE CONSTITUTION OF THE UNITED STATES

THE
CONSTITUTION OF THE UNITED STATES OF AMERICA

LITERAL PRINT

CONSTITUTION OF THE UNITED STATES

We the People of the United States, in Order to form a more perfect Union, establish Justice, insure domestic Tranquillity, provide for the common defence, promote the general Welfare, and secure the Blessings of Liberty to ourselves and our Posterity, do ordain and establish this Constitution for the United States of America.

Article. I.

Section. 1. All legislative Powers herein granted shall be vested in a Congress of the United States, which shall consist of a Senate and House of Representatives.

Section. 2. The House of Representatives shall be composed of Members chosen every second Year by the People of the several States, and the Electors in each State shall have the Qualifications requisite for Electors of the most numerous Branch of the State Legislature.

No Person shall be a Representative who shall not have attained to the age of twenty five Years, and been seven Years a Citizen of the United States, and who shall not, when elected, be an Inhabitant of that State in which he shall be chosen.

Representatives and direct Taxes shall be apportioned among the several States which may be included within this Union, according to their respective Numbers, which shall be determined by adding to the whole Number of free Persons, including those bound to Service for a Term of Years, and excluding Indians not taxed, three fifths of all other Persons. The actual Enumeration shall be made within three Years after the first Meeting of the Congress of the United States, and within

3

4   CONSTITUTION OF THE UNITED STATES

every subsequent Term of ten Years, in such Manner as they
shall by Law direct. The Number of Representatives shall not
exceed one for every thirty Thousand, but each State shall have
at Least one Representative; and until such enumeration shall
be made, the State of New Hampshire shall be entitled to chuse
three, Massachusetts eight, Rhode-Island and Providence Plan-
tations one, Connecticut five, New-York six, New Jersey four,
Pennsylvania eight, Delaware one, Maryland six, Virginia ten,
North Carolina five, South Carolina five, and Georgia three.

When vacancies happen in the Representation from any
State, the Executive Authority thereof shall issue Writs of Election to fill such Vacancies.

The House of Representatives shall chuse their Speaker
and other Officers; and shall have the sole Power of Impeachment.

Section. 3. The Senate of the United States shall be composed of two Senators from each State, chosen by the Legislature thereof, for six Years; and each Senator shall have one
Vote.

Immediately after they shall be assembled in Consequence
of the first Election, they shall be divided as equally as may be
into three Classes. The Seats of the Senators of the first Class
shall be vacated at the Expiration of the second Year, of the
second Class at the Expiration of the fourth Year, and of the
third Class at the Expiration of the sixth Year, so that one
third may be chosen every second Year; and if Vacancies happen by Resignation, or otherwise, during the Recess of the Legislature of any State, the Executive thereof may make tem-

CONSTITUTION OF THE UNITED STATES   5

porary Appointments until the next Meeting of the Legislature, which shall then fill such Vacancies.

No Person shall be a Senator who shall not have attained to the Age of thirty Years, and been nine Years a Citizen of the United States, and who shall not, when elected, be an Inhabitant of that State for which he shall be chosen.

The Vice President of the United States shall be President of the Senate but shall have no Vote, unless they be equally divided.

The Senate shall chuse their other Officers, and also a President pro tempore, in the Absence of the Vice President, or when he shall exercise the Office of President of the United States.

The Senate shall have the sole Power to try all Impeachments. When sitting for that Purpose, they shall be on Oath or Affirmation. When the President of the United States is tried the Chief Justice shall preside: And no Person shall be convicted without the Concurrence of two thirds of the Members present.

Judgment in Cases of Impeachment shall not extend further than to removal from Office, and disqualification to hold and enjoy any Office of honor, Trust or Profit under the United States: but the Party convicted shall nevertheless be liable and subject to Indictment, Trial, Judgment and Punishment, according to Law.

Section. 4. The Times, Places and Manner of holding Elections for Senators and Representatives, shall be prescribed in each State by the Legislature thereof; but the Congress may at

6   CONSTITUTION OF THE UNITED STATES

any time by Law make or alter such Regulations, except as to the Places of chusing Senators.

The Congress shall assemble at least once in every Year, and such Meeting shall be on the first Monday in December, unless they shall by Law appoint a different Day.

Section. 5. Each House shall be the Judge of the Elections, Returns and Qualifications of its own Members, and a Majority of each shall constitute a Quorum to do Business; but a smaller Number may adjourn from day to day, and may be authorized to compel the Attendance of absent Members, in such Manner, and under such Penalties as each House may provide.

Each House may determine the Rules of its Proceedings, punish its Members for disorderly Behaviour, and, with the Concurrence of two thirds, expel a Member.

Each House shall keep a Journal of its Proceedings, and from time to time publish the same, excepting such Parts as may in their Judgment require Secrecy; and the Yeas and Nays of the Members of either House on any question shall, at the Desire of one fifth of those Present, be entered on the Journal.

Neither House, during the Session of Congress, shall, without the Consent of the other, adjourn for more than three days, nor to any other Place than that in which the two Houses shall be sitting.

Section. 6. The Senators and Representatives shall receive a Compensation for their Services, to be ascertained by Law, and paid out of the Treasury of the United States. They shall in all Cases, except Treason, Felony and Breach of the Peace, be privileged from Arrest during their Attendance at the Session of their respective Houses, and in going to and returning

CONSTITUTION OF THE UNITED STATES   7

from the same; and for any Speech or Debate in either House, they shall not be questioned in any other Place.

No Senator or Representative shall, during the Time for which he was elected, be appointed to any civil Office under the Authority of the United States, which shall have been created, or the Emoluments whereof shall have been encreased during such time; and no Person holding any Office under the United States, shall be a Member of either House during his Continuance in Office.

Section. 7. All Bills for raising Revenue shall originate in the House of Representatives; but the Senate may propose or concur with amendments as on other Bills.

Every Bill which shall have passed the House of Representatives and the Senate, shall, before it become a law, be presented to the President of the United States: If he approve he shall sign it, but if not he shall return it, with his Objections to that House in which it shall have originated, who shall enter the Objections at large on their Journal, and proceed to reconsider it. If after such Reconsideration two thirds of that House shall agree to pass the Bill, it shall be sent, together with the Objections, to the other House, by which it shall likewise be reconsidered, and if approved by two thirds of that House, it shall become a Law. But in all such Cases the Votes of both Houses shall be determined by Yeas and Nays, and the Names of the Persons voting for and against the Bill shall be entered on the Journal of each House respectively. If any Bill shall not be returned by the President within ten Days (Sundays excepted) after it shall have been presented to him, the Same shall be a Law, in like Manner as if he had signed it, unless the Congress

8   CONSTITUTION OF THE UNITED STATES

by their Adjournment prevent its Return, in which Case it shall
not be a Law

Every Order, Resolution, or Vote to which the Concurrence
of the Senate and House of Representatives may be necessary
(except on a question of Adjournment) shall be presented to the
President of the United States; and before the Same shall take
Effect, shall be approved by him, or being disapproved by him,
shall be repassed by two thirds of the Senate and House of
Representatives, according to the Rules and Limitations prescribed in the Case of a Bill.

Section. 8. The Congress shall have Power To lay and col-
lect Taxes, Duties, Imposts and Excises, to pay the Debts and
provide for the common Defence and general Welfare of the
United States; but all Duties, Imposts and Excises shall be uniform throughout the United States;

To borrow Money on the credit of the United States;

To regulate Commerce with foreign Nations, and among
the several States, and with the Indian Tribes;

To establish an uniform Rule of Naturalization, and uniform Laws on the subject of Bankruptcies throughout the United States;

To coin Money, regulate the Value thereof, and of foreign
Coin, and fix the Standard of Weights and Measures;

To provide for the Punishment of counterfeiting the Securities and current Coin of the United States;

To establish Post Offices and post Roads;

To promote the Progress of Science and useful Arts, by se-
curing for limited Times to Authors and Inventors the exclusive
Right to their respective Writings and Discoveries;

CONSTITUTION OF THE UNITED STATES   9

To constitute Tribunals inferior to the supreme Court;

To define and punish Piracies and Felonies committed on the high Seas, and Offences against the Law of Nations;

To declare War, grant Letters of Marque and Reprisal, and make Rules concerning Captures on Land and Water;

To raise and support Armies, but no Appropriation of Money to that Use shall be for a longer Term than two Years;

To provide and maintain a Navy;

To make Rules for the Government and Regulation of the land and naval Forces;

To provide for calling forth the Militia to execute the Laws of the Union, suppress Insurrections and repeal Invasions;

To provide for organizing, arming, and disciplining, the Militia, and for governing such Part of them as may be employed in the Service of the United States, reserving to the States respectively, the Appointment of the Officers, and the Authority of training the Militia according to the discipline prescribed by Congress;

To exercise exclusive Legislation in all Cases whatsoever, over such District (not exceeding ten Miles square) as may, by Cession of Particular States, and the Acceptance of Congress, become the Seat of the Government of the United States, and to exercise like Authority over all Places purchased by the Consent of the Legislature of the State in which the Same shall be, for the Erection of Forts, Magazines, Arsenals, dock-Yards and other needful Buildings;—And

To make all Laws which shall be necessary and proper for carrying into Execution the foregoing Powers and all other Powers vested by this Constitution in the Government of the United States, or in any Department or Officer thereof.

10   CONSTITUTION OF THE UNITED STATES

Section. 9. The Migration or Importation of such Persons as any of the States now existing shall think proper to admit, shall not be prohibited by the Congress prior to the Year one thousand eight hundred and eight, but a Tax or duty may be imposed on such Importation, not exceeding ten dollars for each Person.

The Privilege of the Writ of Habeas Corpus shall not be suspended, unless when in Cases or Rebellion or Invasion the public Safety may require it.

No Bill of Attainder or ex post facto Law shall be passed.

No Capitation, or other direct, Tax shall be laid, unless in Proportion to the Census of Enumeration herein before directed to be taken.

No Tax or Duty shall be laid on Articles exported from any State.

No Preference shall be given by any Regulation of Commerce or Revenue to the Ports of one State over those of another: nor shall Vessels bound to, or from, one State, be obliged to enter, clear or pay Duties in another.

No Money shall be drawn from the Treasury, but in Consequence of Appropriations made by Law; and a regular Statement and Account of the Receipts and Expenditures of all public Money shall be published from time to time.

No Title of Nobility shall be granted by the United States: And no Person holding any Office of Profit or Trust under them, shall, without the Consent of the Congress, accept of any present, Emolument, Office, or Title, of any kind whatever, from any King, Prince or foreign State.

CONSTITUTION OF THE UNITED STATES   11

Section. 10. No State shall enter into any Treaty, Alliance, or Confederation; grant Letters of Marque and Reprisal; coin Money; emit Bills of Credit; make any Thing but gold and silver Coin a Tender in Payment of Debts; pass any Bill of Attainder, ex post facto Law, or Law impairing the Obligation of Contracts, or grant any Title of Nobility.

No State shall, without the Consent of the Congress, lay any Imposts or Duties on Imports or Exports, except what may be absolutely necessary for executing it's inspection Laws: and the net Produce of all Duties and Imposts, laid by any State on Imports or Exports, shall be for the Use of the Treasury of the United States; and all such Laws shall be subject to the Revision and Controul of the Congress.

No State shall, without the Consent of Congress, lay any Duty of Tonnage, keep Troops, or Ships of War in time of Peace, enter into any Agreement or Compact with another State, or with a foreign Power, or engage in War, unless actually invaded, or in such imminent Danger as will not admit of delay.

Article. II.

Section. 1. The executive Power shall be vested in a President of the United States of America. He shall hold his Office during the Term of four Years, and, together with the Vice President, chosen for the same Term, be elected, as follows:

Each State shall appoint, in such Manner as the Legislature thereof may direct, a Number of Electors, equal to the whole Number of Senators and Representatives to which the State may be entitled in the Congress: but no Senator or Representative, or Person holding an Office of Trust or Profit under the United States, shall be appointed an Elector.

12   CONSTITUTION OF THE UNITED STATES

The Electors shall meet in their respective States, and vote by Ballot for two Persons, of whom one at least shall not be an Inhabitant of the same State with themselves. And they shall make a List of all the Persons voted for, and of the Number of Votes for each; which List they shall sign and certify, and transmit sealed to the Seat of the Government of the United States, directed to the President of the Senate. The President of the Senate shall, in the Presence of the Senate and House of Representatives, open all the Certificates, and the Votes shall then be counted. The Person having the greatest Number of Votes shall be the President, if such Number be a Majority of the whole Number of Electors appointed; and if there be more than one who have such Majority, and have an equal Number of Votes, then the House of Representatives shall immediately chuse by Ballot one of them for President; and if no Person have a Majority, then from the five highest on the List the said House shall in like Manner chuse the President. But in chusing the President, the Votes shall be taken by States, the Representatives from each State having one Vote; a quorum for this Purpose shall consist of a Member or Members from two thirds of the States, and a Majority of all the States shall be necessary to a Choice. In every Case, after the Choice of the President, the Person having the greatest Number of Votes of the Electors shall be the Vice President. But if there should remain two or more who have equal Votes, the Senate shall chuse from them by Ballot the Vice President.

The Congress may determine the Time of chusing the Electors, and the Day on which they shall give their Votes; which Day shall be the same throughout the United States.

CONSTITUTION OF THE UNITED STATES   13

No Person except a natural born Citizen, or a Citizen of the United States, at the time of the Adoption of this Constitution, shall be eligible to the Office of President; neither shall any person be eligible to that Office who shall not have attained to the Age of thirty five Years, and been fourteen Years a Resident within the United States.

In Case of the Removal of the President from Office, or of his Death, Resignation, or Inability to discharge the Powers and Duties of the said Office, the Same shall devolve on the Vice President, and the Congress may by Law provide for the Case of Removal, Death, Resignation or Inability, both of the President and Vice President, declaring what Officer shall then act as President, and such Officer shall act accordingly, until the Disability be removed, or a President shall be elected.

The President shall, at stated Times, receive for his Services, a Compensation, which shall neither be encreased nor diminished during the Period for which he shall have been elected, and he shall not receive within that Period any other Emolument from the United States, or any of them.

Before he enter on the Execution of his Office, he shall take the following Oath or Affirmation:—"I do solemnly swear (or affirm) that I will faithfully execute the Office of President of the United States, and will to the best of my Ability, preserve, protect and defend the Constitution of the United States."

Section. 2. The President shall be Commander in Chief of the Army and Navy of the United States, and of the Militia of the several States, when called into the actual Service of the United States; he may require the Opinion, in writing, of the

14   CONSTITUTION OF THE UNITED STATES

principal Officer in each of the executive Departments, upon
any Subject relating to the Duties of their respective Offices,
and he shall have Power to Grant Reprieves and Pardons for
Offences against the United States, except in Cases of Impeachment.

He shall have Power, by and with the Advice and Consent
of the Senate, to make Treaties, provided two thirds of the Senators present concur; and he shall nominate, and by and with
the Advice and Consent of the Senate, shall appoint Ambassadors, other public Ministers and Consuls, Judges of the supreme Court, and all other Officers of the United States, whose
Appointments are not herein otherwise provided for, and which
shall be established by Law: but the Congress may by Law vest
the Appointment of such inferior Officers, as they think proper,
in the President alone, in the Courts of Law, or in the Heads
of Departments.

The President shall have Power to fill up all Vacancies that
may happen during the Recess of the Senate, by granting Commissions which shall expire at the End of their next Session.

Section. 3. He shall from time to time give to the Congress
Information on the State of the Union, and recommend to their
Consideration such Measures as he shall judge necessary and
expedient; he may, on extraordinary Occasions, convene both
Houses, or either of them, and in Case of Disagreement between them, with Respect to the Time of Adjournment, he may
adjourn them to such Time as he shall think proper; he shall
receive Ambassadors and other public Ministers; he shall take
Care that the Laws be faithfully executed, and shall Commission all the Officers of the United States.

CONSTITUTION OF THE UNITED STATES   15

Section. 4. The President, Vice President and all Civil Officers of the United States, shall be removed from Office on Impeachment for and Conviction of, Treason, Bribery, or other high Crimes and Misdemeanors.

Article. III.

Section. 1. The judicial Power of the United States, shall be vested in one supreme Court, and in such inferior Courts as the Congress may from time to time ordain and establish. The Judges, both of the supreme and inferior Courts, shall hold their Offices during good Behaviour, and shall, at stated Times, receive for their Services, a Compensation, which shall not be diminished during their Continuance in Office.

Section. 2. The judicial Power shall extend to all Cases, in Law and Equity, arising under this Constitution, the Laws of the United States, and Treaties made, or which shall be made, under their Authority;—to all Cases affecting Ambassadors, other public ministers and Consuls;—to all Cases of admiralty and maritime Jurisdiction;—to Controversies to which the United States shall be a Party;—to Controversies between two or more States;—between a State and Citizens of another State;—between Citizens of different States;—between Citizens of the same State claiming Lands under Grants of different States, and between a State, or the Citizens thereof, and foreign States, Citizens or Subjects.

In all Cases affecting Ambassadors, other public Ministers and Consuls, and those in which a State shall be Party, the supreme Court shall have original Jurisdiction. In all the other Cases before mentioned, the supreme Court shall have appel-

16   CONSTITUTION OF THE UNITED STATES

late Jurisdiction, both as to Law and Fact, with such Exceptions, and under such Regulations as the Congress shall make.

The Trial of all Crimes, except in Cases of Impeachment, shall be by Jury; and such Trial shall be held in the State where the said Crimes shall have been committed; but when not committed within any State, the Trial shall be at such Place or Places as the Congress may by Law have directed.

Section. 3. Treason against the United States, shall consist only in levying War against them, or in adhering to their Enemies, giving them Aid and Comfort. No Person shall be convicted of Treason unless on the Testimony of two Witnesses to the same overt Act, or on Confession in open Court.

The Congress shall have Power to declare the Punishment of Treason, but no Attainder of Treason shall work Corruption of Blood, or Forfeiture except during the Life of the Person attainted.

Article. IV.

Section. 1. Full Faith and Credit shall be given in each State to the public Acts, Records, and judicial Proceedings of every other State. And the Congress may by general Laws prescribe the Manner in which such Acts, Records and Proceedings shall be proved, and the Effect thereof.

Section. 2. The Citizens of each State shall be entitled to all Privileges and Immunities of Citizens in the several States.

A Person charged in any State with Treason, Felony, or other Crime, who shall flee from Justice, and be found in another State, shall on Demand of the executive Authority of the State from which he fled, be delivered up, to be removed to the State having Jurisdiction of the Crime.

CONSTITUTION OF THE UNITED STATES   17

No Person held to Service or Labour in one State, under the Laws thereof, escaping into another, shall, in Consequence of any Law or Regulation therein, be discharged from such Service or Labour, but shall be delivered up on Claim of the Party to whom such Service or Labour may be due.

Section. 3. New States may be admitted by the Congress into this Union; but no new State shall be formed or erected within the Jurisdiction of any other State; nor any State be formed by the Junction of two or more States, or Parts of States, without the Consent of the Legislatures of the States concerned as well as of the Congress.

The Congress shall have Power to dispose of and make all needful Rules and Regulations respecting the Territory or other Property belonging to the United States; and nothing in this Constitution shall be so construed as to Prejudice any Claims of the United States, or of any particular State.

Section. 4. The United States shall guarantee to every State in this Union a Republican Form of Government, and shall protect each of them against Invasion; and on Application of the Legislature, or of the Executive (when the Legislature cannot be convened) against domestic Violence.

Article. V.

The Congress, whenever two thirds of both Houses shall deem it necessary, shall propose Amendments to this Constitution, or, on the Application of the Legislatures of two thirds of the several States, shall call a Convention for proposing Amendments, which, in either Case, shall be valid to all Intents and Purposes, as Part of this Constitution, when ratified by the Legislatures of three fourths of the several States, or by

18   CONSTITUTION OF THE UNITED STATES

Conventions in three fourths thereof, as the one or the other
Mode of Ratification may be proposed by the Congress; Provided that no Amendment which may be made prior to the
Year One thousand eight hundred and eight shall in any Manner affect the first and fourth Clauses in the Ninth Section of
the first Article; and that no State, without its Consent, shall
be deprived of its equal Suffrage in the Senate.

Article. VI.

All Debts contracted and Engagements entered into, before
the Adoption of this Constitution, shall be as valid against the
United States under this Constitution, as under the Confederation.

This Constitution, and the Laws of the United States
which shall be made in Pursuance thereof; and all Treaties
made, or which shall be made, under the Authority of the United States, shall be the supreme Law of the Land; and the
Judges in every State shall be bound thereby, any Thing in the
Constitution or Laws of any state to the Contrary notwith-
standing.

The Senators and Representatives before mentioned, and
the Members of the several State Legislatures, and all executive and judicial Officers, both of the United States and of the
several States, shall be bound by Oath or Affirmation, to support this Constitution; but no religious Test shall ever be required as a Qualification to any Office or public Trust under
the United States.

CONSTITUTION OF THE UNITED STATES   19

Article. VII.

The Ratification of the Conventions of nine States, shall be sufficient for the Establishment of this Constitution between the States so ratifying the same.

The Word, "the," being interlined between the seventh and eighth Lines of the first Page, The Word "Thirty" being partly written on an Erazure in the fifteenth Line of the first Page, The Words "is tried" being interlined between the thirty second and thirty third Lines of the first Page and the Word "the" being interlined between the forty third and forty fourth Lines of the second Page.

done in Convention by the Unanimous Consent of the States present the Seventeenth Day of September in the Year of our Lord one thousand seven hundred and Eighty seven and of the Independence of the United States of America the Twelfth. In witness whereof We have hereunto subscribed our Names,

Attest WILLIAM JACKSON
Secretary

G$^{\circ}$ WASHINGTON—Presid^{t}.
and deputy from Virginia

New Hampshire   JOHN LANGDON
                 NICHOLAS GILMAN

Massachusetts   NATHANIEL GORHAM
                 RUFUS KING

Connecticut   W^M SAM^L JOHNSON
                 ROGER SHERMAN

New York . . . . ALEXANDER HAMILTON

New Jersey   WIL: LIVINGSTON
                 DAVID BREARLEY.
                 W^M PATTERSON.
                 JONA: DAYTON

Pennsylvania   B FRANKLIN
                 THOMAS MIFFLIN
                 ROB^T MORRIS
                 GEO. CLYMER
                 THO^S FITZSIMONS
                 JARED INGERSOL
                 JAMES WILSON
                 GOUV MORRIS

20   CONSTITUTION OF THE UNITED STATES

Delaware   GEO: READ
                  GUNNING BEDFORD JUN
                  JOHN DICKINSON
                  RICHARD BASSETT
                  JACO: BROOM

Maryland   JAMES MCHENRY
                  DAN OF ST THOS JENIFER
                  DANL CARROLL

Virginia   JOHN BLAIR—
                  JAMES MADISON JR.

North Carolina   WM BLOUNT
                  RICHD DOBBS SPAIGHT
                  HU WILLIAMSON
                  J. RUTLEDGE

South Carolina   CHARLES COTESWORTH PINCKNEY
                  CHARLES PINCKNEY
                  PIERCE BUTLER

Georgia   WILLIAM FEW
                  ABR BALDWIN

CONSTITUTION OF THE UNITED STATES   21

In Convention Monday, September 17th 1787.
Present
The States of

New Hampshire, Massachusetts, Connecticut, MR Hamilton from New York, New Jersey, Pennsylvania, Delaware, Maryland, Virginia, North Carolina, South Carolina and Georgia.

Resolved,

That the preceeding Constitution be laid before the United States in Congress assembled, and that it is the Opinion of this Convention, that it should afterwards be submitted to a Convention of Delegates, chosen in each State by the People thereof, under the Recommendation of its Legislature, for their Assent and Ratification; and that each Convention assenting to, and ratifying the Same, should give Notice thereof to the United States in Congress assembled. Resolved, That it is the Opinion of this Convention, that as soon as the Conventions of nine States shall have ratified this Constitution, the United States in Congress assembled should fix a Day on which Electors should be appointed by the States which shall have ratified the same, and a Day on which the Electors should assemble to vote for the President, and the Time and Place for commencing Proceedings under this Constitution. That after such Publication the Electors should be appointed, and the Senators and Representatives elected: That the Electors should meet on the Day fixed for the Election of the President, and should transmit their Votes certified, signed, sealed and directed, as the Constitution requires, to the Secretary of the United States in Congress assembled, that the Senators and Representatives should convene at the Time and Place assigned; that the Senators

22   CONSTITUTION OF THE UNITED STATES

should appoint a President of the Senate, for the sole Purpose
of receiving, opening and counting the Votes for President; and,
that after he shall be chosen, the Congress, together with the
President, should, without Delay, proceed to execute this Constitution.

By the Unanimous Order of the Convention

G⁰: WASHINGTON—Presid^t.

W. JACKSON Secretary.

ACKNOWLEDGEMENTS

Writing a book is a difficult and intense process. It is also rewarding and gratifying. I am so thankful to all of the friends and family who have supported me through all the years.

First and foremost, thank you to my Lord and Savior, Jesus Christ.

Thank you to my mom and dad. Without your love and guidance, none of this would be possible. Thank you to my brother Todd. He is the writer in the family, and his encouragement and friendship made this possible.

Thank you to President Donald J. Trump. I appreciate your faith in me, and I am grateful for everything. I continue to support your efforts to Keep America Great.

To Vice President Pence, thank you for your support and kindness.

Thank you to the members of President Trump's cabinet—it was an honor to serve alongside you.

Thank you to McGregor Scott, America is great because of people like you and Jennifer.

Thank you to Bernadette Serton. I am grateful for the opportunity to work with you on this book and to tell this story. Our meetings were always productive and therapeutic. You are a true patriot, and you and your family are what is great about our country.

Thank you to all of my colleagues at the Department of Justice. All of the Bush 43 former U.S. Attorneys including: Bob Balfe, Eric Peterson, Drew Wrigley, Richard Roper, the late Don DeGabrielle, Chief Justice of the Nebraska Supreme Court Mike Heavican, Chuck Larson, Sr., Kevin O'Connor, Mike Sullivan, Karen Hewitt, Deb Yang, John Ratcliffe, Matt Dummermuth, Judge Eric Melgren, Bud Cummins, Todd Graves, Catherine Hanaway, Paul Charlton, Greg Brower, Matt Mead, Susan Brooks, Brett Tolman, Ed Yarborough, Terry Flynn, John Richter, Johnny Sutton, Mike Battle, John Brownlee, Leura Canary, Bob Corrente, Jane Duke, Troy Eid, John Wood, Jim McDevitt, Robert McCallum, John McKay, Pat Meehan, Bill Mercer, Greg Miller, Matt Orwig, Jeff Taylor, Ron Tenpas, Mary Beth Buchanan, Marty Jackley, Bill Leone, Jim Letten, Guy Lewis, and Scott Schools. The Attorney General's office staff and counselors, you were each invaluable and so important to this story. Thank you to my friend Theresa Watson who kept me on my toes and the trains running on time. Your contributions to the Department of Justice are immeasurable.

I am grateful for the leadership and friendship of current U.S. Attorneys including Bobby Christine, Nick Trutanich, Jay Towne, Zach Terwilliger, Erin Nealy Cox, Maria Chapa Lopez, Ariana Fajardo Orshan, B. J. Pak, John Lausch, Pete Deegan, Marc Krickbaum, Marc Hurst, Tim Garrison, Jeff Jensen, Craig Carpenito, Rich Donoghue, Matt Martin, Justin Herdman, Trent Shores and Mike Stuart. Thank you to Jeff Sessions, Steve Engel, Noel Francisco, Rachel Brand, John Demurs, Brian Benczkowski, and all of the AAGs and DAAGs, staff and lawyers at main Justice and in the U.S. Attorney's Offices across the country, where much of the important work of the DOJ gets done.

Thank you to my friends and patriots, the state Attorneys General. Thank you to my friends in Congress, especially Devin Nunes for writing the foreword for this book. Thank you to Rick Perry for your longtime friendship and support.

Thank you to Attorney General John Ashcroft and Attorney General Ed Meese. You are true examples of leadership, and the Department of Justice owes you a debt of gratitude for your service. Thank you to all of the professionals serving within the law enforcement agencies at DOJ (FBI, DEA, ATF and U.S. Marshals), all of federal law enforcement agents and staff government-wide, and my friends in state and local law enforcement. You have my thanks, and I have your back. A special thanks to all of the FBI Agents that served on my security detail, led by Mike and Ross, while I was Acting Attorney General.

Thank you to all of my friends from Ankeny, Iowa—there is no better place to grow up. A special thank you to my teachers and coaches at Ankeny. To my teammates and coaches at the University of Iowa, I will always cherish our time together. Coach Fry—we all miss you, and there are not enough words to express what an incredible impact you had on every young man that played for you. May God bless your family. Go Hawks!

Thank you to Jack Whitver, Chris Hagenow, and Bill Gustoff. We had many great times together, and I look forward to more to come. Thank you to Kendra Arnold. You are a great friend and colleague. Thank you to Leonard Leo and Jonathan Bunch. Your friendship is invaluable. Thank you to Jeff Roe and everyone at Axiom. Jeff is the best mind in politics, and I am glad to have him as a friend and colleague.

Thank you to all of my former colleagues at the U.S. Attorney's Office in the Southern District of Iowa. You taught me how to wear the white hat of justice. Thank you to my two former First Assistants—Kevin VanderSchel and Stephen Patrick O'Meara, I know it was a project.

Thank you to Dan Scavino, Jared Kushner, Don McGahn, Annie Donaldson, John Kelly, Emmitt Flood, Pat Cipollone, Mick Mulvaney, and everyone at the White House who was always so helpful and supportive. Thank you Dina Powell McCormick for your friendship and advice. David Urban, thanks for your service to America.

Thank you to Greg Mueller, Keith Appell, Victoria Kucharski, and everyone at CRC Public Relations. I am grateful for everything you do. Thank you to all of my friends at Fox News.

Thank you to everyone who helped and supported my political campaigns in 2002 and 2014, including Rory Triplett, Michael Antonopoulos, and Justin Arnold.

Thank you to Matt and Mercy Schlapp for your friendship. Thank you to Senator Chuck Grassley for recommending me for U.S. Attorney and for your long-time friendship. Thank you to President Bush for selecting me to be your U.S. Attorney in the Southern District of Iowa. To Senator Joni Ernst, thank you for your friendship and encouragement.

Thank you to Keith Urbahn and everyone at Javelin, as well as Harry Crocker and everyone at Regnery.

Thank you, Carol and Joe and the Muldoons.

NOTES

Introduction

Justice Triumphant vs. Justice Defeated

1. "Statement of Michael E. Horowitz, Inspector General, U.S. Department of Justice," Office of the Inspector General, Department of Justice, June 18, 2018, https://oig.justice.gov/testimony/t180618.pdf.
2. Adam Goldman, "Comey Is Criticized by Justice Dept. Watchdog for Violating F.B.I. Rules," *New York Times*, August 29, 2019, https://www.nytimes.com/2019/08/29/us/politics/comey-memos-inspector-general.html.
3. "Report of Investigation of Former Federal Bureau of Investigation Director James Comey's Disclosure of Sensitive Investigative Information and Handling of Certain Memoranda," Office of the Inspector General, Department of Justice, August 2019, https://oig.justice.gov/reports/2019/o1902.pdf.
4. Christina Pazzanese, "It's Spy vs. Spy vs. Spy," *Harvard Gazette*, February 20, 2019, https://news.harvard.edu/gazette/story/2019/02/

harvard-expert-says-russian-spying-is-nothing-new-only-the-technology-is/.

5. Evan Perez, Laura Jarrett, and Ariane de Vogue, "Sessions Realized Too Late That Whitaker Was Auditioning for His Job," CNN, November 9, 2018, https://www.cnn.com/2018/11/09/politics/matt-whitaker-jeff-sessions/index.html.

6. Betsy Swan, "'They Hate This Guy': Matt Whitaker Braces for Showdown with Dems," The Daily Beast, February 7, 2019, https://www.thedailybeast.com/they-hate-this-guy-matt-whitaker-braces-for-showdown-with-dems.

7. Peter Holley, "'Brothers in Arms': The Long Friendship between Mueller and Comey," *Washington Post,* May 17, 2019, https://www.washingtonpost.com/politics/2017/live-updates/trump-white-house/trump-comey-and-russia-how-key-washington-players-are-reacting/brothers-in-arms-the-long-friendship-between-mueller-and-comey/.

8. Alan Smith, "Robert Mueller's 'Pit Bull' Is Coming under Intense Scrutiny over Perceived Anti-Trump Bias," Business Insider, December 9, 2017, https://www.businessinsider.com/who-is-andrew-weissman-mueller-trump-clinton-russia-investigation-fbi-2017-12.

9. Kevin Johnson, "FBI's Peter Strzok: Trump Inquiry 'Maybe the Most Important Case of Our Lives,'" USA TODAY, January 23, 2018, https://www.usatoday.com/story/news/politics/2018/01/23/fbis-peter-strzok-trump-inquiry-maybe-most-important-case-our-lives/1058808001/.

10. Robert Mueller, "Re: Report of the Special Counsel on the Investigation into Russian Interference in the 2016 Presidential Election and Obstruction of Justice," Special Counsel's Office, U.S. Department of Justice, March 27, 209, https://assets.documentcloud.org/documents/5984399/Mueller-Letter-to-Barr.pdf.

11. Devlin Barrett, "FBI in Internal Feud over Hillary Clinton Probe," *Wall Street Journal,* October 20, 2016, https://www.wsj.com/articles/laptop-may-include-thousands-of-emails-linked-to-hillary-clintons-private-server-1477854957.

12. Jerry Dunleavy, "Ex-FBI Lawyer: Carter Page FISA Application Approved in 'Unusual' Way by McCabe, Yates, and Baker,"

Washington Examiner, May 22, 2019, https://www.
washingtonexaminer.com/news/
ex-fbi-lawyer-carter-page-fisa-application-approved-in-unusual-way-
by-mccabe-yates-and-baker.

13. Katie Galioto, "'I'm F—-ed': Trump Called Mueller Appointment
'the End of My Presidency,'" *Politico,* April 18, 2019, https://www.
politico.com/story/2019/04/18/
trump-mueller-report-presidency-1281244.

14. See, for instance, Heather Mac Donald's book *The War on Cops:
How the New Attack on Law and Order Makes Everyone Less Safe*
(New York: Encounter Books, 2016).

15. "Honoring the Service of Law Enforcement Officers Who Died by
Suicide," Blue H.E.L.P., 2018, https://bluehelp.org.

Chapter 1

Double Standards

1. Mark Sumner, "Matthew Whitaker's Work as a Scam Artist and
Threatening Bully Makes Him the Perfect Trup AG," Daily Kos,
November 8, 2018, https://www.dailykos.com/
stories/2018/11/8/1811192/-Matthew-Whitaker-s-work-as-a-scam-
artist-and-threatening-bully-makes-him-the-perfect-Trump-AG.

2. Jerry Nadler, "Ranking Member Nadler Statement on President
Trump Firing Attorney General Jeff Sessions," Newsroom, Nadler.
house.gov, November 7, 2018, https://nadler.house.gov/news/
documentsingle.aspx?DocumentID=391454.

3. Charles Schumer, "Dear Mr. President: Your Decision This Week,"
Democrats, United States Senate, November 9, 2018, https://www.
democrats.senate.gov/imo/media/doc/Schumer%20Letter%20to%20
POTUS%20re%20Whitaker.pdf.

4. Dan Spinelli, "Dan Coats' Deputy Is a Widely Respected Intelligence
Professional. Naturally, Trump Wants Her Out," *Mother Jones,*
August 7, 2019, https://www.motherjones.com/politics/2019/08/
dan-coats-deputy-is-a-widely-respected-intelligence-professional-
naturally-trump-wants-her-out/.

5. Chris Geidner, "Matthew Whitaker Is Acting AG Now because Congress Gave In to Bill Clinton," BuzzFeed, December 9, 2018, https://www.buzzfeednews.com/article/chrisgeidner/trump-attorney-general-appointment-congress.

6. "Final Vote Results for Roll Call 538," Clerk.house.gov, October 20, 1998, http://clerk.house.gov/evs/1998/roll538.xml.

7. Olivia Beavers, "Dismissed FBI Agent Changed Comey's Language on Clinton Emails to 'Extremely Careless': Report," *The Hill*, December 4, 2017, https://thehill.com/homenews/administration/363194-former-fbi-agent-changed-comeys-language-of-clinton-email-use-to.

8. Daniel Chaitin, "Davin Nunes: Peter Strzok's 'Insurance Policy' Was about Getting into Trump Campaign Emails," *Washington Examiner*, May 14, 2019, https://www.washingtonexaminer.com/news/devin-nunes-peter-strzoks-insurance-policy-was-about-carter-page-fisa-warrant.

9. Del Quentin Wilber, "Text Messages May Shed Light on Judge's Recusal in Flynn Case," *Wall Street Journal*, March 18, 2018, https://www.wsj.com/articles/text-messages-may-shed-light-on-judges-recusal-in-flynn-case-1521419841.

10. Michael Schmidt, Matt Apuzzo, and Adam Goldman, "In Texts, F.B.I. Officials in Russia Inquiry Say Clinton 'Just Has to Win,'" *New York Times*, December 12, 2012, https://www.nytimes.com/2017/12/12/us/fbi-trump-russia.html.

11. George Parry, "Note to Trump's Lawyer: Do Not Cooperate with Mueller Lynch Mob," *Philadelphia Inquirer*, November 9, 2018, https://www.inquirer.com/philly/opinion/commentary/note-to-trumps-lawyer-do-not-cooperate-with-mueller-lynch-mob-20181109.html.

12. "Dershowitz: Strzok Should Have Recused Himself from Russia Probe and So Should Rosenstein," Fox News Insider, August 14, 2018, https://insider.foxnews.com/amp/article/62837.

13. Adam Goldman and Michael Schmidt, "Rod Rosenstein Suggested Secretly Recording Trump and Discussed 25th Amendment," *New*

York Times, September 21, 2019, https://www.nytimes.
com/2018/09/21/us/politics/rod-rosenstein-wear-wire-25th-
amendment.html.

14. Carrie Johnson and Philip Ewing, "Rosenstein Denies That He
Discussed Recording Trump, Invoking 25th Amendment," *All Things
Considered,* NPR, September 21, 2018, https://www.npr.
org/2018/09/21/650545077/
rosenstein-denies-that-he-discussed-recording-trump-invoking-25th-
amendment.

15. Nicholas Fandos and Adam Goldman, "Former Top F.B.I. Lawyer
Says Rosenstein Was Serious about Taping Trump," *New York
Times,* October 10, 2018, https://www.nytimes.com/2018/10/10/us/
politics/james-baker-rosenstein-secretly-taping-trump.html.

16. "Statement of Michael E. Horowitz, Inspector General, U.S.
Department of Justice," Office of the Inspector General, Department
of Justice, June 19, 2018, https://oig.justice.gov/testimony/t180619.
pdf.

17. Matthew Mussbaum, "WikiLeaks: DOJ Official Gave Clinton Camp
'Heads Up' about Email Filing," *Politico,* November 2, 2016, https://
www.politico.com/story/2016/11/
wikileaks-clinton-justice-department-heads-up-investigation-230643.

18. Matt Flegenheimer, "Andrew Weissmann, Mueller's Legal Pit Bull,"
New York Times, October 31, 2017, https://www.nytimes.
com/2017/10/31/us/politics/andrew-weissmann-mueller.html.

19. Peter Nicholas, Aruna Viswanatha, and Erica Orden, "Trump's Allies
Urge Harder Line as Mueller Probe Heats Up," *Wall Street Journal,*
December 8, 2017, https://www.wsj.com/articles/
trumps-allies-urge-harder-line-as-mueller-probe-
drags-on-1512748299.

20. Flegenheimer, "Andrew Weissmann, Mueller's Legal Pit Bull."

21. Arthur Andersen LLP v. United States, 544 U.S. ___ (2005), https://
www.law.cornell.edu/supct/pdf/04-368P.ZO; David Willman,
"Mueller Deputy Andrew Weissmann Has a Reputation for Hard-
Charging Tactics—and Sometimes Going Too Far," *Los Angeles
Times,* February 16, 2018, https://www.latimes.com/politics/la-na-
pol-trump-weissmann-20180216-story.html.

22. Flegenheimer, "Andrew Weissmann, Mueller's Legal Pit Bull."

23. Victor Davis Hanson, "Holder's Hypocrisy," RealClear Politics, July 15, 2010, https://www.realclearpolitics.com/articles/2010/07/15/holders_hypocrisy_106319.html.

24. Michael Horowitz, "Give Inspectors General Access to the Records They Need to Do Their Jobs," *Washington Post*, October 18, 2015, https://www.washingtonpost.com/opinions/give-inspectors-general-access-to-the-records-they-need-to-do-their-jobs/2015/10/18/54942f30-738a-11e5-9cbb-790369643cf9_story.html.

25. Nicholas Fandos and Maggie Haberman, "Key Moments from Corey Lewandowski's Testimony before Congress," *New York Times*, September 17, 2019, https://www.nytimes.com/2019/09/17/us/politics/corey-lewandowski-testimony-trump.html?action=click&module=Latest&pgtype=Homepage.

26. "Document: IG's Report on IRS Targeting Tea Party," CNN Politics, May 14, 2013, https://www.cnn.com/interactive/2013/05/politics/irs-timeline/index.html.

27. Rich Morin *et al.*, "Behind the Badge," Social and Demographic Trends, Pew Research Center, January 11, 2017, https://www.pewsocialtrends.org/2017/01/11/behind-the-badge/.

28. Christal Hayes, "Eric Holder Says Michelle Obama Was Wrong: 'When They Go Low, We Kick Them,'" *USA TODAY*, October 10, 2018, https://www.usatoday.com/story/news/politics/onpolitics/2018/10/10/eric-holder-says-michelle-obama-wrong-when-they-go-low-we-kick-them/1593189002/.

29. Tal Kopan, "Comey: Lynch Asked for Clinton Investigation to Be Called a 'Matter,'" CNN Politics, June 8, 2017, https://www.cnn.com/2017/06/08/politics/james-comey-loretta-lynch/index.html.

30. Jonathan Easley, "Mueller Lieutenant Sent Email Saying He Was Proud of Sally Yates," *The Hill*, December 5, 2017, https://thehill.com/homenews/administration/363422-mueller-lieutenant-sent-email-saying-he-was-proud-of-sally-yates.

31. Dunleavy, "Ex-FBI Lawyer: Carter Page FIAS Application."

32. "Review of Four FISA Applications and Other Aspects of the FBI's Crossfire Hurricane Investigation," Office of the Inspector General, U.S. Department of Justice, December 2019, https://oig.justice.gov/reports/2019/o20012.pdf.

33. "Interview of: Bruce Ohr," Transcript of Executive Session, Committee on the Judiciary joint with the Committee on the Government Reform and Oversight, August 28, 2018, https://dougcollins.house.gov/sites/dougcollins.house.gov/files/Ohr%20Interview%20Transcript%208.28.18.pdf.

34. Letter from Assistant Attorney General Stephen E. Boyd to Senate Majority Leader Mitch McConnell and Senate Minority Leader Charles E. Schumer, dated December 20, 2018, from author's personal collection.

35. Associated Press, "Whitaker Rejected Advice to Recuse from Russia Probe," *Politico*, December 20, 2018, https://www.politico.com/story/2018/12/20/matthew-whitaker-recusal-russia-investigation-1071488.

36. Jason Breslow, "READ: Mueller's Letter Expressing Concern about Barr's Summary of His Report," Politics, NPR, May 1, 2019, https://www.npr.org/2019/05/01/719004457/read-muellers-letter-expressing-concern-about-barr-s-summary-of-his-report.

37. "Appointment of Special Counsel," Office of Public Affairs, Department of Justice, May 17, 2017, https://www.justice.gov/opa/pr/appointment-special-counsel.

38. "Section 600.1: Grounds for Appointing a Special Counsel," CFR 201, Title 28, Volume 2, Part 600, Govinfo.gov, https://www.govinfo.gov/content/pkg/CFR-2016-title28-vol2/pdf/CFR-2016-title28-vol2-part600.pdf.

39. William Barr, "AG March 24, 2019, Letter to House and Senate Judiciary Committees," Documents, NPR, March 24, 2019 https://apps.npr.org/documents/document.html?id=5779683-AG-March-24-2019-Letter-to-House-and-Senate.

40. Emma Stefansky and Kia Makarechi, "Trump's Firing of U.S. Attorneys Raises Eyebrows, Prompts Conflict," *Vanity Fair*, March

11, 2017, https://www.vanityfair.com/news/2017/03/
trump-us-attorneys-preet-bharara.

41. "Maxine Waters Grills Eric Holder on U.S. Attorneys," User-Created
    Clip, C-SPAN, March 13, 2017, https://www.c-span.org/
    video/?c4660888/maxine-waters-grills-eric-holder-attorneys.

42. Josh Gerstein, "Obama to Replace U.S. Attorneys," Under the Radar,
    Politico, May 15, 2009, https://www.politico.com/blogs/under-the-
    radar/2009/05/obama-to-replace-us-attorneys-018390.

43. Joseph Tanfani, "Ex-U.S. Attorney Patrick Fitzgerald on James
    Comey's Legal Team," *Chicago Tribune,* April 24, 2018, https://
    www.chicagotribune.com/news/breaking/ct-met-patrick-fitzgerald-
    lawyer-james-comey-20180424-story.html.

44. Henry Kerner, "Report of Prohibited Political Activity under the
    Hatch Act," U.S. Office of Special Counsel, June 13, 2019, https://s.
    wsj.net/public/resources/documents/OSC-Report-to-the-President-re-
    Kellyanne-Conway-Hatch-Act06132019.
    pdf?mod=article_inline&mod=article_inline.

45. Peter Baker, "Trump Is Urged to Fire Kellyanne Conway for Hatch
    Act Violations," *New York Times,* June 13, 2019, https://www.
    nytimes.com/2019/06/13/us/politics/kellyanne-conway-hatch-act.
    html.

46. "What Is the Hatch Act? Explaining Why Trump Was Urged to Fire
    Kellyanne Conway," *New York Times,* June 13, 2019, https://www.
    nytimes.com/2019/06/13/us/hatch-act.html?module=inline.

47. Max Greenwood, "Grassley Suggests Deputy FBI Director May Have
    Violated Hatch Act," *The Hill,* December 1, 2017, https://thehill.com/
    homenews/
    senate/362895-grassley-suggests-deputy-fbi-director-may-have-
    violated-hatch-act.

48. Adam Goldman, "Prosecutors Could Ask for Prison Time for
    Michael Flynn," *New York Times,* September 10, 2019, https://www.
    nytimes.com/2019/09/10/us/politics/michael-flynn-prosecutors-
    prison.html.

49. Tom Winter, "FBI Releases Documents Showing Payments to Trump
    Dossier Author Steele," NBC News, August 3, 2018, https://www.
    nbcnews.com/news/crime-courts/

fbi-releases-documents-showing-payments-trump-dossier-author-
steele-n897506.

50. James Comey (@Comey), "DOJ IG 'found no evidence that Comey or
his attorneys released any of the classified information contained in
any of the memos to members of the media.' I don't need a public
apology from those who defamed me, but a quick message with a
'sorry we lied about you' would be nice," Twitter, August 29, 2019,
10:01 a.m., https://twitter.com/Comey/
status/1167074854757163009?ref_src=twsrc%5Etfw%7Ctwcamp%
5Etweetembed%7Ctwterm%5E1167074854757163009&ref_
url=https%3A%2F%2Fabcnews.
go.com%2FPolitics%2Fjustice-dept-inspector-general-releases-report-
scrutinizing-comey%2Fstory%3Fid%3D65265296.

51. "Rep. John Ratcliffe: Former FBI Lawyer Lisa Page Said Obama DOJ
Ordered FBI Not to Charge Hillary Clinton; No Russia Collusion,"
CBS DFW, March 13, 2019, https://dfw.cbslocal.com/2019/03/13/
lisa-page-obama-doj-ordered-fbi-not-to-charge-hillary-clinton-no-
collusion/.

Chapter 2

Presumption of Guilt

1. "Hillary Clinton: Trump's Actions 'Direct Threat' to National
Security," PBS News Hour, October 8, 2019, https://www.pbs.org/
newshour/show/
hillary-clinton-trumps-actions-direct-threat-to-national-security.

2. Sadie Gurman, Byron Tau, and Aruna Viswanatha, "Justice
Department Watchdog Finds Proper Legal Basis, but Errors, in Russia
Probe," *Wall Street Journal,* November 23, 2019, https://www.wsj.
com/articles/inspector-general-alleges-fbi-lawyer-altered-email-
related-to-russia-probe-11574437554; Adam Goldman and Charlie
Savage, "Russia Inquiry Review Is Said to Criticize F.B.I. but Rebuff
Claims of Biased Acts," *New York Times,* November 22, 2019,
https://www.nytimes.com/2019/11/22/us/politics/russia-investigation-
inspector-general-report.html.

3. Jerry Dunleavy, "FBI Lawyer under Criminal Investigation Altered Document to Say Carter Page 'Was Not a Source' for Another Agency," *Washington Examiner*, December 9, 2019, https://www. washingtonexaminer.com/news/ fbi-lawyer-under-criminal-investigation-altered-document-to-say-carter-page-was-not-a-source-for-another-agency.

4. Devlin Barrett, "Surveillance Court Demands Answers from FBI for Errors, Omissions in Trump Campaign Investigation," *Washington Post*, December 17, 2019, https://www.washingtonpost.com/national-security/surveillance-court-demands-answers-from-fbi-for-errors-omissions-in-trump-campaign-investigation/2019/12/17/ 84c72754-210d-11ea-a153-dce4b94e4249_story. html?wpisrc=al_news__alert-politics—alert-national&wpmk=1.

5. George Papadopoulos (@GeorgePapa19), "Kevin Clinesmith, the high ranking official from the FBI currently under criminal investigation, interviewed me in such a bizarre manner that I would not be surprised if there. is a conspiracy charge coming. Read my book and understand why he's the first domino. Good day for [America]!" Twitter, November 22, 2019, 4:47 p.m., https://twitter. com/georgepapa19/status/1197994975977340928.

6. Office of the Inspector General, "Review of Four FISA Applications."

7. Jerry Dunleavy, "FBI Lawyer under Criminal Investigation."

8. Office of the Inspector General, "Review of Four FISA Applications."

9. "A Review of Various Actions by the Federal Bureau of Investigation and Department of Justice in Advance of the 2016 Election," Office of the Inspector General, U.S. Department of Justice, June 2018, https://www.justice.gov/file/1071991/download.

10. Jeet Heer, "Trump Isn't Totally Wrong about the Deep State," *The Nation*, October 25, 2019, https://www.thenation.com/article/ trump-deep-state/.

11. Robert Mueller, "Report on the Investigation into Russian Interference in the 2016 Presidential Election, Volume II," Office of the Special Counsel, U.S. Department of Justice, March 2019, https:// www.justice.gov/storage/report_volume2.pdf.

12. John Durham, "Statement of U.S. Attorney John H. Durham," News and Press Releases, U.S. Attorney's Office District of Connecticut,

December 9, 2019, https://www.justice.gov/usao-ct/pr/
statement-us-attorney-john-h-durham.

13. Morgan Chalfant, "DOJ Watchdog: Durham Said 'Preliminary' FBI
Trump Probe Was Justified," *The Hill,* December 11, 2019, https://
thehill.com/homenews/
senate/474086-doj-watchdog-durham-said-preliminary-fbi-trump-
probe-was-justified.

14. Office of the Inspector General, "Review of Four FISA Applications."

15. "Statement of Michael E. Horowitz Concerning DOJ OIG FISA
REPORT: Methodology, Scope, and Findings," Office of the
Inspector General, U.S. Department of Justice, December 18, 2019,
https://www.hsgac.senate.gov/imo/media/doc/Testimony-
Horowitz-2019-12-18.pdf.

16. While Inspector General Horowitz did not name Kevin Clinesmith
personally in his report on FISA abuse, Senator Lindsay Graham
revealed Clinesmith's name in a December 11, 2019 hearing: Caroline
Cournoyer, *et al.,* "Horowitz Defends His Trump-Russia Report but
Is 'Deeply Concerned' about FBI's Surveillance Failures," CBS News,
December 11, 2019, https://www.cbsnews.com/live-news/
inspector-general-report-michael-horowitz-testimony-justice-
department-russian-investigation-today/.

17. Office of the Inspector General, "Review of Four FISA Applications."

18. Nate Silver, "There Really Was a Liberal Media Bubble,"
FiveThirtyEight, March 10, 2017, https://fivethirtyeight.com/features/
there-really-was-a-liberal-media-bubble/.

19. Cited by Chuck Ross, "FBI Lawyer Who Sent Anti-Trump
'Resistance' Text Message Also Altered Russia Probe Documents:
Report," The Daily Caller, November 22, 2019, https://dailycaller.
com/2019/11/22/fbi-lawyer-kevin-clinesmith-russia/.

20. Quint Forgey, "Pelosi: Attorney General Barr Has 'Gone Rogue,'"
Politico, September 27, 2019, https://www.politico.com/
news/2019/09/27/
nancy-pelosi-attorney-general-william-barr-005221.

21. Ken Dilanian and Julia Ainsley, "CIA's Top Lawyer Made 'Criminal
Referral' on Complaint about Trump Ukraine Call," NBC News,
October 4, 2019, https://www.nbcnews.com/politics/

trump-impeachment-inquiry/
cia-s-top-lawyer-made-criminal-referral-whistleblower-s-
complaint-n1062481.

22. "Memorandum of Telephone Conversation," The White House
Situation Room, July 25, 2019, https://www.whitehouse.gov/
wp-content/uploads/2019/09/Unclassified09.2019.pdf.

23. Miriam Elder, "Joe Biden's Advisers Knew in 2018 His Comments
about Ukraine Would Be a Problem," BuzzFeed, October 5, 2019,
https://www.buzzfeednews.com/article/miriamelder/
joe-biden-ukraine-hunter.

24. Marc Theissen, "Marc Thiessen: Trump, Ukraine, and Democrats'
Double Standard," *Washington Post,* September 25, 2019, https://
www.foxnews.com/opinion/
trump-ukraine-democrats-marc-thiessen.

25. This was Judge Trevor MacFadden's ruling, when Buzzfeed pressed
for my drafts in court: BuzzFeed, Inc. v. U.S. Department of Justice,
1:19-cv-00070, 24, (D.D.C. 2019), https://law.justia.com/cases/
federal/district-courts/district-of-columbia/
dcdce/1:2019cv00070/203320/24/.

26. Igor Derysh, "Former FBI Lawyer Lisa Page Calls Out Trump's 'Vile
Sort of Simulated Sex Act' in First TV Interview," Salon, December
18, 2019, https://www.salon.com/2019/12/18/
former-fbi-lawyer-lisa-page-calls-out-trumps-vile-sort-of-simulated-
sex-act-in-first-tv-interview/.

27. Molly Jong-Fast, "Lisa Page Speaks: 'There's No Fathomable Way I
Have Committed Any Crime at All,'" The Daily Beast, December 17,
2019, https://www.thedailybeast.com/
lisa-page-speaks-theres-no-fathomable-way-i-have-committed-any-
crime-at-all.

28. Tracy Connor, "Rod Rosenstein: DOJ 'Not to Blame' for Lisa Page's
Abuse," The Daily Beast, December 2, 2019, https://www.
thedailybeast.com/
rod-rosenstein-doj-not-to-blame-for-lisa-pages-abuse.

29. David Jackson and Kevin Johnson, "Donald Trump: 'I Don't Know
Matt Whitaker,'" *USA TODAY*, November 9, 2018, https://www.
usatoday.com/story/news/politics/2018/11/09/

donald-trump-says-he-hasnt-talked-acting-bob-
mueller/1940490002/.

Chapter 3

Coastal Elitism

1. Andrew Grossman, "Controversial Professor Links Two Rising Politicians," *Wall Street Journal,* April 28, 2013, https://www.wsj. com/articles/SB10001424127887324482504578451021412889956.

2. Pardes Seleh, "Hakeem Jeffries Battles Whitaker in Fiery Collision: 'How the Heck Did You Become' Head of DOJ?!" MediaIte, February 8, 2019, https://www.mediaite.com/trump/ hakeem-jeffries-battles-acting-ag-whitaker-in-fiery-collision-how-the-heck-did-you-become-head-of-the-doj/.

3. "Coastal Elite," Cambridge Dictionary Online, https://dictionary. cambridge.org/us/dictionary/english/coastal-elite.

4. Dan Hirschhorn, "How Donald Trump Shocked the World," *Time,* November 9, 2016, https://time.com/4563946/ election-2016-donald-trump-victory-how/.

5. Jeffrey Toobin, "How Much Longer Can Rod Rosenstein Protect Robert Mueller?" *New Yorker,* May 22, 2018, https://www. newyorker.com/news/daily-comment/ how-much-longer-can-rod-rosenstein-protect-robert-mueller,

6. "Rosenstein: Whitaker a Superb Choice," CNN Politics, November 9, 2018, https://www.cnn.com/videos/politics/2018/11/09/rosenstein-calls-whitaker-a-superb-choice-laura-jarret-wolf-blitzer-sot-tsr-vpx. cnn.

7. "Senior Justice Dept. Officials Told Whitaker Signing Gun Regulation Might Prompt Successful Challenge to His Appointment," *Washington Post,* December 21, 2018, https://www.washingtonpost. com/world/national-security/senior-justice-dept-officials-warned-whitaker-of-legal-risks-of-signing-gun-regulation/2018/12/21/ ea0d3c04-054b-11e9-b5df-5d3874f1ac36_story.html.

8. Nicholas Fandos and Adam Goldman, "Former Top F.B.I. Lawyer Says Rosenstein Was Serious about Taping Trump," *New York*

Times, October 10, 2018, https://www.nytimes.com/2018/10/10/us/
politics/james-baker-rosenstein-secretly-taping-trump.html.

9. Katie Benner, "Rosenstein Assails Obama Administration, Comey,
    and Journalists in Depending Handling of Russia Inquiry," *New
    York Times,* April 26, 2019, https://www.nytimes.com/2019/04/26/
    us/politics/rod-rosenstein-speech.html.

10. James Comey, "Farewell Address," Archive, Department of Justice,
    August 15, 2005, https://www.justice.gov/archive/dag/speeches/2005/
    dagfarewell.htm.

11. John Bowden, "Comey: Matt Whitaker 'May Not Be the Sharpest
    Knife in Our Drawer,'" *The Hill,* November 27, 2018, https://thehill.
    com/blogs/blog-briefing-room/
    news/418485-comey-matt-whitaker-may-not-be-the-sharpest-knife-
    in-our-drawer.

12. Garrett M. Graff, "Forged under Fire—Bob Mueller and Jim
    Comey's Unusual Friendship," *The Washingtonian,* May 30, 2013,
    https://www.washingtonian.com/2013/05/30/
    forged-under-firebob-mueller-and-jim-comeys-unusual-friendship/.

13. "Read FBI's Strzok, Page Texts about Trump," Fox News, January
    23, 2018, https://www.foxnews.com/politics/
    read-fbis-strzok-page-texts-about-trump.

14. Katie Reilly, "Read Hillary Clinton's 'Basket of Deplorables' Remarks
    about Donald Trump Supporters" *Time,* September 10, 2016, https://
    time.com/4486502/hillary-clinton-basket-of-deplorables-transcript/.

15. Karen Graham, "Ignorant Hillbillies? Loudoun County Officials
    Respond," *Loudoun Times-Mirror,* February 8, 2018, https://www.
    loudountimes.com/news/ignorant-hillbillies-loudoun-county-officials-
    respond/article_6db75cb5-1222-5a52-a1f0-5915e74452d7.html.

16. Kate Rousmaniere, ed., "Overview" in *The American Midwest: An
    Interpretive Encyclopedia*, ed. Andrew R. L. Clayton, Richard
    Sisson, and Chris Zacher (Bloomington, Indiana: Indiana University
    Press, 2006), 799.

17. Julia Shanahan, "Key 1990 Iowa Football Moment Reflects Matt
    Whitaker's Jump to the White House" *The Daily Iowan,* December
    4, 2018, https://dailyiowan.com/2018/12/04/

key-1990-iowa-hawkeye-football-moment-reflects-matt-whitaker-jump-to-the-white-house/.

18. Mark Maremont, "Acting Attorney General Matthew Whitaker Incorrectly Claims Academic All-American Honors," *Wall Street Journal,* December 26, 2018, https://www.wsj.com/articles/acting-attorney-general-matthew-whitaker-incorrectly-claims-academic-all-american-honors-11545844613.

19. Devlin Barrett, "FBI in Internal Feud over Hillary Clinton Probe," *Wall Street Journal,* October 30, 2016, https://www.wsj.com/articles/laptop-may-include-thousands-of-emails-linked-to-hillary-clintons-private-server-1477854957.

20. Ibid.

21. Michael E. Horowitz, "Dear Chairman Grassley," Office of the Inspector General, U.S. Department of Justice, https://www.judiciary.senate.gov/imo/media/doc/2018-04-13%20DOJ%20OIG%20to%20CEG%20-%20McCabe%20with%20ROI.pdf.

22. Betsy Swan and Sam Brodey, "FBI Agents: McCabe Apologized for Changing His Story on Leak," The Daily Beast, December 31, 2019, https://www.thedailybeast.com/fbi-agents-andrew-mccabe-apologized-for-changing-his-story-on-wall-street-journal-leak.

23. Philip Ewing, "Justice Department Details Case against Fired Deputy FBI Director McCabe," NPR, April 13, 2018, https://www.npr.org/2018/04/13/602331134/justice-department-details-case-against-fired-deputy-fbi-director-mccabe.

24. David Halberstam, *The Best and the Brightest,* (New York: Ballantine Books, 1993), xiv.

Chapter 4

The Sovereign District of New York

1. https://www.justice.gov/usao-sdny/prosecuting-corrupt-public-officials-0.

2. Andrew McCarthy, "Andrew C. McCarthy: Why Trump Is Likely to Be Indicted by Manhattan US Attorney," Fox News, December 8,

2018, https://www.foxnews.com/opinion/
andrew-c-mccarthy-why-trump-is-likely-to-be-indicted-by-
manhattan-us-attorney.

3. Nicholas Lemann, "Street Cop," *New Yorker,* November 3, 2013,
https://www.newyorker.com/magazine/2013/11/11/street-cop.

4. Benjamin Weiser, "A Steppingstone for Law's Best and Brightest,"
New York Times, January 30, 2009, https://www.nytimes.
com/2009/01/30/nyregion/30southern.html.

5. Rebecca Ballhaus, *et al.,* "Tense Relationship between Barr and
Giuliani Complicated Trump Impeachment Defense," *Wall Street
Journal,* October 1, 2019, https://www.wsj.com/articles/
tense-relationship-between-barr-and-giuliani-complicates-trump-
impeachment-defense-11569942261.

6. Lemann, "Street Cop."

7. Miranda Green, "On Podcast, Preet Bharara Gives New Details on
Why Donald Trump Fired Him," CNN Politics, September 21, 2017,
https://www.cnn.com/2017/09/20/politics/preet-bharara-podcast-
trump-firing/index.html.

8. Eileen Sullivan, "Takeaways from the *The Times's* Investigation into
Trump's War on the Inquiries around Him," *New York Times,*
February 19, 2019, https://www.nytimes.com/2019/02/19/us/politics/
investigating-trump-administration.html.

9. "Report of Investigation of Former Federal Bureau of Investigation
Director James Comey's Disclosure of Sensitive Investigative
Information and Handling of Certain Memoranda," Office of the
Inspector General, U.S. Department of Justice, August 2019, https://
oig.justice.gov/reports/2019/o1902.pdf.

10. Lemann, "Street Cop."

11. Taylor Dolven, "What You Need to Know about Robert Khuzami,
the Prosecutor Going after Michael Cohen," Vice, April 19, 2018,
https://www.vice.com/en_us/article/qvxaxm/
who-is-robert-khuzami-lawyer-leading-investigation-trump-attorney-
michael-cohen.

12. Morgan Chalfant, "House Dems Ready Subpoena for Acting
Attorney General Whitaker if He Refuses to Testify," *The Hill,*
February 7, 2019, https://thehill.com/policy/

national-security/428939-house-dems-ready-subpoena-for-acting-ag-whitaker-if-he-refuses-to.

13. Jerry Nadler (@RepJerryNadler), "My response to Acting AG Whitaker regarding the use of a subpoena for tomorrow's @ HouseJudiciary hearing," Twitter, February 7, 2019, 5:33 p.m., https://twitter.com/RepJerryNadler/status/1093639032498778112.

14. Aaron Blake, "The Matthew Whitaker Perjury Question," *Washington Post*, February 26, 2019, https://www.washingtonpost.com/politics/2019/02/26/matthew-whitaker-perjury-question/.

15. Dan Friedman, "Trump's Former Acting Attorney General Agrees to Fix His Testimony about Trump Pressure," *Mother Jones*, February 26, 2019, https://www.motherjones.com/politics/2019/02/trumps-former-acting-attorney-general-says-he-will-change-his-testimony-about-trump-pressure/.

16. Jerry Nadler, "Dear Acting Attorney General Whitaker," Committee on the Judiciary, U.S. House of Representatives, February 13, 2019, https://judiciary.house.gov/sites/democrats.judiciary.house.gov/files/documents/Letter%20to%20Mr.%20Whitaker%20%282.13.19%29.pdf.

17. Mark Mazzetti, *et al.*, "Intimidation, Pressure, and Humiliation: Inside Trump's Two-year War on the Investigations Encircling Him," *New York Times*, February 19, 2019, https://www.nytimes.com/2019/02/19/us/politics/trump-investigations.html.

18. Andrew Desiderio, "Lawmakers Clash over Trump's Talks with Whitaker," *Politico*, March 13, 2019, https://www.politico.com/story/2019/03/13/trump-whitaker-cohen-congress-1220961.

19. "Special Counsel's Office Statement of Expenditures October 1, 2018 through May 31, 2019," U.S. Department of Justice, August 2, 2019, https://www.justice.gov/jmd/page/file/1190286/download.

Chapter 5

How the Special Counsel Undermines the Constitution

1. "Full Text: James Comey Testimony Transcript on Trump and Russia," *Politico*, June 8, 2017, https://www.politico.com/

story/2017/06/08/
full-text-james-comey-trump-russia-testimony-239295.

2. Doina Chiacu and Grant McCool, "Trump's Firing of FBI Head
    Comey Triggered Probe: Ex-official McCabe," Reuters, February 14,
    2019, https://www.reuters.com/article/us-usa-trump-russia-mccabe/
    trumps-firing-of-fbi-head-comey-triggered-probe-ex-official-mccabe-
    idUSKCN1Q320M.

3. Kate Sullivan, "Mueller Explains Why His Family Left Trump's Golf
    Club," CNN, April 18, 2019, https://www.cnn.com/2019/04/18/
    politics/mueller-trump-golf-club/index.html?no-st=1573873154.

4. Kyle Cheney, "McCabe Reveals He's the One Who Decided to
    Remove Strzok from Mueller's Team," *Politico*, May 20, 2019,
    https://www.politico.com/story/2019/05/20/
    mueller-investigation-mccabe-strzok-1336694.

5. Reprinted with permission from CNN. Matthew Whitaker,
    "Mueller's Investigation of Trump Is Going Too Far," CNN,
    November 7, 2018, https://www.cnn.com/2017/08/06/opinions/
    rosenstein-should-curb-mueller-whittaker-opinion/index.html.

6. Marisa M. Kashino, "Robert Mueller Is Back in Private Practice at
    WilmerHale," *The Washingtonian*, October 1, 2019, https://www.
    washingtonian.com/2019/10/01/
    robert-mueller-is-back-in-private-practice-at-wilmerhale/.

7. "A Sitting President's Amenability to Indictment and Criminal
    Prosecution," Office of Legal Counsel, U.S. Department of Justice,
    October 16, 2000, https://www.justice.gov/olc/opinion/
    sitting-president's-amenability-indictment-and-criminal-prosecution.

8. Veronica Rocha, Meg Wagner, and Amanda Wills, "Robert Mueller
    Testifies," CNN, July 25, 2019, https://www.cnn.com/politics/live-
    news/
    robert-mueller-congress-testimony/
    h_6abd70907b88b505d8f8efb4f149af88.

9. Preet Bharara (@PreetBharara), "This is very very close to Mueller
    saying that but for the OLC memo, Trump would have been
    indicted," Twitter, July 24, 2019, 8:06 a.m., https://twitter.com/
    PreetBharara/status/1154045092035883008.

10. Natasha Bertrand, "Annotated: Mueller's Second Opening Statement," *Politico*, July 24, 2019, https://www.politico.com/story/2019/07/24/mueller-hearing-annotated-opening-statement-1430662.

11. Aaron Mak, "Who Is Aaron Zebley, Robert Mueller's Sidekick for Wednesday's Testimony?" Slate, July 24, 2019, https://slate.com/news-and-politics/2019/07/aaron-zebley-robert-mueller-sidekick-congress-hearing.html.

12. Bart Jansen, "Attorney General Says Mueller Investigation 'Close to Being Completed,'" *USA TODAY*, January 28, 2018, https://www.usatoday.com/story/news/politics/2019/01/28/robert-mueller-investigation-close-being-completed-whitaker/2702883002/.

13. Tony Mauro, "Mueller Enlists Top Criminal Law Expert for Russia Probe," Law.com, June 9, 2017, https://www.law.com/nationallawjournal/almID/1202789177543/Mueller-Enlists-Top-Criminal-Law-Expert-for-Russia-Probe/?cmp=share_twitter.

14. Robert Mueller, "Letter to Bill Barr," Special Counsel's Office, U.S. Department of Justice, March 27, 2019, https://int.nyt.com/data/documenthelper/796-mueller-letter-to-barr/02499959cbfa313c36d4/optimized/full.pdf

15. Steven G. Calabresi, "US Law Is Not on the Side of Mueller's Appointment as Special Counsel," *The Hill*, June 19, 2018, https://thehill.com/opinion/judiciary/393088-us-law-is-not-on-the-side-of-robert-muellers-appointment-as-special-counsel.

16. Jack Maskell, "Independent Counsels, Special Prosecutors, Special Counsels, and the Role of Congress," Congressional Research Service, June 20, 2013, https://fas.org/sgp/crs/misc/R43112.pdf.

17. Mark Penn, "Mark Penn: Fixing the Special Counsel Statute in 10 Not-So-Easy Steps," Fox News, March 27, 2019, https://www.foxnews.com/opinion/mark-penn-fixing-the-special-counsel-statute-in-10-not-so-easy-steps.

18. "The Future of the Independent Counsel Act," Committee on Governmental Affairs, April 14, 1999, https://www.govinfo.gov/content/pkg/CHRG-106shrg56376/html/CHRG-106shrg56376.htm.
19. "28 CFR § 600.8–Notification and Reports by the Special Counsel," Legal Information Institute, https://www.law.cornell.edu/cfr/text/28/600.8.

Chapter 6

Criminalizing the Political

1. James Walsh, "Fusion GPS Lights a Candle for the 'Pee Tape,'" Intelligencer, November 22, 2019, http://nymag.com/intelligencer/2019/11/fusion-gps-interview-glenn-simpson-on-the-steele-dossier.html.
2. Matthew Continetti and Michael Goldfarb, "Fusion GPS and the Washington Free Beacon," *Washington Free Beacon*, October 27, 2017, https://freebeacon.com/uncategorized/fusion-gps-washington-free-beacon/.
3. Rowan Scarborough, "Bogus, Dem-Funded Dossier Was Lone FBI Source Used to Launch Trump Conspiracy Probe," *Washington Times,* January 12, 2020, https://www.washingtontimes.com/news/2020/jan/12/fbi-crossfire-hurricane-probe-source-trump-conspir/.
4. Michael Isikoff, "Top FBI Officials Were 'Quite Worried' Comey Would Appear to Be Blackmailing Trump," Yahoo! News, May 15, 2019, https://www.yahoo.com/news/top-fbi-officials-were-quite-worried-comey-would-appear-to-be-blackmailing-trump-132955356.html.
5. Liam Quinn, "Bill Barr Vows to Uncover 'Exactly What Happened' with Russia Probe, Says Explanations Have Been 'Inadequate,'" Fox News, May 17, 2019, https://www.foxnews.com/politics/bill-barr-russia-probe-explanations.
6. Eric Tucker, "The Comey Firing, as Retold by the Mueller Report," AP News, April 23, 2019, https://apnews.com/4ff1ecb621884a728b25e62661257ef0.

7. Emily Larsen and Naomi Lim, "Democratic Candidates: Mueller Remarks Were an Impeachment Referral—So Impeach," *Washington Examiner*, May 29, 2019, https://www.washingtonexaminer.com/news/democratic-candidates-mueller-remarks-were-an-impeachment-referral-so-impeach.

8. Jeremy Herb, Katelyn Polantz, and Laura Jarrett, "Mueller: 'If We Had Confidence That the President Clearly Did Not Commit a Crime, We Would Have Said So,'" CNN Politics, May 29, 2019, https://www.cnn.com/2019/05/29/politics/robert-mueller-special-counsel-investigation/index.html.

9. Jonathan Chait, "Mueller: Trump Is Not Not a Criminal," Intelligencer, May 29, 2019, http://nymag.com/intelligencer/2019/05/mueller-trump-is-not-not-a-criminal.html.

10. Alex Swoyer, "Impeachment Threatens to Become Partisan Go-To Weapon," *Washington Times,* December 21, 2019, https://www.washingtontimes.com/news/2019/dec/21/impeachment-threatens-to-become-partisan-go-to-wea/.

11. Tim Hains, "Rep. Al Green: 'I'm Concerned If We Don't Impeach This President, He Will Get Re-Elected,'" RealClear Politics, May 6, 2019, https://www.realclearpolitics.com/video/2019/05/06/al_green_im_concerned_if_we_dont_impeach_this_president_he_will_get_re-elected.html.

12. Darren Samuelsohn, "Meet the Legal Minds behind Trump's Impeachment," *Politico,* December 12, 2019, https://www.politico.com/news/2019/12/12/trump-impeachment-legal-083037.

13. Joe Concha, "NBC Signs Mueller 'Pit Bull' Prosecutor Andrew Weissman as Legal Analyst," *The Hill,* November 15, 2019, https://thehill.com/homenews/media/470727-nbc-signs-mueller-pitbull-prosecutor-andrew-weissman-as-legal-analyst.

14. William Barr, "Attorney General William P. Barr Delivers the 19th Annual Barbara K. Olson Memorial Lecture at the Federalist Society's 2019 National Lawyers Convention," U.S. Department of Justice, November 15, 2019, https://www.justice.gov/opa/speech/

attorney-general-william-p-barr-delivers-19th-annual-barbara-k-olson-memorial-lecture.

15. Jerry Nadler, "Impeachment of Donald J. Trump, President of the United States," Committee on the Judiciary, House of Representatives, December 18, 2019, https://rules.house.gov/sites/democrats.rules.house.gov/files/CRPT-116hrpt346.pdf; Kyle Cheney and Andrew Desiderio, "Judiciary Committee Impeachment Report Alleges Trump Committed 'Multiple Federal Crimes,'" *Politico,* December 16, 2019, https://www.politico.com/news/2019/12/16/judiciary-committee-impeachment-report-trump-committed-multiple-federal-crimes-086096.

16. Jacqueline Thomsen, "The House Is Set to Impeach Trump. These Lawyers Helped Democrats Get there," Law.com, December 13, 2019, https://www.law.com/nationallawjournal/2019/12/13/the-house-is-set-to-impeach-trump-these-lawyers-helped-democrats-get-there/; Sam Dorman, "Harvard Law Professor Blasts Former AG Whitaker after He Defends Trump," Fox News, October 23, 2019, https://www.foxnews.com/media/laurence-tribe-whitaker-ignorant.

17. Debra Cassens Weiss, "Harvard Law Prof Pitched the Idea of Withholding Impeachment Articles; Is It Constitutional?" *American Bar Association Journal,* December 19, 2019, http://www.abajournal.com/news/article/harvard-law-prof-pitched-the-idea-of-withholding-impeachment-articles-is-it-constitutional.

18. "Criminal Law," Legal Information Institute, Cornell Law School, https://www.law.cornell.edu/wex/criminal_law.

19. "A review of Various Actions by the Federal Bureau of Investigation and Department of Justice in Advance of the 2016 Election," Office of the Inspector General, U.S. Department of justice, June 2018, https://www.justice.gov/file/1071991/download.

20. "Exclusive: President Barack Obama on 'Fox News Sunday,'" Fox News, April 10, 2016, https://www.foxnews.com/transcript/exclusive-president-barack-obama-on-fox-news-sunday.

21. John Ratcliffe (@RepRatcliffe), "Lisa Page confirmed to me under oath that the FBI was ordered by the Obama DOJ not to consider charging Hillary Clinton for gross negligence in the handling of

classified information," Twitter, March 12, 2019, 10:33 p.m., https://
twitter.com/RepRatcliffe/status/1105658231198765057?ref_src=twsr
c%5Etfw%7Ctwcamp%5Etweetembed%7Ctwterm%5E110565823
1198765057&ref_url=https%3A%2F%2Fdfw.cbslocal.
com%2F2019%2F03%2F13%2Flisa-page-obama-doj-ordered-fbi-
not-to-charge-hillary-clinton-no-collusion%2F.

22. Laura Jarrett and Evan Perez, "FBI Agent Dismissed from Mueller
Probe Changed Comey's Description of Clinton to 'Extremely
Careless,'" CNN Politics, December 4, 2017, https://www.cnn.
com/2017/12/04/politics/peter-strzok-james-comey/index.html.

23. James Comey, "Statement by FBI Direction James B. Comey on the
Investigation of Secretary Hillary Clinton's Use of a Personal E-Mail
System," Press Releases, FBI National Press Office, July 5, 2016,
https://www.fbi.gov/news/pressrel/press-releases/
statement-by-fbi-director-james-b-comey-on-the-investigation-of-
secretary-hillary-clinton2019s-use-of-a-personal-e-mail-system.

24. Stephen Collinson and Tal Kopan, "FBI Director: Hillary Clinton
'Extremely Careless' but No Charges Recommended," CNN Politics,
July 6, 2016, https://www.cnn.com/2016/07/05/politics/fbi-director-
doesnt-recommend-charges-against-hillary-clinton/index.html.

Conclusion

The Case for a Strong Unitary Executive

1. "The Constitution of the United States: A Transcription," America's
Founding Documents, National Archives, https://www.archives.gov/
founding-docs/constitution-transcript.

2. Eliana Johnson, "The Real Reason Bill Barr Is Defending Trump," *Politico*,
May 1, 2019, https://www.politico.com/story/2019/05/01/
william-barr-donald-trump-mueller-report-1295273.

3. Committee on the Judiciary, United States House of Representatives v.
Donald F. McGahn II, Civ. No. 19-cv-2379 (KBJ 2019), https://ecf.dcd.
uscourts.gov/cgi-bin/show_public_doc?2019cv2379-46.

4. "Congress Is King," *Wall Street Journal*, November 26, 2019, https://www.
wsj.com/articles/congress-is-king-11574814808.

5.   Eric Holder, "Eric Holder: William Barr Is Unfit to Be Attorney General,"
     Washington Post, December 11, 2019, https://www.washingtonpost.com/
     opinions/eric-holder-william-barr-is-unfit-to-be-attorney-
     general/2019/12/11/99882092-1c55-11ea-87f7-f2e91143c60d_story.html.

6.   Elizabeth Winkler, "The CIA's Former Chief of Disguise Drops Her Mask,"
     Wall Street Journal, December 12, 2019, https://www.wsj.com/articles/
     the-cias-former-chief-of-disguise-drops-her-mask-11576168327.

7.   Michelle Cottle, "They Are Not the Resistance. They Are Not a Cabal.
     They Are Public Servants," *New York Times*, October 20, 2019, https://
     www.nytimes.com/2019/10/20/opinion/trump-impeachment-testimony.
     html.

8.   David Agren, "'Mexico Has Become Trump's Wall': How Amlo Became an
     Immigration Enforcer," *The Guardian*, January 26, 2020, https://www.
     nytimes.com/2019/10/20/opinion/trump-impeachment-testimony.
     html?smid=tw-nytopinion&smtyp=cur.

INDEX

Project Safe Neighborhoods
(PSN), 20–21
public servants, 9, 38, 60, 84, 134
Putin, Vladimir, 1, 2, 4, 99, 136

R

Reagan, Ronald, 12, 130
recusal, 11, 12, 27–28, 30, 35–37,
134,
Rehnquist, William, 31
Resistance, the, 2, 19, 23, 32, 34,
45–46, 48–49, 55, 59, 104,
121–22
Richman, Daniel, 67, 87, 93
Roberts, John, 14
Rose Bowl, 72
Rosenstein, Rod, 1, 16–18,
24–25, 29–30, 35–36, 40, 46,
51, 59–60, 65–66, 94–95,
97–99, 102, 104
Rousmaniere, Kate, 71
Russia, 1–6, 11–18, 20, 23–24,
27, 29, 35–36, 39–40, 43, 45,
47–51, 53, 55–58, 64–65, 77,
86, 94, 96, 106–7, 114–17,
119, 121, 133

S

Schiff, Adam, 6, 104, 118, 120,
122, 131, 136
Schumer, Chuck, 24, 26, 29, 32,
36, 38, 85, 128, 136
Scott, McGregor (Greg), 75, 77,
100, 102, 105

Senate Foreign Relations Committee, 27
Sessions, Jeff, 11–12, 14–15, 18,
27, 35–36, 38–39, 41, 54,
64–65, 77, 85, 94, 96, 118,
134–35
Silver, Nate, 53, 57
Southern District of New York,
the, 22, 66, 81–87, 89–92, 102
Special Counsel, 2, 4, 10–11, 16,
18, 22–25, 28–30, 36–37,
39–42, 57, 61, 65, 67, 77, 81,
86, 92–110, 116–19, 121, 137
Special Counsel regulation,
22–23, 37, 40–41, 98, 106–8
Steele dossier, 2–4, 6, 43, 48, 51,
114
Steinbach, Michael, 47
Strzok, Peter, 5, 15–16, 28–29,
39, 47–48, 51, 54–55, 69–70,
95, 106, 125
Supermax, 38

T

Thomas, Clarence, 14
Trump National Golf Club, 95
2016 election, 5, 9, 11–12, 16, 18,
31, 40, 43, 45–47, 53, 55–57,
64, 70, 82, 85, 96–97, 99, 106,
113–14, 117, 120, 124, 134,
136
Twitter bots, 4